Martial Arts and Your Life

The Story of Us
What We Do and Why

Copyright © 2022 by Lawrence A. Kane and Kris Wilder

All rights reserved. No part of this publication may be reproduced, distributed or transmitted in any form or by any means, including photocopying, recording, or other electronic or mechanical methods, without the prior written permission of the publisher, except in the case of brief quotations embodied in critical reviews and certain other noncommercial uses permitted by copyright law. For permission requests, contact Stickman Publications through our website (www.stickmanpublications.com)
email Lawrence Kane (lakane@ix.netcom.com)
email Kris Wilder (kriswilder@kriswilder.com)
or write to the publisher, addressed "Attention: Permissions Coordinator," at the address below:

Stickman Publications, Inc.
Seattle, WA 98126

www.stickmanpublications.com

ISBN-13: 979-8-9855617-1-5

Cover design and interior layout by Kamila Miller (kzmiller.com)

Disclaimer:

Information in this book is distributed "As Is," without warranty. Nothing in this document constitutes a legal opinion nor should any of its contents be treated as such. Neither the authors nor the publisher shall have any liability with respect to the information contained herein. Further, neither the authors nor the publisher has any control over or assume any responsibility for websites or external resources referenced in this book. When it comes to martial arts, self-defense, violence, and related topics, no text, no matter how well written, can substitute for professional, hands-on instruction. These materials should be used *for academic study only*.

Martial Arts and Your Life

The Story of Us
What We Do and Why

Lawrence A. Kane & Kris Wilder

Foreword by
Eric Parsons, Ph.D.

Table of Contents

Foreword (by Eric Parsons, Ph.D.)	xvii
Introduction	1
How does your system organize rank?	13
Martial Artist Profile – Iain Abernethy	19
What is the highest rank you have ever achieved in the martial arts?	23
Martial Artist Profile – Vicky Stormo	29
How many different martial systems have you tried?	33
If you did not practice the martial art you are involved in now, what other martial art(s) would you do?	39
Martial Artist Profile – Christian Wedewardt	45
What is your Myers-Briggs personality type?	49
What is your somatotype, (a) ectomorph, (b) mesomorph, or (c) endomorph?	57
Martial Artist Profile – Tzviel 'BK' Blankchtein	63
Have you ever applied your martial art outside the training hall or competition/tournament ring?	67
If you applied your martial art in real life, how many times?	73
Martial Artist Profile – Gavin Mulholland	79
What's the worst martial arts-related mistake you have ever made?	83
Martial Artist Profile – Jay Matzko	89
Are you a night owl or an early bird?	93
Martial Artist Profile – Martin Stark	99
What attributes do you admire most?	103
What superpower do you wish you had?	109
Martial Artist Profile – Benjamin Dean LaBelle	115
If wrote a book about your life, what would the title be?	119
What is the best compliment you have ever received?	125
Martial Artist Profile – Parul Verma, Ph.D.	131
What is the best single piece of advice you were ever given?	135
If you had to pick one age to be permanently, which age would you choose	143
Martial Artist Profile – Patricia Bolton	149
If you could go back in time, what advice would you give to your teenage self?	153
Martial Artist Profile – Wallace Smedley	159
When you were a kid, what did you want to be when you grew up?	163
Martial Artist Profile – Peter Freedman	171
What energizes you outside of work?	175
What is your favorite weekend activity?	181
Martial Artist Profile – Sarah Jackson	187

What is your guilty pleasure?	191
Would you rather visit the beach or the mountains?	197
Martial Artist Profile – Todd Durgan	201
Have you ever spent a night in jail?	205
What three words would your friends use to describe you?	211
Martial Artist Profile – Shandra Stevenson	217
What is one thing, big or small, that you are truly bad at?	221
Martial Artist Profile – Randy Haskins	227
What is one thing you are currently trying to make a habit?	231
Martial Artist Profile – Alain Burrese, J.D.	237
Who is/was the greatest athlete of all time?	241
What single event of the past changed the world for the best?	247
Martial Artist Profile – Dan Anderson	253
What single event of the past changed the world for the worst?	257
Who is your favorite musician or band?	265
Martial Artist Profile – Dana Abbott	271
What terrifies you?	275
Do you regularly carry a weapon?	281
Martial Artist Profile – Hermann Bayer, Ph.D.	289
Who influenced you the most?	293
Martial Artist Profile – Restita DeJesus	299
Why did you start training?	303
Martial Artist Profile – Josh Amos	309
For good or ill, what was the biggest impact of your martial arts training on your life?	313
If you stopped or took a long break from training, why?	319
Martial Artist Profile – Karl Duff, Ph.D., J.D.	325
How have you made money from your martial arts?	329
Which one of your senses are you most willing to sacrifice?	335
Martial Artist Profile – Thomas Tobin	341
Knowing what you know now, would you do it all over again?	345
Do you recommend your system/style to your friends or family?	351
Martial Artist Profile – Wendell A. Goins, MD, FACS	359
Survey demographics – Gender mix	363
Martial Artist Profile – Steven Almendarez	369
Survey demographics – Affinity group mix	373
Martial Artist Profile – Charlie Lampshire	379
Conclusion	383
Rogues' gallery	391

Appendix A – Survey Methodology	407
Appendix B – Questionnaire	409
Bibliography	419
Thank you!	427
About the Authors	429
Amalgamated Works by the Authors	433

Table of Charts

Chart 1 – Highest Rank Achieved	25
Chart 2 – Number of Martial Systems	35
Chart 3 – MBTI Personality Types	51
Chart 4 – Somatotypes	59
Chart 5 – Skills Used in Real Life	69
Chart 6 – Number of Times Skills Used	75
Chart 7 – Night Owl or Early Bird	95
Chart 8 – Ideal Age	147
Chart 9 – Beach or Mountains	199
Chart 10 – Night in Jail	207
Chart 11 – Carry a Weapon	283
Chart 12 – Sense to Sacrifice	337
Chart 13 – Recommend Your System or Style?	353
Chart 14 – Survey Gender Mix	365
Chart 15 – Survey Affinity Group	375

Table of Figures

Figure 1 – Rank Structure	15
Figure 2 – Martial Arts of Interest	41
Figure 3 – Worst Mistake	85
Figure 4 – Admired Attributes	105
Figure 5 – Superpower	111
Figure 6 – Book Title	121
Figure 7 – Best Compliment	127
Figure 8 – Best Advice	137
Figure 9 – Ideal Age	145
Figure 10 – Advice to Teenage Self	155
Figure 11 – Want to be When You Grow Up	165
Figure 12 – Maslow's Hierarchy of Needs	167
Figure 13 – Energized Outside of Work	177
Figure 14 – Weekend Activity	183
Figure 15 – Guilty Pleasure	193
Figure 16 – Three Word Description	213
Figure 17 – What You're Bad At	223
Figure 18 – Habit	233
Figure 19 – Greatest Athlete	243
Figure 20 – Best Event	249
Figure 21 – Worst Event	259
Figure 22 – Favorite Musician	267
Figure 23 – Terror	277
Figure 24 – Biggest Influence	295
Figure 25 – Why Start Training	305
Figure 26 – Biggest Impact	315
Figure 27 – Break from Training	321
Figure 28 – Money from Martial Arts	331
Figure 29 – Would You do it all Again?	347
Figure 30 – Conclusion	385
Figure 31 – Rogues' Gallery	393

Table of Pictures

Pic. 1 – Eric Parsons, PhD	xvi
Pic. 2 – Eric Parsons, Martial Artist	xix
Pic. 3 Martial Artist 'Icon'	2
Pic. 4 – Iain Abernethy	19
Pic. 5 – Chief Vicky Stormo	29
Pic. 6 – Christian Wedewardt	45
Pic 7 – Tzviel 'BK' Blankchtein	63
Pic 8 – Shihan Gavin Mulholland	79
Pic 9 – Captain Jay Matzko	89
Pic 10 – Martin Stark	99
Pic 11 – Benjamin LaBelle	115
Pic 12 – Parul Verma, Ph.D.	131
Pic 13 – Patricia Bolton	149
Pic 14 – Wallace Smedley	159
Pic 15 – Grandmaster Peter Friedman	171
Pic 16 – Sarah Jackson	187
Pic 17 – Todd Durgan	201
Pic 18 – Shandra Stevenson	217
Pic 19 – Randy Haskins	227
Pic 20 – Alain Burrese, J.D.	237
Pic 21 – Grandmaster Dan Anderson	253
Pic 22 – Life in Every Breath	262
Pic 23 – Shihan Dana Abbott	271
Pic 24 – Hermann Bayer, Ph.D.	289
Pic 25 – Restita DeJesus	299
Pic 26 – Josh Amos	309
Pic 27 – Karl Duff, Ph.D., J.D.	325
Pic 28 – Thomas Tobin	341
Pic 29 – Dr. Wendell Goins	359
Pic 30 – Sergeant Steven Almendarez	369
Pic 31 – Charlie Lampshire	379
Pic 32 – Rogues' Gallery Page 1	395
Pic 33 – Rogues' Gallery Page 2	396
Pic 34 – Rogues' Gallery Page 3	397
Pic 35 – Rogues' Gallery Page 4	398
Pic 36 – Rogues' Gallery Page 5	399

Pic 37 – Rogues' Gallery Page 6	400
Pic 38 – Rogues' Gallery Page 7	401
Pic 39 – Rogues' Gallery Page 8	402
Pic 40 – Rogues' Gallery Page 9	403
Pic 41 – Rogues' Gallery Page 10	404
Pic 42 – Rogues' Gallery Page 11	405
Pic 43 – The Authors	426
Pic 44 – Lawrence Kane	429
Pic 45 – Kris Wilder	431

Citing this book…

This book provides unique insight into the mind of the martial artist—who we are, what we do, and why we do it—that is not available anywhere else. As such, we wish to assure that its valuable contribution to the community can be both broad and deep. We welcome you to quote short passages or summarize these materials for comment, book reviews, criticism, news reporting, education, scholarship, or research as long as you comply with fair use requirements (as defined by Section 107 of the Copyright Act) and cite the source.

If you wish to use longer excerpts of this book for commercial purposes, quote items that speak to the heart of the work as defined under copyright law, or reproduce more than three (3) charts, word clouds, or images contained in the book, please contact the authors for prior permission before doing so. You can contact us through our website (www.stickmanpublications.com) or email Lawrence Kane (lakane@ix.netcom.com) or Kris Wilder (kriswilder@kriswilder.com).

"Today is victory over yourself of yesterday; tomorrow is your victory over lesser men."

Miyamoto Musashi
(1584 – 1645)

Dr. Eric Parsons, Ph.D., is an associate teaching professor of economics at the University of Missouri and is responsible for teaching Principles of Microeconomics to nearly 2,000 students each year. He has received several teaching awards and was nominated as a Professor of the Year candidate by the Mizzou Athletics Department. Dr. Parsons has also researched a wide variety of public policy topics. In addition to having published scholarly articles in well-respected academic journals, he has also served in an advisory capacity with the Missouri Department of Elementary and Secondary Education, the Houston (Texas) Independent School District, the Columbia (Missouri) Police Department, and the Missouri Attorney General's Office, among others. Prior to working at Mizzou, Dr. Parsons taught mathematics, statistics, and economics at a Kansas City-area community college and served for two years as a Peace Corps Volunteer in the East African nation of Uganda. He has trained in the martial arts for over twenty-five years and, upon returning from the Peace Corps, created the Karate for Life Foundation to help provide support for his former students, now primary school teachers, as they work to improve the life skills training and life outcomes of their pupils.

Foreword
(by Eric Parsons, Ph.D.)

"Knowledge is like money: To be of value it must circulate, and in circulating it can increase in quantity and, hopefully, in value."

Louis L'Amour, American novelist

Odds are that if you are reading this book, you are a martial artist (or at least know one). And if that's true, then there's also a good chance that you've always felt that you and your fellow martial artists were perhaps a bit different from other members of the general public. Well, as it turns out, we are (at least in some ways), and the delightful book that you hold in your hands (or are viewing on a screen, if you're not a Luddite like me) is about to illuminate some of these differences for you. Some of the them will have you nodding your head, as the book puts into words and figures thoughts that you've always had or possibly more subtle perceptions that you couldn't quite put your finger on. Other results may surprise you. And to invert Randy's Law (fans of survey participant Wim Demeere will know what I'm talking about), the areas where martial artists aren't different from the population at large are also interesting and important. Because, as it turns out, although there are some common traits that bind us, martial artists are a pretty diverse group of individuals, much like the wide variety of martial arts we practice.

Diving a bit deeper, social science research (I'm an economist by trade) like that presented here generally falls into one of two broad categories—quantitative research and qualitative research. Quantitative research is looking at the numbers. Tabulating data. Identifying trends. Assessing relationships numerically. This type of research can allow us to see connections between seemingly unrelated items and, when done well, can even help us to identify and understand cause and effect. Qualitative research, on the other hand, is the stories and words, the examination of open-ended responses. It provides flavor to the quantitative results but can also help us better understand the mechanisms of how things are working on the ground. Moreover, it is vital in determining what questions we should be asking in the first place.

This book is a wonderful combination of both. There are plenty of charts to keep the quants happy. Want to know the highest rank achieved by survey participants or how many martial arts systems they've tried? There are some nice bar charts for you. How about respondent personality type (the results of which I found fascinating), somatotype (body shape), sleep preference (early bird or night owl), or respondents' experiences using their arts in real world situations? This book's got you covered. It even contains some data that you at first might consider off the beaten path, such as would participants prefer to visit the mountain or the beach, or what superhero power would they choose (it's a rare martial artist whom I've met who's not at least a bit of a comic book or sci-fi geek, myself included), all of which will keep you fascinated and will make you think. And if a book makes you think, it's worth the price of admission.

That said, even though I'm a numbers guy (economist, remember?), where the book really shines is on the qualitative side of the coin. Through a combination of interesting questions and candid responses, you really get a feel for what makes the participants tick. And although not easy to summarize in charts (there are a lot of fun word clouds), these responses, aided by the context, external data, discussion, and reasoned conjecture presented by the authors, really get to the heart of the matter. Of particular interest are the martial artist profiles that tell the participants' stories and also provide a fair bit of wisdom in the process. (One of my favorites – "When faced with two choices… choose the one that will give you the best story.").

All in all, this book's combination of the quantitative and the qualitative, seasoned with the Kane and Wilder's expert and experienced commentary, successfully provides the committed reader with both knowledge and wisdom. And for a book on martial artists, that ultimately seems quite fitting.

Introduction

"The more you sweat in training, the less you bleed in combat"
Commander Richard Marcinko, founder of SEAL Team 6 and Red Cell

When most people hear the term "martial artist," the first thing that pops into their head is a white uniform *gi* tied at the waist with an iconic black belt. Perhaps this image comes from the movie *The Karate Kid* or popular spinoff program *Cobra Kai*. Or, maybe it originated from one of the many practitioners who have displayed their prowess on the silver screen, actors such as Chuck Norris, Bruce Lee, Donnie Yen, Cynthia Rothrock, Steven Seagal, Michelle Yeoh, or Jackie Chan.

But many martial artists don't wear a gi, and martial systems reach far beyond this one-dimensional icon… In fact, martial arts are defined as any system or tradition of combat practiced for competition, cultural heritage, spiritual development, self-defense, military, or law enforcement application. This includes both armed and unarmed techniques which can be useful for a broad range of endeavors spanning from personal growth to physical fitness to self-defense and a whole lot more.

> Martial arts encompass any system or tradition of combat practiced for competition, cultural heritage, spiritual development, self-defense, military, or law enforcement application.

Practitioners may dabble a bit and then move on to other interests, engage long enough to meet specific goals (such as learning certain self-defense skills or earning a black belt), or even make martial arts their lifetime vocation. For example, as of this writing the authors have a combined 92 years of training under their belts. And yeah, we actually wear black belts, though many of our brethren do not.

Derived from the Latin *martialis,* the word martial means "belonging to Mars," a reference to the Roman god of war. As such, it commonly refers to anything relating to war, combat, or military life, including fighting sports. There are hundreds of codified martial systems worldwide, with half a dozen achieving enough global popularity to be featured in the Olympic Games: (1) boxing, (2) fencing, (3) judo, (4) karate, (5) taekwondo, and (6) wrestling. Here's a brief summary of their Olympic origins:

- Boxing premiered during the 648 BC Olympics in Ancient Greece, and has been featured in all modern games (with refashioned rules) since 1904. In 2012, women's boxing was added to the competition in London.
- Fencing was introduced at the 1896 Olympics in Athens and has continued without disruption ever since. Women's fencing was added in 1924 at the Paris Olympics.
- Judo premiered in the 1964 Olympics in Tokyo as a nod to that nation's heritage, with women's competition added in 1992 in Barcelona.
- Karate debuted in the 2021 Olympics in Tokyo, with both men's and women's events, and included both *kata* (forms) and *kumite* (sparring) competitions.
- Taekwondo got its start as a demonstration event at the Seoul Olympics in 1988, becoming a full medal sport in 2000. Women's competition was added in 2021.
- Wresting was featured for the first time in 708 BC Olympics in Ancient Greece. In modern times, Greco-Roman wrestling was introduced in Athens in 1896, with freestyle wrestling getting its start at the 1904 Olympics in St. Louis. The first women's freestyle wrestling event was held in 2004 in Athens.

In addition to these hand-to-hand and sword-fighting competitions, the modern Olympic games have included shooting sports since their inception in 1896, with 15 different firearm events offered today. The biathlon, first held in the Chamonix Winter Olympics in 1924, combines both cross-country skiing and rifle marksmanship, in homage to Scandinavian tradition. Even though bows and arrows have been used in warfare since sometime around 1200 BC, archery was not a part of the ancient games and was not introduced into the Olympics until 1900 in Paris, with contests held in 1904, 1908, and 1920. It disappeared from medal competition for half a decade, and then was reintroduced in 1972 at the Munich Olympic games.

Olympic shooting sports are divided into three categories, (1) rifle, (2) pistol and (3) shotgun, and are additionally segregated into separate programs for male and female athletes, whereas archery competitions include (1) recurve, (2) compound, and (3) barebow contests, again with separate programs for males and females. Here is a brief summary of these contests:

- Rifle and pistol competitions are held on outdoor shooting ranges where marksmen and women aim at targets at distances of 10, 25, and 50 meters. Small bore rifles are loaded with .22 caliber bullets or .177 caliber compressed air pellets, whereas competition pistols are loaded with .22 caliber bullets or .177 caliber compressed air pellets.
- In the shotgun event, competitors shoot at clay targets propelled through the air at a series of different directions and angles. Competition shotguns are loaded with 12-gauge shells.
- In biathlon events, competitors use cross-country skiing skills, while carrying a .22-caliber rifle, in individual, sprint, relay, pursuit, mass start, and team races along a track. They stop at various intervals to shoot at targets from both standing and prone firing positions, with penalties added to the athlete's circuit time for each miss.
- Bow competitions include both indoor and field (outdoor) archery, with competitors aiming at targets of varying sizes and distances based on the category in which they compete. For example, the 50-meter target for compound bows is 80 cm in diameter whereas the barebow target at that same distance is 122 cm in diameter since archers are not allowed to use stabilizers or sight pins on barebows.

Most countries have a longstanding martial tradition, some such as the aforementioned Olympic sports more recognizable than others, yet such things have been pervasive for most of human history. Some of the better-known styles throughout the world include Brazilian *jiu-jitsu* and *vale tudo*, Chinese *baguazhang*, *bajiquan*, kung fu, *shaolin*, *tai-chi-quan*, and *wing chun*, Greek *pankration*, Indian *kalarippayattu*, Indonesian *silat*, Israeli *Krav Maga*, Japanese *aikido*, judo, *jiujitsu. jujutsu*, *kendo*, *kyudo*, and *sumo*, Korean *hapkido* and *taekwondo*, Okinawan karate, Peruvian *bacom*, Filipino *arnis*, *eskrima*, and *kali*, Russian *samozashchita bez oruzhiya* (*sambo*) and *systema*, Thai *Muay Thai*, and United States boxing, Marine Corps Martial Arts Program (MCPAP), mixed martial arts (MMA), and wrestling.

During long periods of unrest that have marked most of human history where tribal factions preyed upon one another and the strong subjugated the weak, such warlike pursuits were imperative, yet even in largely peaceful times millions of people study one or more martial disciplines today. To put this dynamic into perspective, during the Middle Ages (roughly 476 AD ~ 1400 AD) about a quarter of the population lost their lives to violence, whereas by 2017 (the latest data available) a mere 0.7% of deaths globally resulted from homicide according to Our World in Data, an organization devoted to making world-changing problems accessible, understandable, and solvable through research. Clearly there have been ebbs and flows in bloodshed over the last six centuries (e.g., World War I, World War II, Korea, Vietnam, Syrian civil war, Rwandan genocide, Second Congo war, Iraq war, Afghanistan war, Ukraine conflict, Yemeni civil war, Darfur conflict, etc.), but this overall trend represents a 97.2% reduction in worldwide violent deaths from the high point.

> Most countries have longstanding martial traditions, with a variety of hand-to-hand, sword-fighting, archery, and shooting sports competitions gaining enough popularity worldwide to be highlighted in the Olympic games.

Data can be a bit hard to come by, since there is no worldwide monitoring body or ubiquitous definition of the discipline, but the most practiced martial arts in America according to data science community Analytics Vidhya include boxing, Brazilian *jiu-jitsu*, *karate*, *taekwondo*, MMA, kickboxing, *Krav Maga*, *Muay Thai*, *kung fu*, and *aikido* in order of popularity. A Simmons Market Research study demonstrated that 18.1 million Americans, roughly 6% of the population, had practiced some form of traditional martial arts between 2010 and 2011, accounting for 9.4 million adults, 5.5 million teenagers, and 3.2 million children. At that same time, the U.S. Bureau of Labor Statistics reported that there were 1.1 million full-time law enforcement officers, 0.8 million security guards, 1.5

million active-duty military personnel, and 0.4 million military reserves employed in the United Sates. Collectively, that's 21.9 million people involved in some type of martial arts in the U.S. alone, with many times that number participating worldwide.

More recently, research institute IBISWorld conducted an examination that determined that the traditional martial arts industry, which they defined as sports like MMA, karate, taekwondo, *judo*, *kung fu*, and *jiujitsu*, generated about $4.0 billion in global revenue in 2018, with an annualized growth rate of 4.2%. That's pretty impressive for what many consider a niche undertaking. And, despite a downturn during the 2020 to 2021 pandemic, the global market for MMA equipment alone is expected to hit $565 million by 2022.

> A multibillion-dollar industry, the world's most popular martial arts include boxing, Brazilian jiu-jitsu, karate, taekwondo, MMA, kickboxing, Krav Maga, Muay Thai, kung fu, and aikido.

Traditional martial arts are a multibillion-dollar a year industry in their own right, yet world military expenditures are far larger, accounting for another $2.1 trillion or so a year. Advanced weapon systems obviously account for a large component of that expenditure, yet according to The World Bank, military forces represent nearly one percent of the global workforce (0.809% in 2018). Additionally, about 3.37% percent of global Gross Domestic Product (GDP) is spent on public order and safety (e.g., law enforcement and security) annually, which equated to about $2.8 trillion in 2020. Collectively, these are mind-boggling numbers!

Even if you have never studied a martial art, odds are good that you know somebody who does (or has), regardless of whether or not they have told you about their experience. Many martial artists are cautious when it comes to disclosing their training. In fact, when relaying the worst martial arts-related mistake they have ever made on our survey, several respondents simply replied, "Talking about it." This reticence helps stave off needless threats and challenges while reserving the element of surprise should a martial artist be called upon to utilize their skills in defense of themselves or others.

The industry is not just about self-defense or personal safety, however, people take up these fighting arts for a wide variety of reasons, everything from getting in shape to learning discipline to advancing their spiritual development, many of which have little to do with combat, though learning how to defend themselves is a common enough reason for folks get started. Oftentimes people who have suffered from traumatic events such as assault or rape, or survived debilitating illnesses such as cancer or Addison's disease, are able to find solace and build the strength necessary to take back control of their lives through the study and practice of martial arts. Regardless of why people begin their training, improved fitness, mental strength, discipline, grit, determination, and self-confidence are counted among the numerous benefits practitioners achieve from such endeavors.

So, we've teased you with a bit of data and definitions, shown you a measure of our industry, but what is this thing that we do really? Who are the individuals, the community behind those statistics?

Martial arts take on many different uniforms, trappings, and settings. As martial artists, we observe what we do from our own perspective. Sometimes we are able to perceive it as our friends, confidants, family members, or relatives might, but rarely. This pursuit is important to us or we wouldn't waste our time with it, yet it holds little meaning for folks who are not avid practitioners and is actively disdained by some. Outside observers may notice the results of our endeavors, but they do not have the frame of reference needed to truly "get" what we do and why we do it… which is, of course, why we wrote this book.

Think of it this way: both authors like strawberries. We like the taste of strawberries, and you may as well, yet we cannot be certain how a strawberry would taste to you, let alone to each other. We have an estimation, of course, believing that strawberries are sweet and fruity. Nevertheless, we cannot know exactly how the flavor of a strawberry sits upon your tongue unless we ask you about it. Similarly, we cannot know other martial artists' experiences without inviting practitioners to share observations from their martial journeys.

That's exactly what we did here, ask… We didn't just ask, however, we did so systematically, conducting a comprehensive study in order to get the full flavor of the martial arts experience from folks around the world who participate in traditional martial arts, Reality-Based Self-Defense (RBSD), fighting sports, military, and law enforcement disciplines.

> To understand the full flavor of the martial arts experience, with all its depth and nuance, we conducted a comprehensive, worldwide study of practitioners.

Our methodology involved a 40-question survey (which you can find in the back of this book) that was sent to a representative cross-section of practitioners from around the world. These questions included yes/know, multiple-choice, and essay responses to assure a holistic appraisal. We also collected demographic data to better frame the answers we received. Participants were encouraged to tie their name to their inputs, but also had the option of responding anonymously if they so desired. We honor the contributions of everyone who was willing to be counted by name in our rogues' gallery, and included photographs of those survey respondents who provided them, in the back of the book.

There is one chapter devoted to our analysis of each question on the survey, plus a couple of extra chapters on demographics of the participants who completed it. Additionally, interspersed between these chapters are the profiles of some of the more interesting and inspiring martial artists who provided us this information, along with a handful of their individual answers to various survey questions.

The questionnaire might appear somewhat random at first glance, especially in the order in which the queries were presented, yet it was designed to test our theories around a broad range of actions and attributes of martial artists. Some of the survey results were pretty much in line with our hypotheses, while others were truly eye-opening.

For example, we know that martial artists study violence yet wondered if as a community we might become more belligerent or aggressive through our studies. After all, as the old adage goes, "If all you have is a hammer, everything begins to look like a nail." Well, the data we gathered was conclusive. In fact, martial artists do not become more violent as a result of their training, the opposite is true. We are incarcerated at half the rate of the general population. And, as an added benefit, our analysis of this particular subject revealed actionable advice for parents and guardians looking for ways to assure better life outcomes for their children.

> Many of our survey results were eye-opening... For instance, martial artists study violence yet they do not become violent through their studies. In fact, they are incarcerated at half the rate of the general population.

Respondents ranged in age from 15 to 80. Some began training as a way to recover from violence or disease, others were attracted to the arts because of Bruce Lee, Jackie Chan, or the Teenaged Mutant Ninja Turtles (yeah, that's a real answer from our survey), some simply looked to get into better shape, and others started as a way to bond with their children. While these individual circumstances and experiences varied widely, on average these practitioners reported trying 5.79 different martial systems, ultimately achieving an average rank of approximately 3rd *dan* black belt or equivalent thereof (in systems where rank actually exists) in the one that represented their highest level of achievement.

These folks invested significant time and energy to accomplish what they did, sacrificing other ventures in favor of their martial arts training. This says a lot about the value that can be found by participating in these fighting arts.

At every stage in life there are things we wish we had known earlier, lessons that would have kept us from doing something we would later learn to regret as well as lessons that would have enabled us to accomplish something more easily or understand and appreciate it more fully. Whatever route led them into the martial arts, knowing what they know now 94.4% of our survey respondents reported that they would still travel that same path again. This means that there are important lessons for aspiring martial artists to learn from their examples. And, of course, there are also useful insights for more experienced practitioners to gather from their peers' journeys as well.

> Knowing what they know now, 94.4% of respondents stated that they would travel their same path again. There are valuable lessons to learn from their examples.

As you read the results of our analysis and meet some of our fellow practitioners, you may see yourself in the examples and conclusions. Certainly, you will gain a deeper appreciation for these disciplines along with a better understanding of why we in the martial arts community are attracted to these pursuits. And, you will discover some of the tactics that helped us become more successful in our endeavors. In absorbing these materials, you will discover a new light for your own martial arts adventure, one that more clearly illuminates your best path forward.

Whether you are considering trying martial arts for the first time, an experienced practitioner, or anywhere in between, we trust that you will find the results of our study enlightening, the insight into the world of the martial artist profound. You will come to know the mind of the martial artist, learning who we are, what we do, and why we do it in ways that have never been available before thanks to this comprehensive, worldwide investigation.

Ultimately you will discover that while everyone likes to think that they're special, the data indicates that in many ways martial artists actually are. Read on and you'll discover why the personal and societal benefits of our training are legion.

How does your system organize rank?

"When it comes to performance standards, it's not what you preach, it's what you tolerate."
Jocko Willink, American author, retired U.S. Navy SEAL officer

For a seemingly simple question, this one generated some of the widest ranging and most complex responses of our whole survey. Before we discuss our findings, let's set the stage with a short history lesson.

Japanese educator/athlete Jigoro Kano (1860–1938), the founder of judo, codified a system of wearing colored sashes or belts which was subsequently adopted by many other art forms around the world. His classifications distinguished between advanced practitioners and different levels of beginning and intermediate students. The *dan* (black belt) indicated advanced proficiency, whereas *kyu* (colored belts) indicated lower levels of expertise.

In Japanese-influenced martial arts, those who have earned black belt rank are called *yudansha* (which means *dan* recipients). The *kyu* degrees represent the varying levels of competency below *dan*, and are called *mudansha* (those not yet having received a black belt rank). Kano believed that students should appreciate that one's training was in no way complete simply because they had achieved a coveted black belt, emphasizing that the attainment of the *dan* rank merely symbolized the beginning of a practitioners true training. In other words, reaching black belt level simply meant that you had completed the foundational requirements necessary to embark upon a lifelong journey that would ultimately result in self-mastery.

> While there is no universal rank classification that spans across all martial arts systems, the belt system commonly used today was codified by professor Jigoro Kano in 1907.

After establishing his *Kodokan Dojo* (school) in Tokyo's Bunkyo ward, Kano distributed black sashes, which were worn around the training uniform of that era to his *yudansha*. Around 1907, this black sash was replaced with the *kuroi-obi*, or black belt, which became the standard that is still used in most martial systems today, even ones that historically did not have belts, sashes, or badges of rank. This is where that iconic image of a white uniform *gi* tied at the waist with a black belt actually came from.

In the beginning there were only white belts and black belts. Later addition of green and brown belts rounded out Kano's traditional ranking system. Nowadays it has become far more complicated with the addition of multiple colors, stripes, and gradations. While combinations are wide-ranging, and vary significantly amongst martial systems, the most common progression is white, yellow, green, blue, brown, black, *akashiro* (red/white), and red belts.

Let's contrast Kano's system with traditional Chinese *kung fu* programs like those utilized in *baguazhang, bajiquan, shaolin, tai-chi-quan, wing chun*, and their ilk. Historically, status in Chinese society was achieved through age, with the older practitioners generally held in higher regard than the younger ones. This was not codified, so there was no guarantee that any given individual would receive a certain status at some particular age, but there was usually a connection between age and rank.

In *shaolin*, for example, there were three stages of training: (1) secular disciple, (2) martial monk, and (3) master. Even though some schools use colored sashes now, none of these levels came with a distinctive indicator of rank on the practitioner's uniform back in the day. There were private distinctions that denoted the relationship between the teacher and individual students or groups of disciples. Generally, these distinctions were known within the school, but not indicated publicly. In certain instances, master martial artists would present signed scrolls that attested the skills and abilities of their students however.

> A structure of merit, such as a belt or rank system, helps in creating standards by which the skill progression of martial artists can be tracked.

Military and law enforcement organizations all use formal hierarchical systems too, with enlisted, non-commissioned officer, and commissioned officer ranks and various gradations within those categories. Fighting sports such as boxing, wrestling, and MMA, on the other hand, look to win and loss records rather than some sort of rank hierarchy. Since they segregate participants by weight class (e.g., flyweight, bantamweight, featherweight, cruiserweight, heavyweight, etc.) and gender to help assure competitiveness and safety, athletes can be graded according to their accomplishments, say landing in the top ten fighters in one's weight division. These sports also crown champions by division.

Turning to academia for a moment, doctoral degrees represent the highest educational levels attainable, providing graduates with the tools and training necessary to become involved with research that expands their chosen field of study. Doctor of Philosophy (Ph.D.) degrees are recognized for theoretical research whereas Doctor of Management (D.M.) degrees represent applied research. Students typically achieve these levels by completing ten or more years of advanced exploration. They may both represent the pinnacle of academic study, but can we really compare a Ph.D. in Medieval Portuguese Literature to a D.M. in Organizational Effectiveness? Likely not.

Similarly, we cannot truly compare a black belt in Brazilian *jiu-jitsu* with a *guru* in Filipino *eskrima*. For a field that encompasses any system or tradition of combat practiced for competition, cultural heritage, spiritual development, self-defense, military, or law enforcement applications, this whole rank thing can quickly become overwhelming.

There is no perfect benchmark with which to accurately compare across systems, styles, and schools. Nevertheless, by following a structure of merit such as a rank or belt system, senior practitioners have a way of monitoring the development and skill progression of their students, teaching them according to set standards. That's goodness despite our inability to precisely compare things from one martial art to another. So, while the question of rank is complex, the existence of rank in these various systems can be beneficial.

Martial Artist Profile – Iain Abernethy

Iain Abernethy is 50 years old and been training in karate since childhood. Iain's focus is on the modern-day application of the traditional art. He travels widely to teach seminars on kata *application, functional karate, and self-defense. Iain currently holds the rank of 7th* dan *black belt with the English Karate Federation, British Combat Association, and World Combat Association. One of the world's leading exponents of applied karate, Iain regularly writes for the United Kingdom's leading martial arts magazines and he is a member of the Combat Hall of Fame. He has written several books on applied karate and produced numerous instructional videos. Iain lives in northwest England, very close to the border with Scotland. His website is www.iainabernethy.co.uk.*

When you were a kid, what did you want to be when you grew up?

"According to my mum, I originally wanted to be a tramp because homeless people did what they wanted and didn't have to go to work. A somewhat idealistic view of life on the streets, but I have stuck true to the idea of living life on my own terms. Aged 16, I wanted to be a fulltime martial arts instructor. I got another job to pay the bills while I grew up and developed my skills. Aged 32, I finally felt ready enough to make the step. The last 18 years have been awesome. There's no other job I'd rather have."

What's the worst martial arts-related mistake you have ever made?

"Taking it way too seriously as a child/teenager. My self-esteem, at that point in my life, was hugely dependent on my performance at the previous training session. Martial arts were the first thing in my life I can recall being good at, and therefore my self-worth became totally bound up in them. It was not healthy, and I am pleased to say I eventually learnt that the key thing is consistency over time so that your bad days are not as bad and good days are better."

What is the best single piece of advice you were ever given?

"My grandfather told me, 'When making anything, the first thing you need to make is the mess.' He was a carpenter of some local renown and said it referring to the sawdust, offcuts, etc. that would be all over the place when making anything. However, I saw a life lesson in it. Whenever I completely mess up something new, I hear his words and think, 'Great! That's the mess out of the way! Now onto step two.' It helped me try new things without worrying about the initial outcome."

For good or ill, what was the biggest impact of your martial arts training on your life?

"The people I have met through them and the richness they have given to my life. The martial arts have given me a social circle of very special people who I have learnt lots from and who are fun to spend time with. Furthermore, martial arts have a very wide appeal and hence don't just attract people from a given part of society. It's good to spend time with people with very different backgrounds, outlooks on life, professions, lifestyles, aspirations, etc."

> "The martial arts have given me a social circle of very special people who I have learnt lots from and who are fun to spend time with... people with very different backgrounds, outlooks on life, professions, lifestyles, aspirations, etc."

What single event of the past changed the world for the worst?

"I think I'd have to defer to my grandfather's experience and hard-won wisdom. A super tough guy who was at both Dunkirk and D-Day, he was wounded numerous times and was the sole survivor of one encounter. He was a great storyteller who was never coy about sharing the horrors of war along with the tales of comradery and bravery. He once said to me, 'Whoever invented the gun should have had the thing blow up in his face (profanities omitted).' He was not a pacifist, and neither am I. However, I would agree that the industrialization of war has led to horrors undreamed of in the days of swords and spears."

Knowing what you know now, would you do it all over again?

"Definitely! The bottom line is that it has been, and continues to be, great fun! That's not to say it's all been fun, well not at the time at least. After the hardship there is a sense of triumph and accomplishment, which is also fun. I'd not be who I am without the martial arts. While friends work the '9 to 5' with the same people, doing the same things every day, I have met people from all walks of life from all over the globe, I have travelled widely, and I have plenty of good stories to tell. I owe it all to the martial arts."

What is the highest rank you have ever achieved in the martial arts?

"Your art is what you do when no one can tell you exactly how to do it. Your art is the act of taking personal responsibility, challenging the status quo, and changing people."

Seth Godin, American author

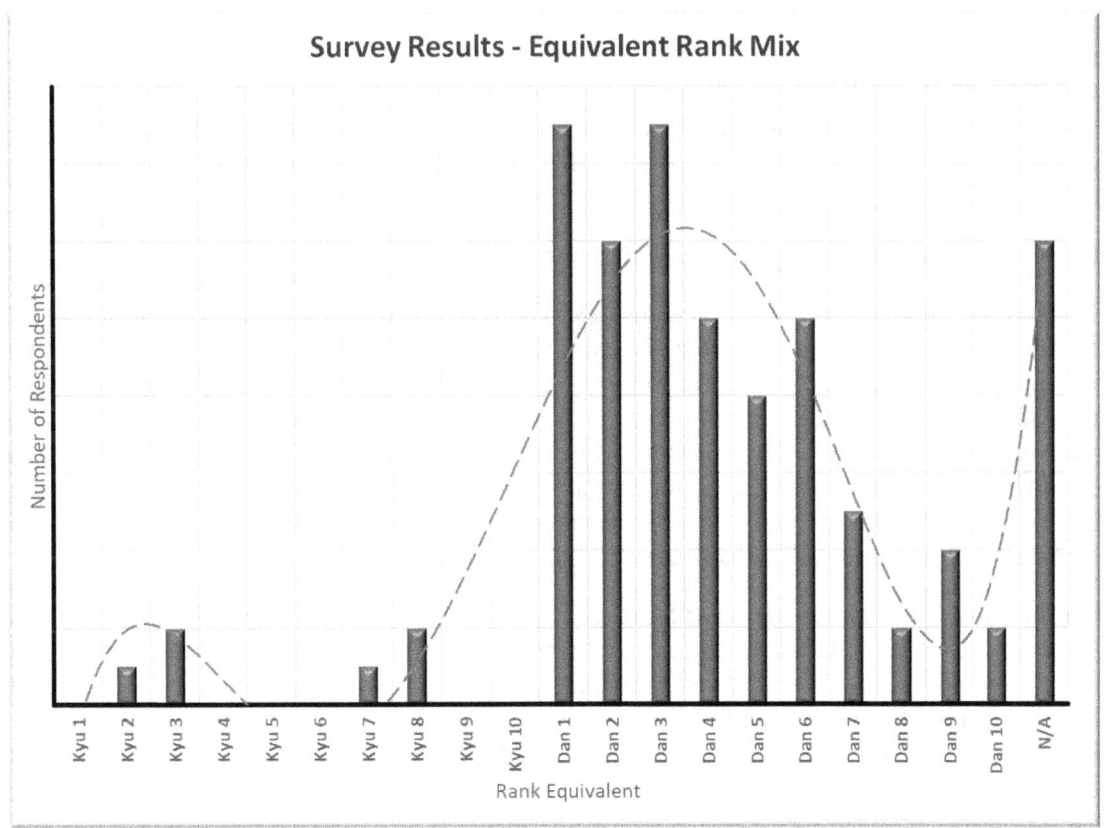

If we look to any given martial arts school or franchise that uses a rank system, we tend to find a pyramid when it comes to levels achieved by the practitioners who train there. The majority of students will be counted in the lower ranks, often white and yellow belts or equivalent thereof. As folks ascend through the ranks, and the colors of their signifiers such as belts or patches get darker, the population gets smaller and smaller, with only a handful of instructors or single individual holding the highest rank at the top.

This clustering of larger numbers at lower ranks is not unique to martial arts. We can perceive this same dynamic in any organization. In the army there are far more privates and non-commissioned officers than generals. In the business world too, there more frontline workers than vice presidents and in most instances only a single CEO (Chief Executive Officer).

Part of the reason for this dynamic is that white/yellow belts, privates, and frontline workers have more turnover than brown belts or black belts, generals, and vice presidents.

The second group, those holding higher rank, is comprised of people who are dedicated to a path. These folks aren't dipping their toes in the proverbial water, searching for a direction or profession, or dabbling in something that might be interesting for a moment or two, they have figured out exactly what they want and have a reasonable understanding of how to earn it. And, once identified, they are willing to pay the price necessary to achieve their goal.

Let's use a historical example to tease this out…

Thomas Jonathan "Stonewall" Jackson (1824 – 1863) served as a Confederate General during the United States Civil War. Jackson was beloved by his commanders, adored by his men, and feared by the Union forces he fought against. He played a prominent role in a majority of the engagements that took place in the Eastern Theater of Civil War. Jackson reportedly earned his nickname at the First Battle of Bull Run in July 1861 when he rushed his troops forward to close a gap in the line against a ferocious Union attack. Upon observing Jackson, one of his fellow generals exclaimed, "Look men, there is Jackson standing like a stone wall!" and the moniker stuck.

Unlike most generals of that era, Jackson was born of simple means. Beyond a lack of finances growing up, Jackson experienced several deaths in his family. When he was just two years old, his six-year-old sister and father both died of Typhoid fever. His mother Julia was forced to sell off their family processions to pay off their considerable debts before dying of the disease herself, leaving the remaining three children orphaned. Jackson was raised by an uncle in the town of Jackson's Mill, located in present-day West Virginia.

In 1842 Jackson was accepted to the United States Military Academy at West Point. His acceptance there was based on the advocacy of a member of the United States Congress to whom Jackson had ridden several days on horseback to plead his case for endorsement. Upon entry into West Point, it became clear Jackson was academically and socially behind the majority of his classmates. To solve this problem, he studied more and worked harder than his peers, applying himself to rigorous memorization after being shamed in the classroom for his lack of knowledge. He was even mocked by other cadets for using his personal time to practice formation marching by himself, yet managed to graduate because of these extraordinary efforts.

Like Jackson struggling through West Point, martial artists with longevity in the training hall know what they want and are willing to do whatever it takes to achieve it. They relentlessly pursue their goals, paying attention in every class, practicing outside of school hours, studying books and videos to learn about their art, keeping notes and training journals, work through injuries, and overcoming plateaus in their training in order to advance. It's arduous work, but this approach assures achievement irrespective of the practitioner's inherent physical talent or athletic ability.

> **Survey participants reported achieving an average rank of approximately 3rd degree black belt (or equivalent) in the system representing their highest level of achievement.**

The people who stay in the martial arts beyond their first black belt rank experience a similar fall-off in participation. In other words, the advanced practitioner population is similar to the colored belts population in its pyramidal shape. There are more practitioners in the lower levels of these advanced ranks such that the number of *shodan* (first degree black belts) is significantly larger than the number of *nidan* (second degree black belts), which in turn has more membership than *sandan* (third degree black belts), and so on up the ladder.

Most traditional martial arts top out at *judan*, the 10th degree of black belt, with ranks above *godan* (fifth degree black belt) bestowed to honor a practitioner's lifetime of contribution to their system or style. Oftentimes there are special titles such as master, senior master, chief master, or grandmaster that come with the higher ranks too. For example, in Japanese-influenced martial arts these honorifics often include *shihan* (master instructor), *renshi* (polished expert), *kiyoshi* (teacher of teachers), *hanshi* (head master of a style), and *shodai-soke* (founder of a style).

Practitioners in our survey reported achieving an average rank of approximately 3rd *dan* black belt or equivalent thereof (in systems where rank actually exists) in the one that represented their highest level of achievement. This rank denotes at least nine to ten years of experience in most systems, sometimes considerably more.

You see, most systems have minimum time requirements between each rank. For example, while it is possible after four years of studying karate to earn *shodan* rank, the lowest level of black belt, separation between black belt ranks is based on years equivalent to the next rank. For example, the minimum time between *shodan* and the second degree of black belt, *nidan*, is two years. The minimum time between *nidan* and *sandan*, the third *dan* rank, is three years. So, to go from *shodan* (1st degree) to *sandan* (3rd degree) takes a minimum of five (2+3) years, typically a lot longer unless you are a gifted athlete who has a lot of time to train both inside and outside the *dojo* (training hall). Using the minimum time between ranks formula, a *karateka* who started training at age twenty would be eligible for *rokudan* (6th degree black belt) at age forty-five. *Judan* (10th degree black belt), the highest rank attainable, could happen somewhere around age seventy.

Given the length of time it takes to earn advanced rank, and the high dropout rate we tend to find in the lower levels of progression, we expected to observe the same pyramid shape in ranks achieved by our survey respondents as we find in the broader community. Nevertheless, we discovered that while results varied widely, they were skewed pretty far to the right as can be seen in the chart at the beginning of this chapter. While it could be that we oversampled overachievers, and in some instances clearly did, this appears to be related to the length of time our survey respondents spent training in the martial arts too. When we participate long enough, strive hard enough, advanced rank eventually comes with the undertaking.

Law enforcement and military service does things similarly. For example, if one were to join the United States Army as an enlisted soldier, that person would graduate basic training at the rank of E-1. To achieve promotion to E-2, private second-class, takes six additional months of service. Another year of service is required to receive promotion to E-3, private second class. Two more years of service and at least six months of time in paygrade is required to become an E-4 specialist.

The rank of corporal is level E-4 too, but simultaneously the lowest noncommissioned officer rank, and to qualify for that promotion takes 24 months in service and six months of time in grade, though in some instances a commanding officer could expedite the promotion and award it in only 18 months. From there, promotions become harder and a bit more complicated, requiring completion of certain educational requirements and leadership courses, time in grade, time in service, promotion point scores, and unit commander recommendations. Under this formula, minimum time to be promoted to E-5 sergeant is 36 months, and E-6 staff sergeant 84 months, and so on up the chain… Commissioned officer ranks have similar time in service, time in grade, educational, leadership, and other advancement requirements.

In any martial system that uses ranks, be it a traditional style, law enforcement agency, or modern military, promotions are only awarded to those demonstrating certain competencies and capabilities. In other words, advancement takes significant investment. It is earned through hard work, dedication, and mastery. The fact that our survey respondents have achieved the levels they did reflects an unusual level of commitment and perseverance for which they should be applauded.

Martial Artist Profile – Vicky Stormo

Before retiring from law enforcement after 35 years of service, Vicky Stormo was Chief of Police at the University of Washington Police Department. She previously worked as a consultant and Deputy Chief for the Oregon Health Science University Department of Public Safety as well as a Lieutenant in the Albuquerque Police Department. Still active in the community, she is President of the Behind the Badge Foundation (https://behindthebadgefoundation.org/), an organization whose mission is to honor law enforcement officers who have died or suffered serious injury in the line of duty. The foundation provides immediate and ongoing support to families, agencies, and communities in times of critical need, and also maintains the Washington State Law Enforcement Memorial which commemorates the lives and dedication of officers who died in service to citizens of that state. Vicky holds a Bachelor's of Science degree in Criminology from the University of Albuquerque and Masters in Public Administration from the University of New Mexico, and is also a graduate of the Leadership Albuquerque program. She earned the New Mexico YWCA Woman on the Move Award and the New Mexico Commission on the Status of Women Trailblazer award. She is also a past president of the National Association of Women Law Enforcement Executives. A black belt in Chinese Kenpo, she taught karate from 1973 to 1996.

What is the best compliment you have ever received?

"I was told I was like a glacier rider, from an executive coach. I had become a law enforcement executive, a chief of police. The executive coach listened to my story as a small female in a male-dominated occupation, moving through the ranks and now as a chief of police. Karate gave me confidence that no matter my size, with courage, determination, self-discipline and perseverance I could do anything. I was taught to be patient, assess, analyze, and consider the consequences. I used that in making major changes in a department, but also learning to adjust if results did not meet the goals. Change was slow, like a glacier, moving to make changes without most people realizing the terrain was changing. The coach pictured me on that glacier with ropes guiding the way."

What's the worst martial arts-related mistake you have ever made?

"I honestly don't have any martial arts-related mistakes. I gained confidence in myself through my training to avoid any mistakes. Through my personal life and law enforcement experience of 35 years, I never used my martial arts in a way that would reflect poorly on myself, my *dojo*, or the law enforcement agencies I worked for. I never had a complaint of excessive use-of-force filed against me while working in law enforcement. The skills I obtained through my training allowed me to properly assess the situation and respond appropriately. Yes, in some situations it required physical force, but it was done efficiently and effectively with little or no injuries and no injuries to myself nor others."

For good or ill, what was the biggest impact of your martial arts training on your life?

"I am a small female who had a desire to help others though law enforcement and life experiences. I wanted to be skillful, have confidence in my abilities, learn my strengths and weaknesses, and be ready to handle any conflicts without resorting to physical violence and causing injury to myself or others. I knew that I would have challenges functioning and being accepted in a male-dominated occupation. I wanted to be as prepared and as strong as I could be to meet the challenge. After getting lessons and teaching for 5 years, I was accepted into my dream occupation and served 35 years. I never had a complaint of excessive use of force. I learned to treat people with dignity and respect no matter their circumstances. Martial arts made me whole as a person. I taught martial arts for about 23 years and hope that I helped others."

Why did you start training?

"I started training to build self-confidence, avoid victimization after having been raped, develop skills to protect myself and others, and discipline."

> "I started training to build self-confidence, avoid victimization after having been raped, develop skills to protect myself and others, and discipline... Martial arts made me whole as a person. I taught martial arts for about 23 years and hope that I helped others."

If you could go back in time, what advice would you give to your teenage self?

"Things that you do as a teenager do have an impact on you later in life! I was a pretty tough cookie and I was out there to dispel any disbelief in my skills and abilities. Even though I was a small female, I was very active and athletic. I rode motorcycles, worked five jobs at one time to pay for college, ran long distance, did push-ups and sit ups daily, coached a girls track team, and more. I was reckless at nineteen and ended up being raped. That's how I ended up taking karate. The rape affected my relationships with men. I didn't tell anyone until I met my late husband (in my mid-40s). I never asked for help. I didn't want anyone to think I was vulnerable. I still do a lot of risky things, but I think about the consequences of whatever I do."

Knowing what you know now, would you do it all over again?

"I would not have changed anything. Martial arts gave me skills and confidence to be the best person I could be in my personal life and career in law enforcement. I had no lows in my training. Being a small female, I had to overcome any misperceptions that to be a good martial artist or police officer meant that you had to be able to conquer all through fighting skills, no matter their size. Obviously, that is not realistic and definitely would not work for me. It was much more than that, such as learning there are ways to solve potential threatening situations through other means than just hands on. It was also about respecting others and helping them overcome life's challenges. It is about being disciplined and in control of yourself. Being involved in martial arts, not just training, but teaching as well, was the best thing I ever did."

How many different martial systems have you tried?

"I nonetheless caught myself and realized I had always devoted my time and attention to people who fascinated me and were pleasant, who engaged my sympathy, and that as a result I was seeing society like the moon, always from one side."

Aleksandr Solzhenitsyn, Russian novelist, philosopher, and historian

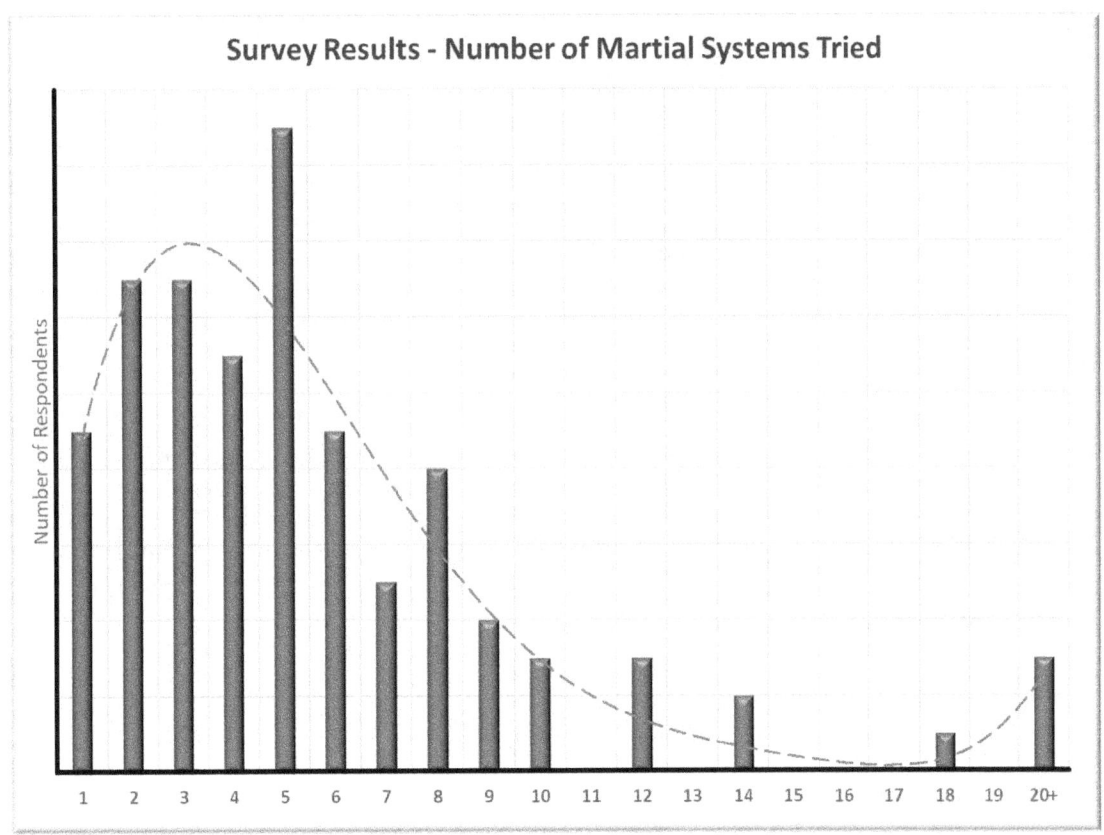

Most martial artists who achieve rank at the higher levels have experience with several different systems and styles. In fact, practitioners in our study reported trying 5.79 different martial systems on average. Sure, some folks find a great fit in the first school they try and stick with it for their entire career, but since our needs and interests tend to evolve over time and many schools struggle to stay in business, it is unusual to do so. We could not find reliable worldwide statistics, but according to the U.S. Census Bureau people in the United States can expect to move 11.7 times during their lifetime, which in many instances necessitates changing systems not just finding a new instructor or school simply due to options available in one's new location.

In much the same way as a thirty-year-old woman tends to have a stronger immune system than a two-year-old child, volume comes from time and exposure. In other words, the longer we participate, the more martial arts we are going to be exposed to. Even if we do not lose interest, move, change schools, or whatever, most of us participate in seminars, tournaments, and other activities where we are able to get to know folks who perform different arts which we may find interesting enough to try for some period of time.

Within the same art, we may experience multiple different styles too. For example, there are more than 75 different types of karate practiced today, with *Chito Ryu*, *Goju Ryu*, *Gosoku Ryu*, *Isshin Ryu*, *Kyokushin*, *Shindo Jinen Ryu*, *Shito Ryu*, *Shorin Ryu*, *Shotokan*, *Shukokai Ryu*, *Shuri Ryu*, *Uechi Ryu*, and *Wado Ryu* counted among the more popular styles. While they all perform punching, kicking, grappling, throwing, and other empty-hand techniques, some include weapons forms in their curriculum while others do not. And, virtually every instructor will have a slightly different focus even when sticking to the same general lesson plan too. It's a matter of brain chemistry and teaching style, among other factors.

Further, since many of these disparate martial systems are similar, they immediately become more accessible. Once we understand the fundamentals of one, we can more readily approach another. These systems often get explored outside of a practitioner's core practice where they are considered "shoulder" styles. This means that they are not primary, they are not the head or the core, but rather lie to the left or the right on a shoulder, so we do not have to give up our current system or style in order to give them a try. There can be great value in this.

> Martial artists rarely stick with a single system or style throughout their journey. Survey participants reported trying 5.79 different arts on average.

An example might be a karate practitioner not choosing another karate style to study, but rather choosing a stick-fighting system such as *arnis*. *Arnis* would be the shoulder style. Karate originated in Okinawa and Japan whereas *arnis* comes from the Philippines, yet these two martial arts styles overlap. They are similar enough to be comprehensible to practitioners, but different enough to be complementary. In other words, we're looking at empty-hand karate versus weapon-first *arnis*, yet many karate systems include *kobudo* weapon forms and *arnis* has empty-hand drills in its curriculum.

Variety is an important component of the learning process. Even if a martial artist's instructor is an excellent teacher, their students will often reach important epiphanies or break through plateaus in their training after experiencing another instructor or peer's perspective on how things could or should be done. No matter what our level of experience, we can benefit from exposure to a variety of teaching styles and systems, so visiting other schools or taking broad-based seminars from time to time is beneficial.

While we may move around a bit until we find a martial system that both resonates and helps us fulfill our learning goals and objectives, and then stick to our core for the remainder of our martial journey, adoption of shoulder styles is valuable. After all, to paraphrase English poet William Cowper (1731–1800), variety is the very spice of life, that gives it all its flavors.

If you did not practice the martial art you are involved in now, what other martial art(s) would you do?

"The only journey is the one within."
Rainer Maria Rilke, Austrian poet and novelist

Our hypothesis in asking this question was that since martial artists strive to continuously challenge and improve themselves, we would find that most respondents would select a shoulder style, a system that was different than the one they currently practiced. For example, strikers, that is folks who practice striking arts like karate, taekwondo, or boxing, might branch out into a grappling art like judo, Brazilian *jiu-jitsu*, or wrestling to gain a broader skillset. In large part, this proved to be the case.

We also found some linkage between respondents' age and a preponderance toward exploring softer styles or internal arts like *qigong, taijiquan* or yoga, which may be related to overall wear and tear on the body, or a desire to focus more on fitness and health. Certainly, when we looked into what superpower survey respondents wished they had in a later chapter, we found that many of the older practitioners wanted various types of healing powers, though evidence of correlation here is somewhat less clear.

As discussed in the previous chapter, practitioners may change systems or styles because of evolving interests or desires, or simply because they settled on practicing the only martial art they could find in their local area after their school went under or they or their instructor moved. This means that some respondents answered this question by reverting back to a style they had previously enjoyed but for whatever reason were unable to continue practicing.

Valuable insight into this question came from *Black Belt Magazine* Hall of Fame member Hock Hochheim who wrote in his survey response, "After decades, I find all martial arts to be one or two-dimensional, therefore I am not interested enough to fully 'do,' other ones, just filter and experiment with for essentials." This demonstrates that more experienced practitioners seek value, often adopting techniques that can fill gaps in their knowledge or shore up deficiencies in their skill rather than looking to any particular art or system. Part of this is because martial styles are legion, with significant commonality and overlap amongst strategies, methods, and tactics.

> **Striving to improve themselves, martial artists often seek out contrasting systems. Their goal in doing so is to shore up of weaknesses in their training.**

Combat arts have existed throughout the history. The highest purse sport in ancient Greece's first Olympic Games in 776 B.C. was *pankration*, a martial art that translates as "all powers fighting." Alexander the Great's *pankratiasts* spread their fighting form throughout the many regions that his armies conquered such as Egypt, Persia, Syria, Babylonia, Media, and India.

Over time diverse fighting arts took on unique characteristics of different cultures, especially in Egypt, Turkey, and central Asia. The principles behind Asian martial arts are believed to have spread from Turkey to India, where they were further developed into sophisticated arts. Once codified, these principles spread through from China to Okinawa and then to Japan and beyond, heavily influencing the indigenous fighting arts in those regions. Eventually they spread out into the Western world as well.

Karate, for instance, was first brought to the United States and Europe after World War II. Military personnel stationed in Okinawa during that period were among the first

Westerners to learn the art. Returning home after their tours, they were anxious to teach the exciting new fighting system that they had learned and helped popularize it. Modern combatives and RBSD often adopted and evolved from these traditional styles, incorporating shooting, knifework, stick fighting and the like to create a more holistic curriculum.

Martial arts are not exclusively an Asian practice, of course. Western styles evolved separately yet with many parallels, starting in ancient world with Olympic arts like wrestling and boxing, before growing to encompass codified systems for swords, daggers, darts, staffs, bows, and various other forms of armed and unarmed combat over time. In fact, one of the oldest surviving manuscripts covering the art of self-defense was a sword-and-buckler manual written by a German priest in the early 13th century.

Looking to Europe for a moment, Donald McBane (1664–1732) was one of Scotland's greatest warriors. He served in the military, fought over 100 duels, and founded a school of swordsmanship, leaving behind a manual called *The Expert Sword-Man's Companion* which he wrote in 1732 shortly before he died. Another interesting character of that time period was Joseph Bologne, Chevalier de Saint-Georges. Even though he was born the son of a white nobleman and an African slave, he grew up to became the most celebrated fencing master of 18th Century France.

Martial arts were popular with both commoners and aristocrats alike, with former U.S. Presidents, Abraham Lincoln (1809–1865), Andrew Jackson (1767–1845), Chester Arthur (1829–1886), Franklin Pierce (1804–1869), George Washington (1732–1799), James Garfield (1831–1881), Ulysses S. Grant (1822–1885), and Zachary Taylor (1784–1850) all being accomplished wrestlers. Theodore Roosevelt (1858–1919) studied judo, Howard Taft (1857–1930) was a Yale wrestling champion, Dwight D. Eisenhower (1890–1969) both boxed and wrestled, and Gerald Ford (1913–2006) was a boxing coach in the Navy during World War II. Russian President Vladimir Putin holds black belts in Kyokushin and judo, former Canadian Prime Minister Pierre Trudeau (1919–2000) was a black belt in judo, Croatian President Zoran Milanovic is a skilled boxer, and Jamaican's first female Prime Minister Portia Simpson Miller is also an accomplished boxer.

Clearly martial arts are both bread and deep, with hundreds of systems and styles to choose from And, as our survey demonstrates, there is value in spending time with more than one.

Martial Artist Profile – Christian Wedewardt

Christian was born in 1974, started to learn karate with age of 13, and never stopped training. In 2022 this added-up to 34 years. In the beginning he was a competition fighter and won some titles. Years later he decided to become a teacher. This is what he does today and love so much, spreading the fire for our martial art: karate! In 2008 he established Karate Praxis (www.karatepraxis.com). He and his team teach worldwide a karate system which is based on traditional roots yet offered in a modern way, as he says, in modern tradition. He and his team transfer the usual "3k" structure (kihon, kata, and kumite), which translates as fundamentals, forms, and fighting/sparring) into a wholistic program based on practical application of every aspect in the syllabus. Christian firmly believes that karate should be back on the shortlist for all those who want to learn a martial art. Karate is an original and immensely valuable martial art, which is unfortunately widely outperformed by new hybrid-systems.

What is the best single piece of advice you were ever given?

"My best friend and karate-teacher, Ludwig, told me to slow down in my race for changes in karate and every now and then to take look back, relax and see how little seeds have already become plants. Then he said the most important thing: 'You've got friends around you. Dare to ask for help if needed. You don't have to do everything and always alone!'"

When you were a kid, what did you want to be when you grew up?

"I wanted to become a policeman. Doing good. Serving the community. I did everything to fulfill this dream. I was best in class in school and did great in the assessment-center for becoming a policeman. After this 2-day assessment it was the doctor who told me, my left eye was to poor for getting access to this job. So, I became a salesman."

For good or ill, what was the biggest impact of your martial arts training on your life?

"Being a black belt has provided me two chances for good employment. I became aware later that the Human Resources departments chose me because they thought a rather young blackbelt in karate would be diligent, honest, and reliable. And I meet my wife on a seminar!"

What is the best compliment you have ever received?

"Hmm… Okay, there are two sides to answer. Personal life: My wife once said, 'I love you anyway!' and my son said, 'I want to be like you!' In my martial arts life, someone said to me after a seminar, 'Having seen this kind of karate you taught today, there is no way back to 3k (*kihon, kata, kumite*) karate. Thank you so much!'"

> "I became aware later that the Human Resources departments chose me because they thought a rather young blackbelt in karate would be diligent, honest, and reliable."

What is your guilty pleasure?

"As a typical German, I like beer a lot. So, I do drink beer probably too often, but not too much in quantity. Knowing about the danger I do always keep an eye on my consumption."

Knowing what you know now, would you do it all over again?

"I did my 6th degree blackbelt test within the German karate organization and tried to deliver everything in a 20-minute timeframe. Of course, I didn't good on this path. It was too much information I wanted to transfer, too much application… Just too much. If I had to do it again, I would concentrate on some examples keep it short and easy and instead of trying to cover everything just show some highlights and leave room for questions."

What is your Myers-Briggs personality type?

"Odd about humans: they've been trying to categorize and understand themselves ever since ever. Know what? When it comes to personalities, almost every philosophizer has decided on four dominant types. For Hippocrates it was Sanguine, Choleric, Phlegmatic and Melancholic. Jung decided on Feeler, Thinker, Sensor and Intuitor. Keirsey calls them Idealists, Rationals, Guardians and Artisans."

Future Now, a consulting group

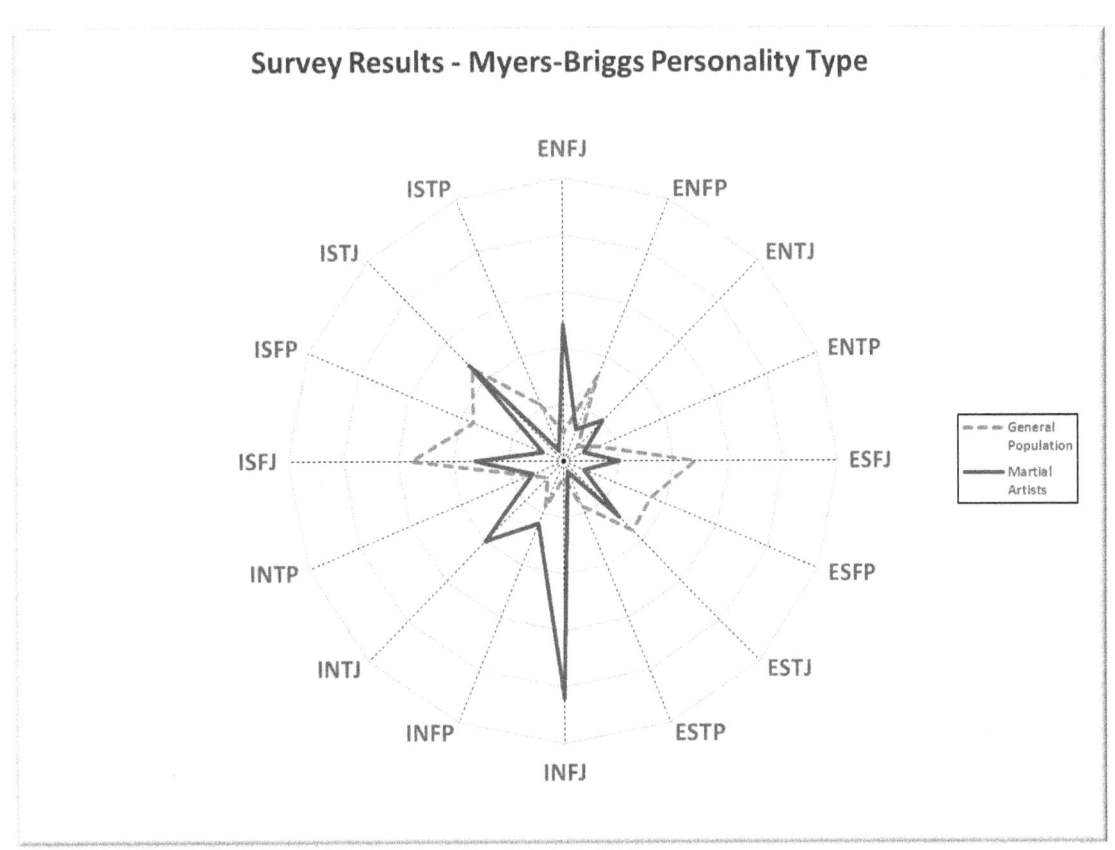

The Myers-Briggs Type Indicator (MBTI), created by Katherine Cook Briggs (1875–1968) and Isabel Briggs Myers (1897–1980) is a useful tool to help us understand the role of individual differences in personality type and the implications thereof. Leveraging an understanding of our personal predilections can help supports our emotional well-being, athletic performance, and professional goals by leveraging scientific insight into our strengths and weaknesses. This information can also be used better communicate with those we regularly interact with such as family, friends, bosses, coworkers, students, and teachers.

Scores obtained from the MBTI analysis indicate a person's preference on each of four dichotomous dimensions, leading to sixteen individual combinations which can then be summarized into four affinity groups. These dimensions include Extraversion (E) versus Introversion (I), Intuition (N) versus Sensing (S), Thinking (T) versus Feeling (F), and Perceiving (P) versus Judging (J). If you do not already know your personality type and care to find out you can take a free test and gather insight into your results at www.16personalities.com.

Our respondents represent every personality combination imaginable, yet weigh in more heavily toward the Intuition (N) side of the N-S continuum and the judging (J) side of the P-J scale. Since intuition and judgement are important attributes of situational awareness and rapid decision-making under stress, it makes sense that folks with these proclivities might be attracted to martial arts. In fact, as a community we appeal to a higher than the normal distribution of Diplomat and Analyst personality types, but fewer than average Sentinel and Explorer personality types. Here's a quick, high-level summary to get the gist of what this means:

- **Diplomats** (share N and F traits) – Compassionate and caring, these personality types are driven to better understand themselves and others. They would rather cooperate than compete in most things. These folks tend to be motivated by principles over practicality, often striving to make a lasting difference in the world. Martial artists exceed the general population in this category by 25.5%.

- **Analysts** (share N and T traits) – Logical, enterprising, and introspective, these personalities are relentless self-improvers who are driven to learn, understand, and create. These folks tend to be independent and socially selective, with a small circle of close friends rather than numerous acquaintances. Martial artists exceed the general population in this category by 9.6%.

- **Sentinels** (share S and J traits) – Hardworking and dutiful, these personality types are self-motivated, seeking order, security, steady progress, and stability. These folks can be counted upon to deliver results, but prefer to avoid unpredictable situations, chaos, or drama. The general population exceeds martial artists in this category by 14.1%.

- **Explorers** (share S and P traits) – Curious and fun-seeking, these personality types find impulsiveness thrilling, live for change, and are drawn to uncertainty. These folks prefer group activities over individual pursuits. The general population exceeds martial artists in this category by 21%.

These four categories are further broken down into four personality types each. We are only skimming the surface of what each means here when we summarize as follows:

Diplomats:

- Advocates (INFJ) – Having a deep sense of idealism and integrity, these individuals stand up for what they believe is right and take concrete steps to leave their mark on the world. Martial artists exceed the general population in this brain type by 19.5%.

- Mediators (INFP) – Idealistic and empathic, these individuals are true to their authentic selves and often feel a call to help others. Martial artists exceed the general population in this brain type by 1.6%.
- Protagonists (ENFJ) – Born leaders, these individuals channel their passion and charisma to inspire others, speaking in ways that resonate and create action. Martial artists exceed the general population in this brain type by 9.5%.
- Campaigners (ENFP) – Free spirits, these individuals are outgoing, upbeat, and open-minded, devoted to enriching relationships in their lives. Martial artists are 5.1% less than the general population in this brain type.

Analysts:

- Architect (INTJ) – Rational, strategic, and quick-witted, these individuals have a thirst for knowledge, deriving esteem from mental acuity. Martial artists exceed the general population in this brain type by 7.9%.
- Logician (INTP) – Vigorous intellectuals, these individuals love to analyze patterns and contemplate deep questions, feeling at home in the realm of logic and rationality. Martial artists are 0.3% less than the general population in this brain type.
- Commander (ENTJ) – Charismatic and confident, these individuals project authority, believing that with time and resources they can accomplish near any goal. Martial artists exceed the general population in this brain type by 3.2%.
- Debater (ENTP) – The ultimate "devil's advocates," these individuals look at arguments from all sides, questioning prevailing thought, and thriving on a quest for knowledge. Martial artists are 1.2% lower than the general population in this brain type.

Sentinels:

- Logistician (ISTJ) – Known for integrity, practical logic, and tireless dedication to duty, these individuals use facts and data to determine their course of action. Martial artists exceed the general population in this brain type by 0.4%.
- Defender (ISFJ) – Desiring above all to do good, these individuals are altruistic perfectionists who are driven to do everything they can to support and secure those they care about. Martial artists are 5.8% lower than the general population in this brain type.
- Executive (ESTJ) – Drawn toward tradition and order, these individuals are eager to help, taking pride in bringing people together to accomplish worthy goals. Martial artists are 1.7% less than the general population in this brain type.
- Consul (ESFJ) – Social creatures, these individuals have a strong moral compass, taking responsibility to do the right things in an altruistic way. Martial artists are 7.0% less than the general population in this brain type.

Explorers:

- Virtuoso (ISTP) – Known for their strong sense of realism, these individuals are drawn to examination and experimentation, exploring the world through their sense of vision and touch. Martial artists are 4.4% lower than the general population in this brain type.

- Adventurer (ISFP) – Often pushing the limits of social convention, these individuals are inspired by new experiences with colors, sensations, and connections. Martial artists are 6.8% lower than the general population in this brain type.

- Entrepreneur (ESTP) – Smart and energetic, these individuals are known to leap before they look, often adopting risky behaviors in search of passion, pleasure, and drama. Martial artists are 3.3% less than the general population in this brain type.

- Entertainer (ESFP) – Encouraging, and generous with their time, these individuals are exceedingly passionate, often getting caught up in the excitement of the moment. Martial artists are 6.5% less than the general population in this brain type.

> A higher than the normal distribution of Diplomat and Analyst personality types, but lower than average number of Sentinel and Explorer personalities are attracted to pursuing the martial arts.

While anyone can become a martial artist, folks who are drawn to our community more often than not set high expectations for themselves and others. We are introspective, aware of our shortcomings. We relentlessly pursue self-improvement, and are more driven than the norm to learn, understand, and create. We tend toward measured risk-taking, balancing between stability and impulsiveness. Truly unpretentious, we oftentimes have trouble bragging about ourselves and our accomplishments, believing that our actions speak for themselves even when they go unnoticed. We are independent-minded and motivated by principles, with a strong sense of right and wrong, often seeking to serve causes that are bigger than ourselves.

This brain chemistry is why the qualities found in the ancient samurai code of conduct, the *bushido*, often resonate with martial arts practitioners irrespective of what system(s) or style(s) they practice or the country in which it originated. Created by the Japanese warrior class, with influence from Buddhism and Confucianism, the *bushido* evolved and morphed a bit over time, ultimately teaching that, among other things, warriors should train not only in warfare but also in civility. Aspiring to the virtues of the *bushido* such as courage, honor, justice, compassion, respect, integrity, loyalty, and self-control is good advice for practitioners of any fighting art. And that, in large part, is exactly what we do.

What is your somatotype, (a) ectomorph, (b) mesomorph, or (c) endomorph?

"Imperfections are beautiful details viewed from a negative perspective."
Etheria Divine, Finnish artist

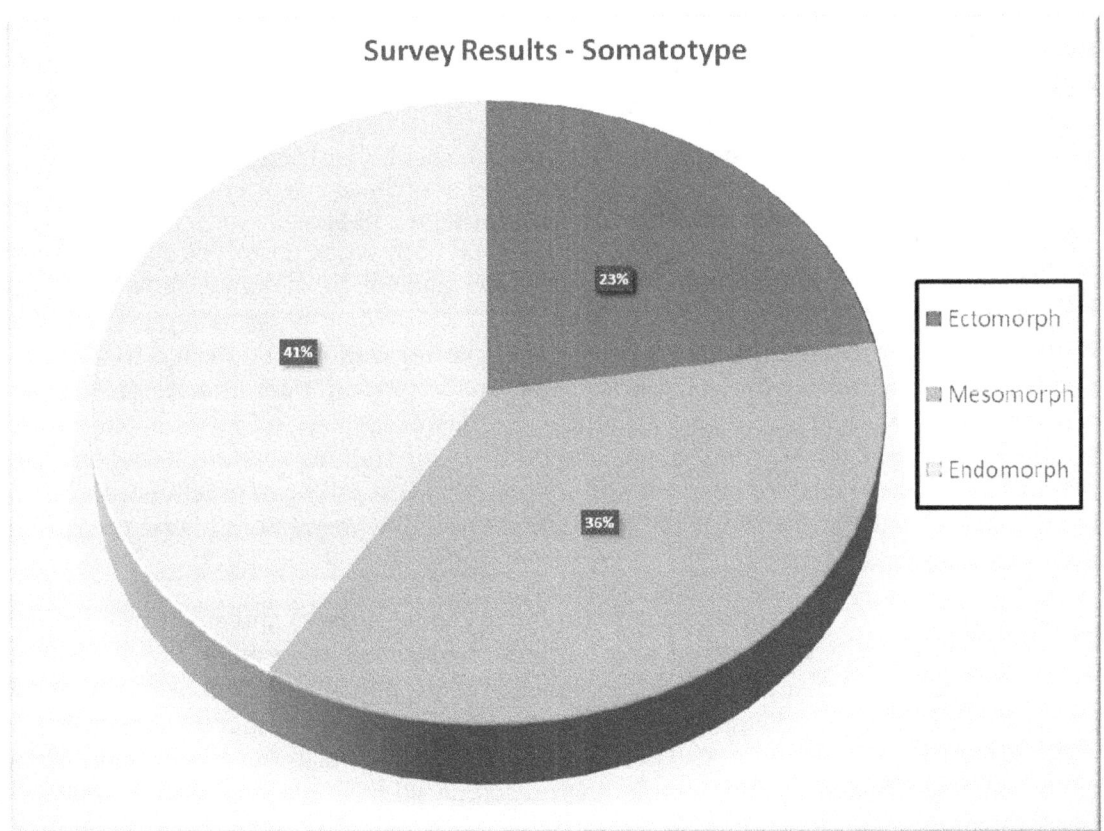

These three somatotypes, or body types, were categorized in the 1940s by psychologist William Herbert Sheldon (1898–1977). While some aspects of his work have long since been discredited, modern research shows that a person's body type impacts their athletic performance and can help determine how best to achieve their fitness goals. These body types can be summarized as follows:

- **Ectomorphs** – (slim/linear type) tend to be naturally lean, with narrow shoulders and hips, and faster metabolisms, and often struggle to gain muscular weight or body fat. They tend to have excellent thermoregulation but may be more susceptible to injury than the other somatotypes. While there is a wide range of ectomorph body types, prototypical examples include marathon/distance runners, cyclers, pole vaulters, and tennis players.

- **Mesomorphs** – (muscular type) tend to have wider shoulders, narrower waist/hips, small joints, and long limbs, and fit in the middle between the other two somatotypes. They can often gain or lose weight quickly. While there is a wide range of mesomorph body types, archetypal examples include gymnasts, sprinters, soccer players, bodybuilders, and triathletes.
- **Endomorphs** – (round/fat type) tend to have heavier bone structures, wider waist/hips, squarer torsos, and slow metabolisms, and often have an easier time gaining both muscular weight and body fat. This body shape is not ideally suited for speed and agility. While there is a wide range of endomorph body types, prototypical examples include *sumo* wrestlers, powerlifters, shot-putters, and discus/hammer throwers.

With the exception of fighting sports, where artificial separations are created to improve safety and competitiveness, martial arts rarely divide practitioners into weight or size classes. For example, traditional martial arts like *iaido*, karate, and *kobudo* often have both adult male and female practitioners attend the same training sessions based on rank, *mudansha* (colored belts) vs. *yudansha* (black belts), so that folks can practice with, learn from, and discover how to effectively fight against people who are both bigger or smaller than themselves.

In other words, once you put on your *gi* (uniform) and *obi* (belt) and step into the *dojo* (training hall) in many ways your gender becomes irrelevant, you're a *budoka* (student of the martial way) and treated accordingly. Since practitioners who have not yet earned a black belt are still internalizing the fundamentals, they tend to not have the knowledge, skill, ability, or control necessary to keep up with the black belts, though black belts often attend *mudansha* classes to help perfect their teaching skills.

In large part, this practice has become commonplace because good technique can overcome any inherent physicality discrepancies amongst combatants, especially when artificial safety rules such as eliminating eye gouges or groin strikes are taken off the table or weapons are involved, as we tend to find in self-defense, law enforcement, and military scenarios. Because skill trumps size and strength in martial arts, this means that unlike many other forms of athletic endeavor, everyone who is interested can not only participate but also excel. As expected, we found this in our survey results.

Although there is a slightly larger distribution of endomorphs in our respondent community, the results are more-or-less evenly split three ways. In fact, our analysis shows that the lower number of ectomorphs is primarily related to the underrepresentation of females in martial arts (which we discuss in the survey demographics section on gender mix) more than to any other factor. When cross-referenced with reasons that practitioners stopped or took a break from training for a long period of time, we discovered that ectomorphs had a 3.8% greater likelihood to have pointed to injuries for pausing their training than the other two somatotypes.

> Unlike many sports, it's not the participant's body type that matters. With effective training, anyone with enough desire and commitment can become a successful martial artist.

Let's compare and contrast this martial arts somatotype mix with what we find in track and field events. Ectomorphs tend to dominate in certain competitions such as hurdles, long jump, and pole vault. Endomorphs, on the other hand, excel at events like the hammer throw and shotput. If we were to transpose these two body types into each other's specialty, they would fail. The endomorph would not medal in the pole vault nor would the ectomorph win a shotput event. By the very nature of these track and field activities, equipment, and governing rules, certain body types have an inherent advantage in reaching peak performance in the sport.

We find this same specialization in American football when we compare wide receivers or cornerbacks with linebackers or linemen. No matter how athletic you are, how desirous and driven, there are certain positions where it is virtually impossible to perform at the highest levels if you were born the wrong somatotype.

This dynamic in other sports made us wonder if there was something to this whole specialization factor that might not be found in martial arts at the macro level but that could apply at the micro level. In other words, martial arts encompass such a wide range of styles and systems, we wondered if the breadth of the field might be camouflaging our results. For instance, might endomorphs be drawn toward and perform better in grappling sports such as judo, Brazilian *jiu-jitsu*, or wrestling, or might ectomorphs do better in striking arts such as karate, boxing, or taekwondo?

When we cross-correlated our survey respondents' body types with the martial art that they currently practice or want to perform, we still found no data to substantiate the theory that body type impacts a person's ability to excel in any of the martial arts.

Unlike team sports where those who are less athletically gifted might make the team yet ride a bench (and not start a game or have much if any playing time) throughout their career, everyone participates in martial arts. In many ways the fighting arts can be thought of as individual contests practiced in a group setting, everybody gets to play. All things being equal, the superior athlete will still win a fighting sports competition like boxing, wrestling, or point-sparring, yet with good training, skill, and experience we are able to build quickness and power that can overcome most discrepancies in strength and speed once artificial safety rules are removed from the equation or weapons are introduced into the mix.

When it comes to brain chemistry, on the other hand, we discovered a different outcome. As we discussed in the prior chapter on the Myers-Briggs personality type (and will delve a little deeper into later on in the what did you want to be when you grew up chapter), martial artists are predisposed toward process and service. Although the field is not dominated by one single brain type, several categories such as Adventurers, Entertainers, Logicians, Mediators, and Virtuosos are conspicuous by their comparatively low numbers when compared to the general population.

Pulling these survey findings together, all evidence indicates that practitioners do not self-select into or out of the martial arts using body type as a discriminator as they might for other types of physical endeavors, but rather by having a brain type which sparks their interest and desire. In other words, mental temperament supersedes physical characteristics. So, it's not the body type that matters, anybody with the right desire and determination can become a successful martial artist.

Martial Artist Profile – Tzviel 'BK' Blankchtein

Tzviel 'BK' Blankchtein was born and raised in Israel. He served a total of 21 years in the Israeli Defense Forces, mostly in Special Operations. BK's specialties include counterterrorism, maritime operations, plain clothes operations, intelligence and counter-intelligence operations, small weapons, and tactical operations in austere environment. BK holds a Bachelor's Degree in Counterterrorism, and a Master's Degree in Security Management. Along the way he earned advance degrees in several martial arts and defensive tactics systems, and in 2007 opened Masada Tactical (https://masadatactical.com) to fill a much-needed gap in realistic and practical training for professional warriors and civilians alike. Programs offered include defensive tactics, Israeli combat-shooting and tactical handgun, active threat/shooter response, executive protection, edged weapon tactics for law-enforcement, tactical emergency medicine, Israeli approach to urban counterterrorism, Special Weapons And Tactics (S.W.A.T.) maritime operations, and Maryland-compliant firearms classes. BK is a sworn police officer in the State of Alabama, and is Commission on Peace Officer Standards and Training (P.O.S.T.) certified instructor in over thirteen states in the United States.

If you could go back in time, what advice would you give to your teenage self?

"Stop quitting on things. I grew up in an upper middle-class home, where everything was given to me with little effort on my end. As a result, whenever I took on any endeavor, from Boy Scouts to martial arts training, from schooling to working out, and it would get too hard, I'd just quit. There were no consequences to that. When I got into the military, I found out that one cannot just coast through the service. Poor performance and more quitting, was not an option. It was one of the hardest lessons for me to learn, and likely the most valuable."

What's your guilty pleasure?

"Cheesecake. As someone who grew up fat and always struggled with weight and body image, cheesecake is something that I crave but reserve for special occasions (birthdays, etc.)."

What's the best compliment you have ever received?

"One of my students who earned his black belt under our system and went on to become a Marine officer (he's a captain now), was quoted answering during his Officer Candidate School (O.C.S.) training, when asked 'who influenced you the most,' my name. The realization that I have helped change someone's trajectory in life, helped them grow, and made such an impact was mind-blowing."

> "During his Officer Candidate School training, when asked 'who influenced you the most,' he provided my name. The realization that I have helped change someone's trajectory in life, helped them grow, and made such an impact was mind-blowing."

What is the best single piece of advice you were ever given?

"Make time for yourself. I moved to the United States of America on my own with $500 in 1999. I struggled for a long while, and was facing many hardships. I thought that working 24/7 would solve that, but in reality, it made things more stressful and less manageable. During one of my phone conversations with my father he asked if I was doing anything for me, such as going on a hike, finding a hobby, reading, anything… I said 'no.' But after the call I decided to follow that advice. I block time every week for me. I go hiking, kayaking, shooting, anything that I can do alone, be in my own mind for a while without outside distractions. It has been probably the single biggest positive influence in my life."

What single event of the past changed the world for the worst?

"Being Jewish I naturally think to the holocaust. The mass genocide, not only of jews, but also gypsies, homosexuals, and so many other groups and ethnicities, highlighted the darkest side of human behavior and evil capabilities, while depriving the world from the contributions all of those murdered could have made."

For good or ill, what was the biggest impact of your martial arts training on your life?

"Martial arts gave me so much. It provided me with tools to deal with daily events by becoming aware of ways to deal with adversaries. It helped improve my self-esteem. It connected me to thousands of other people I wouldn't have known otherwise. But likely most important is the fact that I teach self-defense today as my primary occupation, a job I wouldn't have had if it weren't for my martial arts training."

Have you ever applied your martial art outside the training hall or competition/tournament ring?

"The fury of a demon instantly possessed me. I knew myself no longer. My original soul seemed, at once, to take its flight from my body; and a more than fiendish malevolence, gin-nurtured, thrilled every fiber of my frame."

Edgar Allan Poe, American author

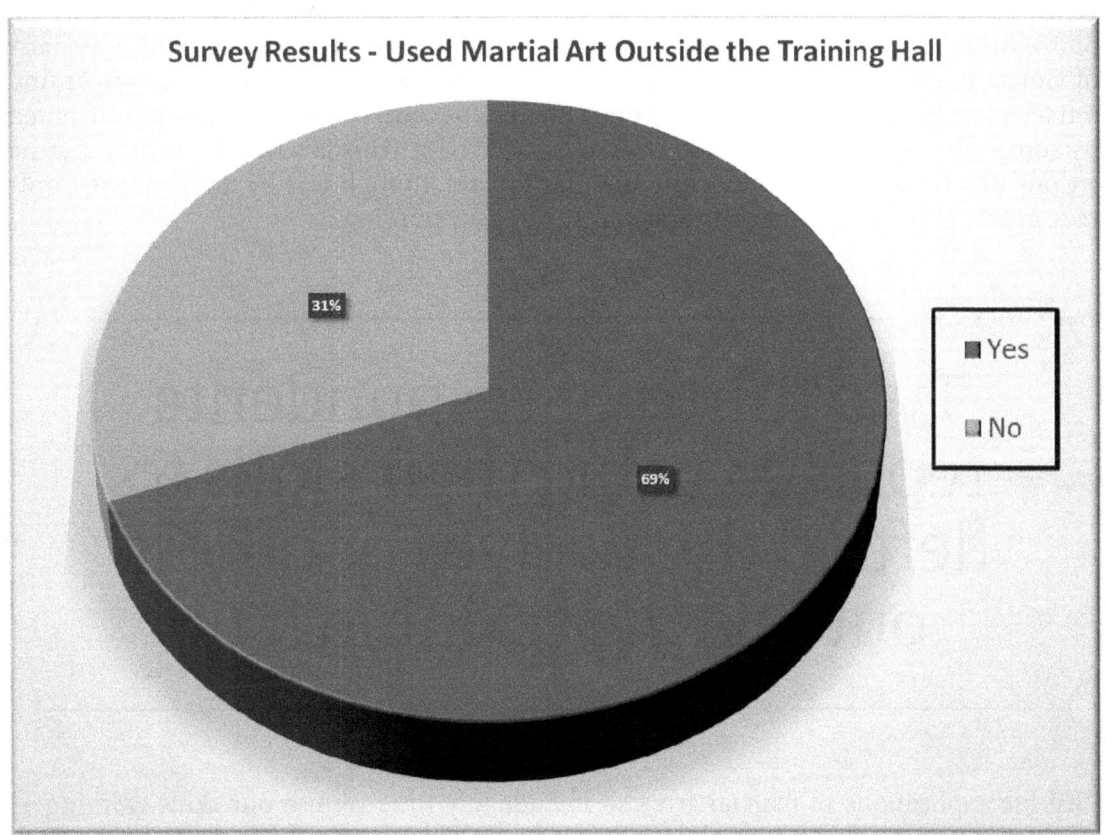

This is another area where reliable international data is simply not available so we had to revert to information from the United States. According to the U.S. Bureau of Justice Statistics, less than half (41%) of violent victimizations are actually reported to law enforcement authorities. Nevertheless, based on the best data we can uncover from crime victimization surveys, somewhere between 1.1 and 1.4 million people a year are seriously physically assaulted (generally feloniously) and an additional 4.0 million people a year become the victims of simple assault (generally misdemeanors) in the United States. This equates to about 743,000 rapes/sexual assaults, 573,000 robberies, 1,058,000 aggravated assaults, and 4,019,000 simple assaults a year, a rate of around 22.2 victimizations per 1,000 people in the country. Additionally, there are another 15.8 million property crimes like burglaries, trespassing, and motor vehicle thefts a year or 118.6 per 1,000 people in the country. Violence from strangers outnumbers violence from intimate partners by a rate of about 2.5 to 1.

While these numbers appear relatively small as a percent of the population, and we live in one of the safest times in all of human history, any time we find ourselves in the crosshairs of violent intention these statistics become far less meaningful than the situation we find ourselves in. In other words, statistics don't matter one iota if we find ourselves confronted by someone who thinks we would make a good victim. This is why self-defense can be a draw that brings practitioners into the martial arts, though it is by no means the only reason that people embrace the opportunity to begin training.

> Two thirds of respondents reported using their skills to defend themselves or others outside the training hall.

Real life applications of martial arts can include any time we use our skills working as a bouncer, security professional, law enforcement officer, or military operative as well as in street fights, barroom brawls, assaults, and other endeavors that do not include a specified venue with codified safety rules and supervision or referees. Actions span a range from doing nothing skillfully all the way up to taking a human life, and everything in-between, though survey participants did not count instances where their physical presence or situational awareness staved off violence without resorting to physical contact when responding to this question.

When we consider the full range of martial arts encompassed by our definition, the fact that many people are drawn toward the arts after encountering violence up close and personal, as well as the odds of finding ourselves in physical danger from a criminal assailant, it's unsurprising that about two thirds of our respondents have found the need to use their skills outside the training hall. Incidents can span a wide range of situations, from a drunkle uncle or inebriated roommate acting the fool at a party up to a carefully orchestrated home invasion robbery or professional contract hit. Survey respondents have dealt with this full range of events, even including professional contract hits, and lived to tell the tale.

We must note, however that several respondents chose not to answer this question or the next one on how many times they found a need to use their skills in real life. They simply skipped over it and moved on to the rest of the survey. Since they responded to other subjects it leads to a strong likelihood that this question was deliberately avoided even though we promised not to attribute responses to certain questions like this one back to individuals but rather present them in aggregate. This of course leads to the question of why this subject was avoided.

Since many martial artists are reticent to tell their friends and business associates about their training, we were disappointed but not surprised or taken aback by their excessive caution in answering here. This likely means that the percent of respondents who needed to use their skills to defend themselves or others has been somewhat underreported. Nevertheless, we will delve deeper into these findings in the next chapter on how many times martial artists have had to use their skills in real life.

If you applied your martial art in real life, how many times?

"An eye for an eye will only make the whole world blind."
Mahatma Gandhi, Indian attorney and political ethicist

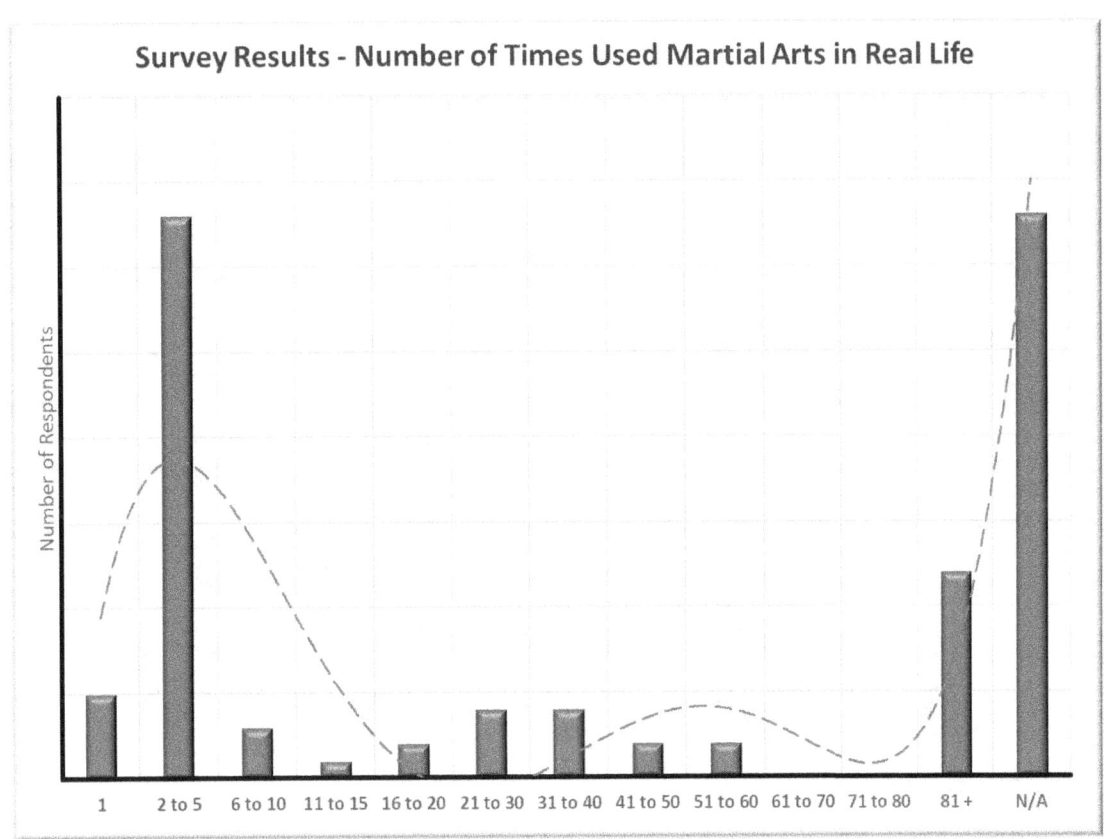

Altercations are normal, they are part of life. As a rule of thumb, however, run-ins with the law, violence, and crime tend to reduce as people age. As Marc MacYoung wrote, "One of the harder things for a young man to hear is that many of the things that he is willing to fight for aren't worth fighting for. In fact, often all you seem to hear from older people is 'don't fight.' Unfortunately, that is kind of hard to do. As a young man, you have many opportunities to get involved in violence. And in the heat of the moment, it really does seem like the only way to handle the problem."

Young people, especially males, tend to have a long list of things to prove, whether they are conscious of them or not. Oftentimes motives are instinctive because they are based on biological patterns of the human species. Much of what we think and feel is actually based in these subconscious patterns, and this especially applies to territoriality and status.

Further, younger people rarely understand or fully appreciate the physical, psychological, and legal costs of violence. They often feel immortal, never considering the possibility of becoming maimed, crippled, or even killed in a confrontation. Consequently, they will fight for any number of reasons—affiliations, self-esteem, social status, revenge for some perceived slight, or just to blow off a little steam, to name a few. For instance, it's possible that one of the authors may have attended a hockey game or two in college just to find an excuse to pick a fight… but that would have been entirely inappropriate.

> It is common to engage in 2 to 5 fights over a lifetime. Reporting 81 or more altercations represents practitioners who work in the violence profession (e.g., security, military, or law enforcement).

As we grow older and more established in our careers and relationships, however, the desire to fight is reduced with time. That does not mean that we can avoid all conflict, only that we are far less likely to participate in causing or escalating it. It is interesting, therefore, that the two-thirds of martial artists responding to our survey who had found themselves in a physical altercation effectively answered the question, "Yes, a little," or "Yes, a lot," as we can see displayed in the trendline on the chart above.

"Yes, a little," falls into the category of 2 to 5 times. "Yes, a lot" is 81 times or more. The category of 2 to 5 times looks to be a common number when applied over a lifetime whereas 81+ appears extraordinary until we look into the background and vocation of the respondents. People who replied at the higher end of the scale are those who chose employment in careers that regularly placed them in hazardous or confrontational situations. Examples include law enforcement officers, security guards, doormen, bouncers, bodyguards, and military personnel.

So, while it may be possible to go a lifetime without facing any type of physical violence, most folks have a reasonable chance of needing to use their expertise to defend themselves at some point. This means that we should not only train to become proficient in using our martial arts skills, but also know when and under what conditions it is appropriate to fight because all physical confrontations have consequences, some of which could be life-altering. And, importantly, we must discover ways to keep out of danger, using tactics like awareness, avoidance, and de-escalation to identify what may be coming and remain safe. After all, the only fight we're guaranteed to walk away from is the one we don't get in.

Martial Artist Profile – Gavin Mulholland

Alongside his three brothers, Gavin began training under his father who was teaching judo and unarmed combat in the British Forces throughout the 1960s. After witnessing a Goju Ryu *karate demonstration in the late 70s he became an immediate convert. Gavin has travelled extensively throughout Asia experiencing a wide diversity of martial arts. However, as a holistic fighting art,* Goju Ryu *already incorporates elements from virtually every other fighting system and Gavin has remained within the* Goju *framework. He is a member of the Combat Association Hall of Fame and was awarded the rank of* godan *in 2002 by the one-time student of Eiichi Miyazato, Shihan Rick Woodhams.* Kiyoshi *Kim of the* Sobo Bugei No Kai *subsequently awarded him the title* Shihan. *In 2009, Gavin was awarded the rank of* rokudan *and in 2019 he was promoted to* nanadan *(7th degree black belt) by the Chairman of the Okinawan Martial Arts Association (OMAA), Shihan Roger Sheldon. Gavin spent many years on the door and was a regular instructor for Meido Ltd., a company specializing in door supervisor, security, and close protection. He has made television and film appearances, published regular articles, and wrote the highly acclaimed book* Four Shades of Black. *He is Joint Chief Instructor of DKK, Daigaku Karate Kai (www.goju-karate.co.uk), and was a regular on the United Kingdom's MMA scene with his team DKK Fighters who compete successfully in Cage Rage, Ultimate Challenge, BAMMA, and Bellator. One student even made it as far as the UFC.*

What's the worst martial arts-related mistake you have ever made?

"I think my worst mistake in the martial arts is a very common one. Mild paranoia. We spend an awful lot of time focusing on violence and violent encounters and if we are not careful, that can start to take over too much of our lives. I was training karate 3 or 4 times a week, working on doors in the evenings, and teaching training courses to security personnel at the weekends and I did not notice that my view of the world was becoming very narrow and not very pleasant. I definitely reached the point where I could no longer enjoy a night out with friends as I would constantly be scanning for trouble, seated with my back to the wall, checking for exits, etc. etc…. Now, don't get me wrong; all of these things are vitally important, as is the awareness and mindset that goes hand-in-hand with dealing with violence, but there needs to be an off switch and I didn't yet have it. I have since achieved a much better balance and have come to see that this on/off switch is a big part of what we are trying to teach our students."

What is the best compliment you have ever received?

The compliment that really stands out for me would be my long-term instructor bestowing on me the title of *shihan*. I had taken every grade from 9th *kyu* to 4th *dan* under his guidance, but for a number of reasons, my 5th *dan* was taken under somebody else. I did not know how he would respond to this news and, despite the relatively high grade, was somewhat nervous about telling him. So, I took the courageous way out and didn't mention it! Of course, he was always going to find out and his response was very gracious. In addition to congratulating me on the award, he gave me the title of *shihan*, literally 'Teacher of Teachers.' It actually meant more to me that the grade and I think that I had been kidding myself about how much his opinion actually mattered to me."

> "'When faced with two choices, all other things being equal, choose the one that will give you the best story.' I love this advice and have tried to live by it. It has resulted in many dodgy scenarios, but I survived them all and, best of all, I have stories to tell!"

What single event of the past changed the world for the worst?

"We have always had wars, and we will always have wars, but gunpowder changed the scale of the potential for slaughter exponentially. Gunpowder was the ultimate death of the warrior. Decades of training were no longer needed to become a competent killer of men. A relatively unskilled man, could defeat a highly trained warrior with ease. And killing could be done from a distance which makes it easier to do. Even today death sits so easily on the squeeze of a trigger."

If you could go back in time, what advice would you give to your teenage self?

"I would give myself the second-best bit of advice I was ever given—again from my father. And it is this: 'When faced with two choices, all other things being equal, choose the one that will give you the best story.' I love this advice and have tried to live by it. It has resulted in many dodgy scenarios and a good many scrapes, but I survived them all and, best of all, I have stories to tell!"

What is the best single piece of advice you were ever given?

"'Go. This not the last job you will ever have. This is not the last house you will ever own. It's always nice to be able to look over the edge, and see where you will land, but sometimes you just have to jump, and trust that you will.' In the mid '80s I was an engineer with a good job and my own house. I decided that I wanted to pack it all in and go travelling. I was nervous about telling my mum and dad and the above was my dad's response. Due to that advice, I headed off to India for a three-month trip. But three-months spilled into four, into five, into six… I ended up hitch-hiking the length of Japan, and finally returned to England two years later. Sometimes you just have to jump."

For good or ill, what was the biggest impact of your martial arts training on your life?

"The biggest impact for me has probably been where I find myself in the world. Before travelling I had barely met anyone with a degree, so when I did, I was shocked to find that they were not the geniuses I'd expected. So, I decided to go. I was in Australia but applied to go in England. My stipulations were; any course, any university—with just one exception. Not London! Well, you can't say those things because the Gods hear you and laugh. So, I ended up in London, started the karate club that became *Daigaku Karate Kai*, there, and never left! I used to feel guilty because not only did I chose locations based on karate, I chose my jobs based on how easily I could get to karate. I don't feel guilty anymore and have come to realize that that is exactly why you should live where you live, and do what you do for a living."

What's the worst martial arts-related mistake you have ever made?

"Have no fear of perfection, you'll never reach it."
Salvador Dali, Spanish artist

This is a quality question not a quantity question. We did not ask how many times a survey participant joined a martial arts organization only to find that it was unsatisfactory, unsafe, or cultlike. We did not ask how many times a practitioner knocked the teeth out of their sparring partners' head before they learned that such behavior was bad form. We did not ask about how many barfights it took for any given martial artist to appreciate that the value of minding their tongue. We didn't even ask how long it took to realize that one can enjoy a hockey game without throwing a punch at someone, discovering that the tougher we are the less we should need to prove it. The responses were broad and interesting, yet they can be boiled down into two categories: (1) individual mistakes and (2) organizational mistakes.

Although we suppose that one could argue that these mistakes are ultimately the same, since the individual making the mistake had autonomy, hence responsibility for his or her actions, we make a distinction because it adds to our analysis. You see, these two types of mistakes form a Venn diagram. Each classification can stand on its own yet may also have overlapping attributes of the other. For example, "I made a choice that was not consistent with who I aspired to be," or "I thought the organization was a good fit, but they pressured me into actions I don't believe in." The overlap is a conflict of values, yet in one instance it was the individual who did the wrong thing and in the other it was organizational misconduct.

Individual mistakes included such things as losing perspective, overfocusing on training, or needlessly injuring oneself or others. Most of the injuries listed by our respondents occurred through accident, lack of focus, or simple immaturity. They were not generally purposeful misconduct, which makes sense when we overlay these findings with our analysis of the question about spending a night in jail in a later chapter. Martial artists may have an occasional lapse in judgement or understanding, but tend to be both well-intended and law abiding.

Organizational mistakes, on the other hand, can be born of an ill fit, conflicting agendas, or mismatched expectations. You see, organizations have a plan. That plan centers around how to survive, and grow as an enterprise. And, the plan is manifest in its agenda. Oftentimes we discover that our training objectives are not met (or are no longer being met) by the organization, and that will spur us to move on in search of a better fit.

In certain circumstances we may even find that the organization will publicly say one thing yet do another. All organizations are capable of making such mistakes when facing misaligned priorities, especially when the moral and ethical considerations of actions are not properly taken into account. A common, business example of this is a manufacturing company that posts a sign in their shop proclaiming, "Safety First!" That's a great slogan, and likely well intended, but in reality, safety is often not the top priority, especially when it stands in the way of profitability.

Remember the Ford Pinto debacle of the 1970s? A case often cited in college business ethics classes, the short version is that failure by Ford executives to spend an extra $11.00 to install a part that would have made their cars safer led to the recall of 1.5 million automobiles, massive lawsuits, and a criminal indictment. According to Ford's estimates, their unsafe fuel tanks were projected to cause 180 burn deaths, 180 serious injuries, and the destruction of 2,100 vehicles per year. They calculated that the company would have to pay $200,000 per death, $67,000 per injury, and $700 per vehicle, which made for a total of $49.5 million. This was compared against the cost of $11.00 per vehicle to implement the fix which calculated out to $137 million per year, roughly three times the cost of doing nothing.

Clearly it was cheaper for Ford to let their vehicles burst into flames and their customers burn to a crisp, but was that the right thing to do? Obviously not, but that's the decision they made anyway. Safety lost out to profitability, and it backfired spectacularly, taking decades to repair the damage to their brand reputation alone not to mention the personal and financial ramifications of that shortsighted thinking.

> Most martial arts mistakes stem from mismatched expectations, lack of focus, accidents, or immaturity rather than from malicious intent.

Most of the mistakes brought up in response to this question had a rational analysis to them; respondents didn't just report what they did but attempted to explain why. The classic statement goes, "Hindsight is 20/20." This phrase means that a review of an action after some time has passed loses its emotional charge. From this distance we gain perspective of the content and the context, hence are better able to determine the optimal response to any given situation than we may have discovered in the moment.

Martial artists weren't designing unsafe vehicles, but they did report doing a lot of injudicious and irresponsible things. In retrospect these actions led to regrets, but they simultaneously created opportunities to discover lessons from the mistakes and grow. After all, anything we live through we are able to learn from if we chose to do so.

It can be tough to work past guilt and self-loathing when we discover that we have done something reprehensible, even accidentally or carelessly. This is especially true once we determine the level of pain we may have caused, discover the corresponding harm to our reputation or standing in the community, and discern the full repercussions of what we have done. Oftentimes we beat ourselves up over and over again as we relive our failings from the past. We obviously cannot change history, but psychologists have identified proven strategies for getting over our regrets and responsibly moving on.

To begin, we must accept that humans are fallible, that there is a difference between who we are and what we do. If we're good people who have done something bad, there is no benefit from self-hatred, only from correcting the mistake to the extent feasible and using the agony it caused to grow into better human beings.

Begin with a genuine apology, a wholehearted attempt to set things right. Depending on the magnitude of what we did, the person or organization we wronged may not forgive us, and we may not be able to wholly rectify the damage we caused, but if we're honest in our intent the incident can be the spark that allows us to forgive ourselves and in doing so reshape of actions and intentions moving forward.

Whenever we find ourselves in situations that trigger negative self-talk, we must consciously evaluate what we are telling ourselves about ourselves, as feelings affect behaviors. In many ways we are the sum of our thoughts. For example, saying "I'm an idiot" is completely different than thinking "I could have done better by doing X instead of Y."

We can use this inner voice to empower ourselves to do better in the future rather than to continue to beat ourselves up about the past. Oftentimes it helps to use a journal, reflect on our regrets, put pen to paper (it's better to do this with handwriting than on a keyboard), and write down why we did what we did. Then, document what we will do differently in the future when faced with a similar situation or challenge. The very act of writing things down often helps us let go of the past, particularly when we do so honestly yet compassionately.

The power to shape our intentions and behaviors going forward can be brought to fruition via the brain-body connection of our handwriting. This is a responsible way to learn from our past shortcomings and take a giant first step toward becoming a better human being.

Martial Artist Profile – Jay Matzko

Jay Matzko was seven when his dad died in a TA-4 crash that he was piloting, which turned out to be a seminal event in his life. He, his mom, and younger sister moved to Phoenix where he lived until college, and that was where he first practiced martial arts. His martial arts journey spans 30 years and includes training in judo, Shuri Ryu, Shorin Ryu, and he eventually attained the rank of shodan in Goju Ryu. After he graduated from the United States Naval Academy, Jay spent 27 years in the Navy as an operational pilot and test pilot with a five-year stint in Navy weapons systems program management where he earned the rank of Captain. As a Commander in the U.S. Navy, Jay was featured in an episode of Air Warriors (Season 2, Episode 2, "Prowler Growler") on the Smithsonian Channel (https://www.youtube.com/watch?v=XD72WdJxI2E). That episode tells the story of the Navy's newest airborne electronic attack aircraft, the EA-18 G Growler. He retired from the Navy in 2020 and currently works for defense contractor Northrop Grumman in Washington State. His hobbies include karate, road biking and SCUBA diving, and he and his 8-year-old son plan to build a replica Shelby Cobra in 2022.

If you could go back in time, what advice would you give to your teenage self?

"Live in the present. I've just finished my first career as a Navy pilot. For many of the 27 years I was in I was constantly looking ahead to the next rank, the next job and the next time I was going to move to the next duty station. We moved 14 times in 27 years and just about everywhere we lived felt temporary, which made it difficult to become part of the community and make civilian friends. The same was true with my time in the *Goju Ryu dojo* I attended. I was constantly looking to learn the next *kata* and associated applications or the next rank. I would advise my teenage self to not be so worried about the future, it will come. Instead appreciate the really cool things you'll get to do, whether it is attending a *gasshuku* (training camp) in Okinawa or landing on an aircraft carrier."

What is the best single piece of advice you were ever given?

"My mother advised me before I went to college to pay off my credit card bill in full every month. Perhaps a strange thing to say for a book about martial arts, but this bit of advice shaped a lot of the decisions I made as a young adult that set me up for success today. It forced me to be disciplined in my purchases and taught me to live within my means, which afforded me the luxury of never having to worry about money. That's not to say that I've been able to purchase or experience everything I desired, but as Joe Walsh wrote, 'Life's been good to me so far...'"

What's the worst martial arts-related mistake you have ever made?

"Buying into the idea that my style was the only 'true' form of the art, and was the wellspring that all other forms of karate came from. When I moved away from my *Goju Ryu dojo* in

2009 I continued practicing on my own until 2012 when I moved to Maryland and started at a *Shorin Ryu dojo*. My previous experience was immediately discounted by the *sensei*. Near the same time, I began following Iain Abernethy, which led me to Kris Wilder and Lawrence Kane. I attended two seminars with Iain and his message of effectiveness over style resonated with me. His interpretations of *kata* regardless of style in person and in his book *Bunkai-Jutsu*, and the similar breakdown of *kata* in Wilder and Kane's *The Way of Kata* have completely changed my thinking. Even though it is a game, the message is self-evident in the UFC. UFC fighters use what works and ignore everything else."

What energizes you outside of work?

"Home improvement projects and wood working. I like making a plan to alter some aspect of my house and seeing it become a reality, whether it is renovating a bathroom, adding a screened in porch or building a home entertainment center."

For good or ill, what was the biggest impact of your martial arts training on your life?

"The biggest impact that the martial arts have had on me is the fulfillment of my desire to constantly be learning in order to make myself better. Participating in martial arts has enhanced personal traits that I may have already had such as discipline, respect, being punctual and dedication to name a few. I can't think of too many areas of my life that were not boosted by my practice, including solo training which I've done for the past three years. I mentioned in question 36 that I became disillusioned; I became disillusioned with certain people and the politics within different karate organizations, not the art form itself. I continue to appreciate what karate has done for me and am content to train solo for now."

> "My worst martial-arts related mistake was buying into the idea that my style was the only 'true' form of the art, and was the wellspring that all other forms of karate came from."

Knowing what you know now, would you do it all over again?

"I love learning. I love seeing a master of his or her craft do something that I can't do. This has been my martial arts journey, whether it was stepping into a *Shuri Ryu* karate *dojo* for the first time at age 12 or an *aikido dojo* at age 38. The mysteries of the martial arts have captivated and intrigued me, instilling in me focus, discipline and a determination to make myself better. It was a joy to ride my bike to the *dojo*, and for the three years I trained at my *Goju Ryu dojo* in California I took just about every class that was available to me, sometimes two in a day. There were times when I was either the only student or one of two that would go to the 0500 Wednesday morning class and it was a gift. I would absolutely do it all over again."

Are you a night owl or an early bird?

"The early bird may get the worm, but it's the second mouse that gets the cheese."
Jeremy Paxman, English broadcaster, journalist, and author

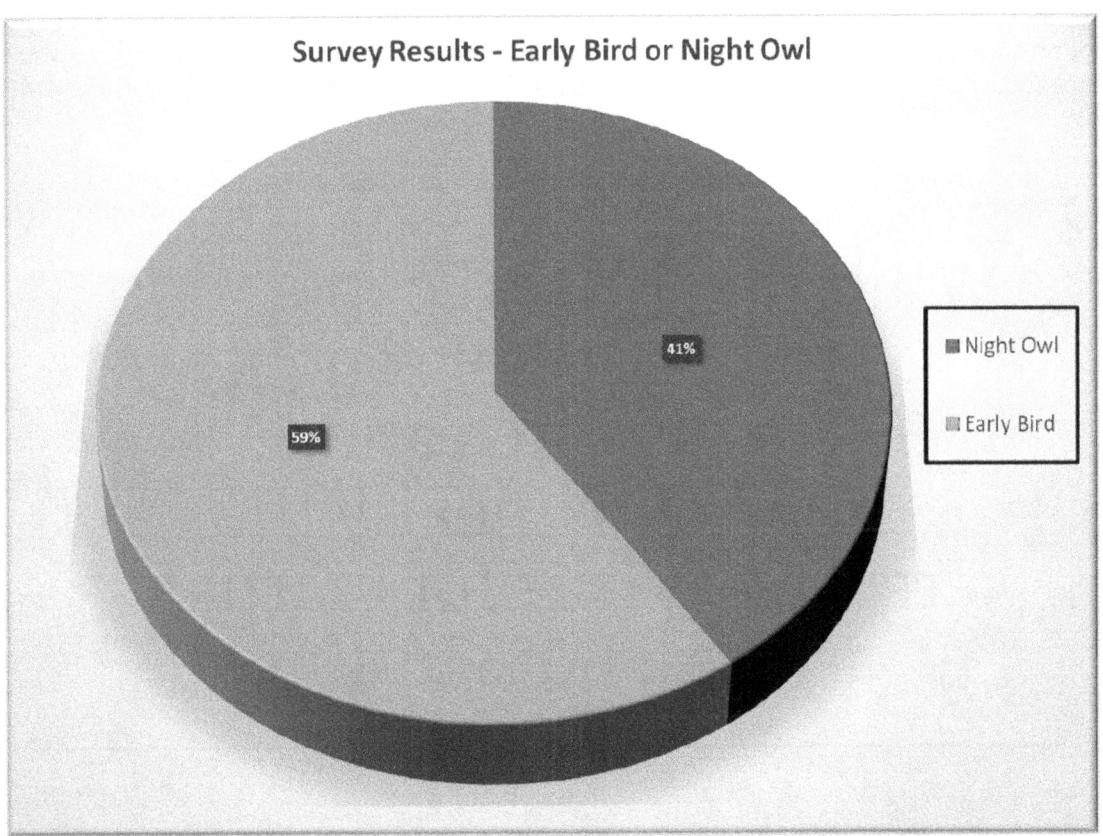

For optimal health, adults need roughly 7 to 9 hours of sleep a night. A good night's sleep helps lower our blood pressure, relax and repair our muscles, regulate our body temperature, rejuvenate our skin, and boost our infection-fighting T-cells, among a host of other benefits. This rest could theoretically come at any hours of the day or night as long as they're contiguous and consistent, though scientific evidence suggests that early risers, who often go to bed early as well, are more likely than night owls to actually get enough sleep on a regular basis. This leads to more energy, higher productivity, and a generally more positive outlook on life.

A 2019 study from the University of Exeter Medical School did a genomic analysis of 250,000 people to evaluate the impact of their body clocks on their mental and physical health. A small group of brain cells, called *suprachiasmatic nuclei*, emit signals to the body that synchronize the time of day. This biological clock runs two hours ahead in morning types (early birds) and two hours later in evening types (night owls). This analysis presented in this study showed strong evidence that night owls are at higher risk of physical and mental health problems, although they reported that further studies were needed to fully understand this link so the findings were not definitive.

> While the general population is comprised of roughly 35% early birds and 65% night owls, nearly the reverse is true for martial artists (~ 60% to 40%).

Certainly, many famous and successful individuals like Darrell Cavens (Zulily CEO), Howard Schultz (Starbucks CEO), Indra Nooyi (PepsiCo CEO), Jack Dorsey (Twitter and Square CEO), Jeffry Immelt (GE CEO), Kevin O'Leary (Shark Tank investor), Mary Barra (General Motors CEO), Michelle Obama (former First Lady of the United States), Paul English (Kayak cofounder), Richard Branson (Virgin Group founder and Chairman), Sallie Krawcheck (Ellevest CEO), Sergio Marchionne (Fiat Chrysler CEO), Tim Armstrong (AOL CEO), Tim Cook (Apple CEO), Tim Gunn (Project Runway cohost), Ursula Burns (Xerox CEO), and Vittorio Colao (Vodafone CEO) are early risers. They report waking up with more vigor, better able to plan their days, accomplish their goals, and still find time for family, exercise, and relaxation than later-waking peers. And, they do far better in structured environments like corporate culture or martial arts, which is why so many CEOs are on this list.

An argument can be made for the night owl side of the equation too. A 2006 study conducted by the Catholic University of the Sacred Heart in Milan showed that those with a penchant for staying up late also exhibited the most creativity. While those who wake up early may be better able to start their day off productively, people who stay up late tend to have higher and more sustainable level of alertness throughout the day. And, a 2009 Elsevier study on personality and individual differences concluded that night owls are more intelligent on average and also have better reasoning skills than their earlier-awaking peers.

Famous night owls include President Barak Obama, Bill Gates (CEO of Microsoft), Charles Darwin (evolutionary scientist), Elvis Presley (American singer and actor), James Joyce (Irish avant-garde novelist), Jennifer Lopez (American actress and singer), Keith Richards (English musician and songwriter), Leonardo da Vinci (Italian polymath, engineer, architect, and artist), Marcel Proust (French novelist), Stephen King (American author), and Winston Churchill (former British Prime Minister). These folks thrive in unstructured, creative environments which is why there are so many artists on this list.

While we asked a binary question, it turns out that science shows that this subject isn't quite that simple. Sleep experts believe that there are actually five or six chronotypes, depending on which study we accept, with about 13% – 15% of the population who are actual early birds (or larks as some call them), 24% – 28% firmly in the night owl category, and everyone else somewhere in-between.

Without muddying the question or the research overmuch, we are able to apportion the remaining chronotypes into one of these two categories and discover that are far less early birds in the general population than night owls, a roughly 35% to 65% split, which is nearly the exact reverse of the 59% to 41% mix that we find in the martial arts community. This finding is entirely consistent with MBTI personality profiles of the survey respondents as well as the fact that martial artists in general are far more process-focused than creative. Due to our brain chemistry, we tend to be healthier, more energetic, more productive, and a hold a more positive outlook on life than the norm too.

Martial Artist Profile – Martin Stark

Martin Stark is a CEO, Keynote Speaker, LGBTQI+ Advocate, Courage Champion, and Inclusion Practitioner. He is passionate about inclusion, diversity, equity, social justice, and fairness. Martin is a seasoned commercial negotiator and supplier diversity expert with 15-years' experience as an IT strategic sourcing leader. He was diagnosed with Addison's disease shortly after surviving being placed in two induced comas and a tracheotomy. Martin believes in health and wellness, staying active and has the words "Courage" and "Fear Nothing" tattooed on his back. He is the Founder and CEO of the not-for-profit company World Gay Boxing Championships Limited (www.worldgayboxingchampionships.org) and plans to hold the inaugural world LGBTQI+ boxing championships in Sydney in February 2023 coinciding with the city hosting World Pride and Mardi Gras. Martin has been interviewed by CNN, The Guardian, Reuters, BBC World Service, BBC Sport and has been featured in prestigious Australian and international LGBTQI+ media.

What is the best single piece of advice you were ever given? Who was it from?

"In my 2016 annual employment review I was rated a high achiever exceeding all my performance objectives and targets my manager wrote 'I would like to Martin be more courageous.' This simple piece of advice transformed my life where I was able to channel my doubts and fears turning my part time confidence to self-belief and embracing courage."

When you were a kid, what did you want to be when you grew up?

"I wanted to be a translator and interpreter and studied French and German at University. After graduating my first job was a Team Manager in a Contact Centre for British Telecom (BT). I visited Australia a few times and knew I wanted to live there. BT had an office in Sydney where I was able to transfer creating a new life and career path."

Why did you start training?

"To recover from Post-Traumatic Stress Disorder (PTSD) after almost dying from Addison's disease which reminded me of my experience of two induced comas and a tracheotomy."

For good or ill, what was the biggest impact of your martial arts training on your life?

"Boxing has transformed my life, helping me recover from PTSD and the experience of almost dying several times including from Addison's disease. It has given me a new sense of purpose where I can make a positive social impact through the World Gay Boxing Championships disrupting homophobia and hatred in sport."

> "Boxing has transformed my life, helping me recover from PTSD and the experience of almost dying several times... It has given me a new sense of purpose where I can make a positive social impact."

Who influenced you the most?

"My husband who was a tower of strength and support as I woke up from second induced coma and came to terms with almost dying."

What single event of the past changed the world for the worst?

"The horrific murders, human rights abuses, racism and the crimes against humanity committed through slavery. I learnt more about the horrors and crimes against humanity committed by Europeans through looking around a building opposite the family home of my husband than I did in school. My husband grew up a few hundred meters away from the entrance of Cape Coast Castle one of forty 'slave castles' built in West Africa. We should all be born into a system that validates and reaffirms we are individuals with the same rights and freedoms. We are still dealing with the consequences of slavery and today there are tens of thousands of victims of modern slavery who have no basic rights or freedom."

What attributes do you admire most?

"The secret of happiness is to admire without desiring."
F. H. Bradley, British philosopher

This was an unstructured question in which we asked survey respondents to reflect on admirable qualities they have seen in their fellow martial arts practitioners. We asked them to consider values (e.g., honesty, integrity, courage, etc.), principles (e.g., coaching, perseverance, giving back to the community, etc.), and skills (e.g., ability to break bricks with a punch, hit a target from a mile away with a rifle bullet, consistently win a tournament), or anything else they felt was appropriate to identify the characteristics that they admired most.

Instead of identifying 1 or 2 attributes, most of our survey respondents listed many. Some used a few words, others narrative sentences, and it was not uncommon for answers to include as many as eight different attributes in one response. Because the characteristics were important enough to contextualize, many provided commentary on why they felt the way that they did too.

When we parsed through these responses, we were able to combine common elements which may have been worded differently but meant much the same thing, such as "humble," "humility," "unpretentious," "modest," and "self-effacing" by way of example, to better affinitize the top attributes that were admired by the martial arts community. In this examination, the qualities of integrity (23%), honesty (17%), and perseverance (11%) topped the list. In fact, words alluding to these three characteristics combined made up a little over half of the responses (51%). Other top responses, in order of priority, included humility, courage, patience, compassion, empathy, loyalty, and dedication. One does not have to be a martial artist to venerate qualities like the ones on this list.

Classic memes such as, "Karate begins and ends with respect," dominate martial arts social media. Interestingly enough, however, the attribute of respect came in 11th in the overall listing of importance on our respondents' list. Another common meme, "A black belt is just a white belt who never quit," falls in the bucket of our number three choice, perseverance. This makes for an interesting disconnect between familiar maxims and what is or is not actually valued by the martial arts community. Respect, hard work, adaptability, discipline, calmness, and open-mindedness are all highly regarded human characteristics, and while reported by some respondents in their answers these qualities did not make our top ten list.

The famous Jordan Peterson aphorism, "Sort yourself out," is not a martial arts meme yet it is popular among many martial artists because it speaks to being a good person, to orienting yourself to the highest possible good you can conceive of. This is reminiscent of Confucian saying, "To put the world in order, we must first put the nation in order; to put the nation in order, we must first put the family in order; to put the family in order; we must first cultivate our personal life; we must first set our hearts right." Sorting ourselves out, setting our hearts right, these notions resonate deep in the human psyche, and our respondents in this study appear to agree. In fact, integrity and honesty are internal choices that flow outward to others.

Integrity, honesty, and perseverance are characteristics that the martial arts community treasures. This finding could be boiled down into one simple sentence: Be truthful, be trustworthy, and never give up.

To put this into perspective, lets shift gears for a moment... Talking points are pre-established messages designed to elicit a response. The talking point principle is used by pundits, politicians, advertising executives, broadcasters, and administrators to drive a point home to their audience. These talking points keep spokespeople on message, helping create validity in their listener's mind.

> The ten traits martial artists admire the most are integrity, honesty, perseverance, humility courage, patience, compassion, empathy, loyalty, and dedication.

The tactic is simple; when people hear the same phrase, words, or ideas from many disparate sources the talking point becomes accepted as truth irrespective of whether or not it actually is factual. This is a simple and persuasive form of propaganda. To help assure success, the keywords used in these talking points are often pre-tested with various affinity groups for impact and stickiness. In other words, to resonate best they need to be both hard-hitting and memorable.

Martial artists' responses to this survey question were far from being talking points, quite the opposite in fact. The diversification of similar responses, such as "humble," "unpretentious," and "self-effacing," were all speaking to the same idea, one that came from the heart. This use of different words to convey similar meaning demonstrates a multiplicity of expression of a single idea rather than some sort of propaganda. The use of such a wide range of different words to describe the same concept demonstrates that the thought was not being parroted or listed by rote.

In fact, when different words are used to express a singular idea, that notion is more likely to have been ingrained in the minds of the respondents who wrote them. In other words, the attributes listed and their value to the martial artists reporting them is genuine.

While it's one thing to come up with a list of nice words, it's another thing to aspire to live by them. Analysis demonstrates, that our survey respondents were not just parroting memes, they were revealing what they truly believed important and commendable. Traits like integrity, honesty, perseverance, humility courage, patience, compassion, empathy, loyalty, and dedication are worthy of both our esteem and ambition.

What superpower do you wish you had?

"Sometimes things become possible if we want them bad enough."
T.S. Eliot, American poet, playwright, and publisher

In job interviews employers often ask candidates questions designed to assess their judgement, creativity, self-reflection, and ability to think on their feet. To provide useful insight, these questions cannot be too formulaic. They need to be both unexpected yet personal to the candidate answering them. And, of course, they cannot have a singular right or wrong answer, as their value lies in understanding how the candidate thinks as much as in analyzing what they say.

One of the more interesting of these "trick" interview questions is, "What superpower do you wish you had?" Here are some common responses from the Society of Human Resource Management and what personnel professionals believe they might mean about the person aspiring to have them:

- **Flying**: adventurous, willing to take risks, and favors a global perspective.
- **Mindreading**: values emotional intelligence, interpersonal relationships, and empathy.
- **Shapeshifting**: enjoys multitasking, variety, and embraces change.
- **Speed**: values efficiency, time management, and continuous improvement.
- **Strength**: enjoys challenge, seeks out opportunities to grow.
- **Teleportation**: values efficiency, prioritization, and time management.
- **Telekinesis**: enjoys finding ways of doing things better, faster, and more effectively.
- **Time travel**: values learning from the past, uses experience to make better decisions.
- **X-ray vision**: enjoys attention to detail and thorough analysis before making decisions.

While the list above puts a positive spin on things, the opposite could easily be true as well. Folks who wish for invisibility might have social anxiety disorders, those who aspire for telekinesis could be unrepentant pranksters, and people hoping for mindreading abilities could easily be into office politics or blackmail. Both context and content are necessary when evaluating questions like this.

Interestingly, when one of the most successful businessmen in the world, Warren Buffet, was asked this question, his response was more bounded in reality, "I'd like the ability to read faster."

In surveying martial artists, the majority of the responses to the survey fell into the realm of the usual selections we might find in comic books and superhero movies, things like flight, invisibility, teleportation, or time travel. Nevertheless, among the plethora of possible superpowers one could aspire to, better healing is one of the more enlightened choices. Consider its value in battle, recovery, and longevity. In analyzing our survey data, we discovered that the older the martial arts practitioner, the more likely they were to wish for an ability to heal faster and more effectively, with responses such as "super healing," "healing touch," "ability to heal faster," and "mutant healing powers like Wolverine" common answers.

> The desire to be more than what we are lies deep in the human psyche, and martial artists are no different in this regard. The older we get, the more we wish for super healing powers like Wolverine from the X-Men comics.

Clearly martial arts create wear and tear on practitioners' bodies, especially when we have accidents, injuries, fail to warm up, stretch, or cool down properly, or use poor body mechanics. Beyond ubiquitous bumps and bruises, dislocations, broken bones, and concussions are pretty common injuries from the fighting arts, which is why so many of us wish we were more like comic book legends Wolverine, Deadpool, Wonder Woman, Superman, The Flash, X-23, Elixir, Incredible Hulk, and Blade, all of whom have super healing abilities.

The desire for such powers existed long before the invention of comic books, however. They have been pervasive throughout human history, spanning all ages and cultures. The Roman demigod Hercules is a good example. His superpower was his strength; he had physical prowess unmatched by any mortal and most immortals. Legend states that bespelled by his jealous stepmother, the goddess Hera, Hercules went temporarily insane and murdered his beloved wife and children.

In order to reach absolution and achieve immortality Hercules performed twelve heroic labors, including slaying the Nemean lion, killing the nine-headed Lernaean hydra, snaring the man-eating Erymanthean Boar, driving away a flock of carnivorous Stymphalian birds, capturing the rampaging Cretan bull, catching the four man-eating horses of Diomedes, stealing the Amazon queen Hippolyte's armored belt, appropriating the cattle of the monster Geryon, acquiring the golden apples of Hesperides, and finally traveling to Hades to kidnap Cerberus, the three-headed dog that guarded the entrance to the underworld. In his story we discover both the classic hero's journey and the creative use of one's superpower to overcome seemingly impossible odds.

Hercules is but one example. History is full of stories and legends of those with superhuman abilities. Some were heroic, others tragic. Consider for example the tale of Cú Chulainn, whose name translates as "the hound of Culann," a medieval Irish warrior of the Ulster (Ulaid) cycle. A demigod and Knight of the Red Branch, his exploits were in many ways comparable to the better-known Greek hero Achilles, yet in battle he was overcome with a berserker rage that left him monstrous and uncontrollable. In this state he unknowingly murdered his own son and best friend in separate battles. Tricked by Medb (Maeve), queen of Connaught, he was lured into an ambush where he was murdered by his foes, yet in his final moments tied himself to a stone spire with his own intestines so that he could die on his feet. His foes were so afraid to approach him that they shied away until a death crow landed on his shoulder indicating that he had passed.

Clearly the story of Cú Chulainn's was designed to stir warriors to courage in battle, prevailing whenever possible yet dying on their feet rather than on their knees when necessary. Other ancient examples of superheroes include the Sumerian legend Lugalbanda, whose kindness to animals resulted in the gift of super speed from the gods. Lugalbanda's chronicle reportedly inspired modern day comic heroes Flash and Quicksilver. The epic Mesopotamian poem Gilgamesh is said to have been the inspiration behind Incredible Hulk. And, the historical Norse god Thor inspired the modern comic character of the same name.

Whether it is the legends of yesteryear or the comic book superheroes of today, the desire to be more than what we are lies deeply embedded in the human psyche, and martial artists are no different in this regard.

Martial Artist Profile – Benjamin Dean LaBelle

Benjamin started training for real in April 2004 walking into Nikko Dojo (Danzan Ryu Jujutsu) *with the attitude I will do this until I am dead or not able to walk. With* Sensei Tom Westfall, *he learned so much and got a firsthand experience with mapping nerves, feeling pain so bad all you can do is laugh. In 2008 he wanted to improve his striking, so he reached out to a friend who hit harder than anyone he knew. Sensei* Zach Zinn *started to train him and his striking improved immensely. As a result, he really fell in love with* Goju Ryu. *They paired very well and he incorporates both in his training and teaching to this day, even naming his own school* JuTe dojo *as an homage to both. Over the years he has been lucky and learned many things from many different systems (Krav Maga, aikido, iaido, judo, jodo, silat, Escrima, Wing Chung, etc.). His website is http://jutedojo.com.*

When you were a kid, what did you want to be when you grew up?

"Well, I wanted to be a superhero or a police officer. I knew I was going into IT when I was in high school though. I was really into building computers and at the same time I loved physics, science in general, philosophy, and wood- and metalworking. It was kind of easy to rule those out. I knew the things I loved like woodworking and metalworking was going to be likely very low paying and I knew I couldn't afford 8 years of collage for the other interests and to be honest not sure I could stand being in school that long. I didn't have good grades except for physics and a few other things. So off to community college for IT I went, I liked it and knew that it was the biggest earner for least amount of education and I liked it. I did really struggle for the first part of IT career with it starting at the end of the dot com bubble and not really finishing my 2-year degree. I then almost became a police officer, went as far as taking the Washington State Patrol entrance exam (I went in dry and didn't pass, close though). I landed my first career job right around that time and I was off to the races in IT..."

What is your guilty pleasure?

"I love reading comic books, manga, and watching anime. I will still watch pro wrestling from time to time. I love to make just weird terrible-for-you food with anything we have in the pantry or in the fridge. I have made from truly horrible stuff that tasted so good, but probably shortened my life by 5 years."

For good or ill, what was the biggest impact of your martial arts training on your life?

"It has been a huge positive influence in my life. It has made me a better, kinder, more self-aware person. I think people assume training in violence makes you more violent, I find it is very much the opposite. I know the risks and possible outcomes of those poor decisions and the have the confidence to not let myself get pulled into silly games of ego and status. Martial arts training has a profound effect for me giving me the courage to do things that

I have found intimidating. Since childhood I have been afraid to be in front of crowds, but after years of martial arts training and teaching, I rather like the rush now. I always tell people at least when I make mistake during a presentation, I don't end up spitting up teeth. I have also found on the far end of martial arts if you want to get better (post black belt) you must self-correct, which is truly a superpower in life."

> "Since childhood I have been afraid to be in front of crowds, but after years of martial arts training and teaching, I rather like the rush now."

What is the best compliment you have ever received?

"I got one that was more of what I think the person was pointing out as a flaw. I was once told by a boss that my ambition far outweighed my ability. I walked away and thought yeah that's how you get better, you see what you want, and you don't have the tools right now but down deep you know you got more in the tank. To this day I still think about that as I have pushed past so many martial art obstacles and professional ones. I am sure a lot of people don't know I have a couple of learning disabilities and was in remedial reading for a good part of elementary school. If you don't dream it, and don't think you can get there, guess what you don't get there. I value myself knowing if I want something bad enough, I can find way to get there."

If you could go back in time, what advice would you give to your teenage self?

"I wouldn't because it would change who I am and risk everything around me. That said, if we are purely talking outside of that I would tell myself, 'Don't rush to fast enjoy the ride and spend more time with the people you won't have one day. Help people where you can and don't let people use you. Don't focus on the bad focus on the good and don't sit on the bad stuff lean in deal with it. Enjoy school do as many activities you can even if they seem silly or not cool as you only will get this once and above all learn to love yourself and be who you really are and don't compare yourself. It's going to be hard and shit is going to hurt but you got some amazing people and things coming to you be ready for them (people will need you). And most of all remember we never stay down.'"

What energizes you outside of work?

"I get excited to share ideas and talk about anything fun or intriguing. I really like learning things to make me a better person like martial arts or even sharing ideas and points of view. I like to just learn about the world and traveling seeing different cultures and food (yes love that food)."

If wrote a book about your life, what would the title be?

"'Classic,' a book which people praise and don't read."
Mark Twain, American novelist

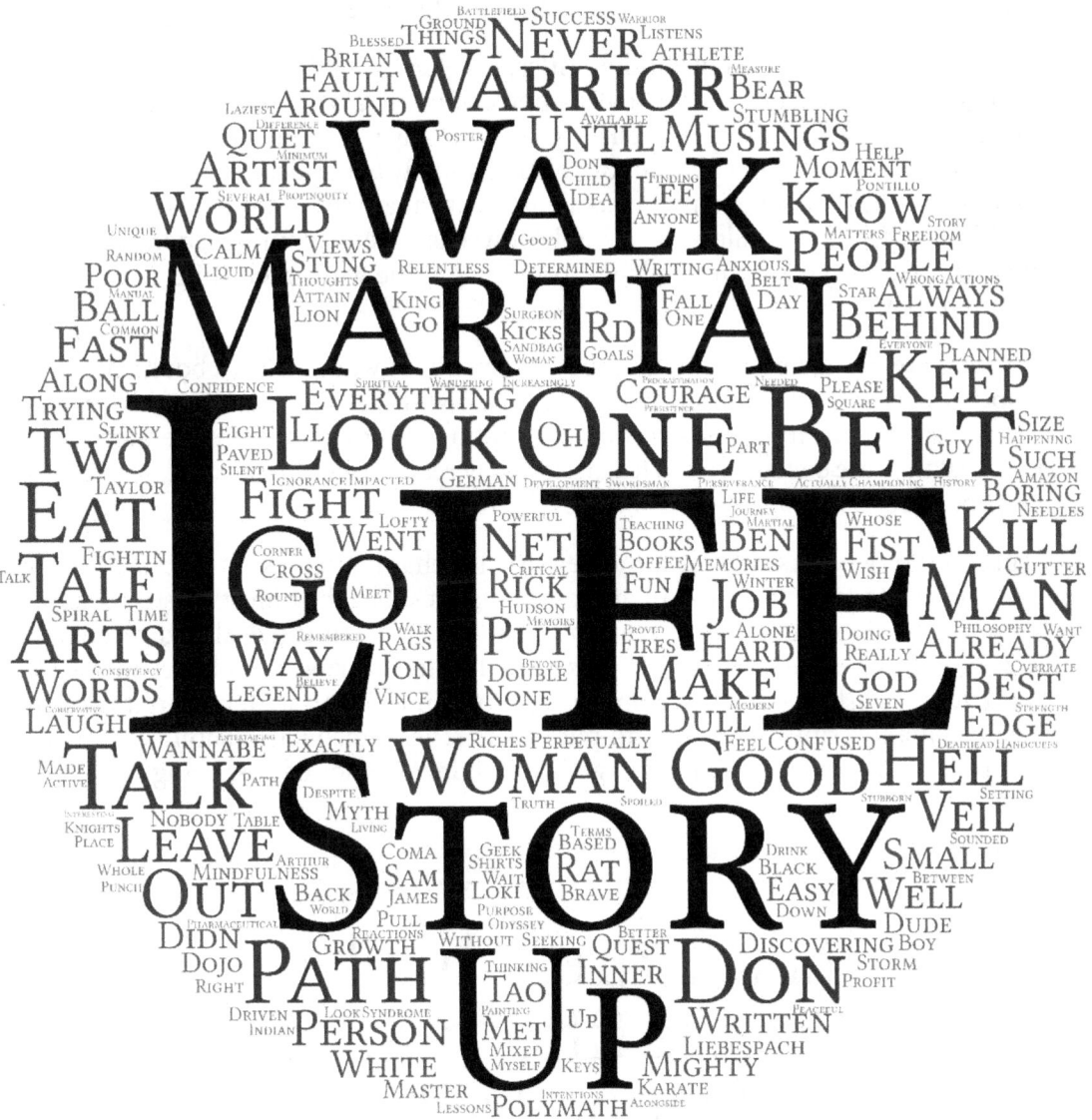

According to Bowker, the world's leading bibliographic information provider, there were more than 1.68 million self-published and "non-traditional" books released in 2018. That is roughly 5.5 times as many as the 305,000 or so books released by traditional publishing houses that same year. Despite this explosion of new titles, the average book sold less than

250 copies that year and is expected to sell under 2,000 copies over its lifetime. In fact, less than 5% of all books ever published have actually sold more than 5,000 copies.

Books that sell tend to have outstanding titles, excellent cover art, and stellar marketing. While a great title won't necessarily make a book sell well, a bad one will almost certainly sink its viability in the marketplace. That dynamic is why publishers use focus groups and advanced analytics, spending millions of dollars annually to perfect their authors' titles. So, we thought it would be interesting to challenge martial artists to come up with a title for their life's story while only allowing a couple of weeks to return our questionnaire. Oddly enough, they stepped up to the challenge, providing some truly interesting, amusing, and insightful responses.

Before we share our favorites, let's talk about more about what makes a book's title worth the paper it's printed on (or electrons it's displayed with). An outstanding title resonates with potential readers. It piques their interest, capturing enough of their attention for long enough that they are encouraged to learn more, say read the back cover text, search inside, look at online reviews, or whatever inspires them to buy.

We can think of a book's title, or a movie's title for that matter, as it's resume. Resumes are not enough to land you a job in and of themselves, but they must be strong enough to get us in the door or we will never have a shot at closing the deal and receiving an offer during the interview process. In this same fashion, boring titles linger in the slush pile. The term "slush pile" comes from the days when aspiring writers would mail their typewritten manuscripts to agents and publishers. These unsolicited submissions would be dumped into a pile of unread work, with a marginal chance of ever being reviewed.

> Like a great book or movie title, martial artists tend to describe themselves in memorable, attention-grabbing, and informative ways.

Book titles can be tough to write, but well worth effort. According to Scribe Media, an agency that helps entrepreneurs publish and market their books, great titles are attention-grabbing, memorable, informative, easy to say, and (in most instances) not embarrassing or problematic for someone to say them. The ones we received from our survey respondents covered a very wide range of styles; some were circumspect, others humorous, and many hinted about or outright spoke to overcoming difficulties along the contributor's life journey.

Some of them made us groan, others made us laugh, and a select few piqued our interest enough to make us wish they had actually been written so that we could peruse them. Those top titles include the following:

- *Pull Up a Sandbag: Martial Lessons from the Battlefield* (Sergeant Chris Webb)
- *Liquid Handcuffs: Life as a Pharmaceutical Poster Child* (Steve Jacobson)
- *Don't Fight the Tao* (Sifu Restita DeJesus)
- *Setting Fires for Fun and Profit* (John Leylegian)
- *I Punch People for a Living* (Iain Abernethy)
- *But… You Don't Look Like a Martial Artist!* (Patricia Bolton)
- *Journey of a Spiritual Warrior Surgeon* (Dr. Wendell Goins)
- *From Fist to Mindfulness* (Master Alessandro Morgante)
- *Musings of a Wannabe Polymath* (Captain Jay Matzko)
- *How to Make God Laugh* (Sifu Stephen Browne)
- *Oh, Him?* (Vaughn Hyslop)
- *Woman Behind the Veil* (Veena Grover)
- *How It Took Me 30 Years to Become an Overnight Success* (Mike Canonica)
- *Please, Just Leave Me Alone Until My 3rd Coffee Kicks In* (Charlie Lampshire)
- *The Calm After the Storm* (John Springer)

What is the best compliment you have ever received?

"If you live for compliments, you'll die by criticism."
Charlamagne tha God, American radio host, television personality, and author

We all like to be complimented, yet all compliments are not created equal. Generalized praise can come across as insincere whereas when we hear about specific behaviors or actions that others appreciate, we are more apt to believe that the accolade is genuine. Paradoxically, many people are uncomfortable receiving compliments and have a hard time simply saying "thank you" rather than trying to explain or change the subject when one is received. For this reason, we thought it would be interesting to find out where martial artists stand when it comes to praise.

Some of the more meaningful phrases culled from survey respondents included, "You really care," "You made a difference in my life," "You are the most compassionate and caring instructor I ever met," "You've got this sort of Zen thing going on," and "You are kind." This is interesting, but not particularly useful. So, rather than broadly analyzing keywords for trends in response to this question, we find it more valuable to pass along some of stories we received in our survey. They're far more enlightening.

Sometimes great compliments are related to our personal attributes. Captain Jay Matzko wrote, "A friend of mine several years ago remarked to me that he saw me as a 'humble leader.' That made me feel good because it was a long steady journey from the hint of arrogance I carried when I was young. I've been humbled a lot in my life's journey, both in and out of the *dojo*. At the risk of sounding like my younger self, karate has heightened my humility and I am better for it. I have come to realize that accolades I have received are fleeting. In the latter part of my first career and into the present I realize that the way I interacted with the people I worked with had a noticeable impact on them and me. I get a kick out of helping people realize their potential while getting the mission done. Karate has played a big role to help me understand that."

When we hear the term compliment, we often thing of what someone else has to say to us, but oftentimes the best commendation stems from other people's actions which can speak far louder than their words. Richard Liebespach wrote, "The best compliment I ever received was that over a dozen people volunteered to help me recover from my having a bone marrow transplant. These are people who are willing to give up days of their lives to ensure that I will have the 24/7 care, for over 2 months, that I will need to survive and recover from my leukemia."

Sometimes complements stem from acknowledgement that we are willing to do the right thing, even when it is much easier to duck responsibility. David Chapman wrote, "There was a difficult person at work who made people uncomfortable, talking about things that should not have been discussed in a work environment. Everyone was afraid of this person, especially management and union leadership. As a supervisor I was presented with the concerns of one of my employees, so I confronted this difficult person on it and kindly reminded them to keep non-work-related conversations at home and focus on work while in the office. Five minutes later I received a call from the union president accompanied by the compliment 'You've got balls man,' which led to further promotions. I don't shy away when things are not right."

> The best compliments martial artists receive speak to their character and contribution to the community.

Some of the most heartfelt praise we can receive stems from how we touch the lives of the people around us. Chris Hanson wrote, "As a school teacher and martial arts coach, I receive countless compliments (good and bad) every year from students, teachers, clients, etc. The one that stood out the most so far was from a parent who genuinely thanked me for inspiring them to make sure that their child did not give up, to continuously check over their work for detail, and to seek out martial arts training. This parent said that their child was inspired by my level of energy in the classroom, and open-hearted sharing of important life lessons. It put a huge smile on my face and motivated me to keep going. I, lately, have been also been getting compliments for the unity-based work I am doing online and for the martial arts community, bringing people together, and fostering open discussions on the martial arts."

The best compliments can be as simple as they are profound. Responding to this question, Emmanuel Rivera modestly wrote, "I trust you."

Many martial artists adopt aspects of the culture of the system or style the practice. Compliments in this arena can stand out in remarkable ways. Don Roley, a Caucasian American wrote, "One night in Japan the teacher asked if any of us were going to the head of the art's training, which was popular with visitors from other countries. I quipped that the place currently was 'lousy' with non-Japanese and would be staying home. One of the senior students turned to me to rebuke me for using a rude term for non-Japanese and stopped when he faced me. Then he murmured, 'I keep forgetting you're not Japanese.'"

Sometimes accolades are tied to our teaching or presentation style, praise for the experience that others enjoy when they come to us for help or advice. Iain Abernethy wrote, "I once read a seminar review that said, 'It was two days of stand-up comedy, with some great martial arts thrown in.' That delighted me because it was clear they had really enjoyed themselves. Life is really hard, and it always means loads to me to know I've given people a little break from it all."

And, given our industry, sometimes compliments reflect on our character in somewhat unusual ways. Marc "Animal" MacYoung wrote, 'You don't know Animal. He'll kill you, but he won't rip you off. If he doesn't show up (with the day's receipts in the morning) that means he's dead. And odds are the people who tried to take it from him are too."

All in all, martial artists aren't much better or worse at receiving or giving compliments than anyone else, but he best compliments they received speak to their character and contribution to the community. This demonstrates that the things we value and aspire to are consistent with our actions, and we appreciate when others notice.

Martial Artist Profile – Parul Verma, Ph.D.

Parul Verma is a postdoctoral researcher in the field of neuroscience at the University of California San Francisco. She studies brain function as well as different brain health-related diseases. She originally hails from India. She learnt Goju Ryu *style karate at a dojo at Purdue University, recognized under* Hanshi *Tino Ceberano. She also trained with* Sensei *Kris Wilder for some time. Currently, she is at shodan level. Apart from karate, she has represented her undergraduate school in basketball in India, and plays squash occasionally. She also regularly practices breathing exercises and has done multiple spirituality-related courses.*

What is the best compliment you have ever received?

"The best compliment I received was, 'You are a superwoman.' It was because the person (who gave the compliment) saw that I was working hard at work as well as practicing my martial art regularly. I was also being active in exploring spiritually and regularly practicing some breathing/meditation exercises. At the same time, I tried to be there for my close ones as much as I could."

What is the best single piece of advice you were ever given?

"The most applicable piece of advice I got was, 'Learn to say no.' It has been advised by many people (because I struggle so much with it!) but emphasized most by my dad."

What's the worst martial arts-related mistake you have ever made?

"When I was a kid, I was very aggressive while practicing my martial art. Once, I hit someone badly during sparring, out of both excitement and rage. Martial arts had become a tool to vent out my anger back in those early days. I later learned the importance of equanimity and mindfulness as an integral part of martial art training."

When you were a kid, what did you want to be when you grew up?

"I wanted to be a doctor. I did not end up being a clinician, but I got a Ph.D. degree, so I have a 'Dr.' title in my name now, and I work in the field of biology. So, it is still close enough. In my early days, I decided not to become a medical doctor because I loved mathematics too much, so I chose engineering instead."

For good or ill, what was the biggest impact of your martial arts training on your life?

"Martial arts training improved my understanding of human body in general and my body in particular. Consequently, I have become more aware of potential self-defense strategies that are more suited for my body type. Because of this, my confidence has increased, and I am able to handle my fears better. There are many other subtler aspects that are practiced in training and have impacted my philosophy in general. One in particular is seeking perfection, which I try to practice in my professional as well as personal life."

> "Martial arts had become a tool to vent out my anger back in those early days. I later learned the importance of equanimity and mindfulness as an integral part of martial art training."

Knowing what you know now, would you do it all over again?

"Yes! In fact, I do want to learn other forms of martial arts from the scratch. I think the training is very beneficial both for physical as well as mental well-being. These trainings are focused on attaining perfection, which requires being calm from within because that is when we can focus on every little detail about every technique. And attaining perfection is a life-long journey."

What is the best single piece of advice you were ever given?

""Bad advice will blind you; good advice will instruct you; excellent advice will enlighten you, and transcendent advice will elevate you."

Matshona Dhliwayo, Zimbabwean philosopher

One of the best pieces of advice in human history came from Greek philosopher Aristotle (384 BC–322 BC), when he wrote, "Know thyself." His words seem so simple, but they mean so much… In many ways he is speaking to emotional intelligence, a concept which wouldn't even be formulated for another couple millennium. Truly, when we know who we are, we can be wiser about our dreams, our goals, our standards, and our convictions. Knowing who we really are allows us to live a life with purpose and meaning. This is nothing new, the founder of the Lyceum, one of the great centers of learning in the ancient world, has been dead for over 2,300 years, yet how many people actually listen to Aristotle's sage suggestion?

Both giving and receiving good advice requires a high level of emotional maturity, since we must move past deeply-ingrained biases, preference for our own opinions over the thoughts of others, and actually have a real dialogue instead of talking past each other. Inquisitiveness, mindfulness, open-mindedness, and active listening are all required.

Rare as these types of conversations may be, there is a difference between telling somebody what to do and giving them advice too. Telling somebody what to do is can be seen in employer-employee relationships. "Hey Bill, move those boxes from here to there, log them into the system, and tell Lynn to expedite shipping." This conversation comes from a hierarchical relationship, given by a person with authority to someone of lower status. This doesn't make the employee inferior as an individual, but when working for others we are being paid to do what they tell us to do.

We do not always listen or act simply because somebody outranks us on an org chart, even when their commands are legal and ethical to carry out and they have license to tell us what to do. Although authority can be a part of any relationship, we are more likely to take advice from those we perceive as having more wisdom, experience, or expert knowledge than we do ourselves.

There are four different types of advice, (1) guidance, (2) counsel, (3) coaching, and (4) mentoring. While these may overlap to small degree, each one has a unique purpose and benefit. For example:

- **Guidance** – asking for discrete recommendations, such as soliciting our supervisor's advice on which one of our subordinates we should promote into management.
- **Counsel** – asking for expert advice in how to approach an unfamiliar challenge, such requesting a real estate agent to help us understand how best to negotiate the purchase of a new home during a hot housing market when we're competing with multiple bidders.
- **Coaching** – asking for help in increasing specific skills, such as requesting a karate, kung fu, or taekwondo instructor to show us how best to perfect our back kick.
- **Mentoring** – asking for advice about personal or professional growth from someone we respect, such as whether or not it makes sense to quit our job and pursue an advanced degree in hopes of creating better opportunities after graduation.

Of all the various types of advice we receive, much of it is ignored no matter how good it is. Consequently, the best advice we have ever been given may have been something we followed or something we ignored to our detriment and subsequently wished that we had followed.

One of the things that helps us both receive and take action on good advice is by carefully defining the problem. This includes setting the stage by describing enough background so that the person we're seeking advice from can understand our dilemma. Then, we must be clear and concise about what guidance, counsel, coaching, or mentoring we're actually looking for. Sometimes we may just wish to vent whereas other times we actually want someone to help us solve our problem.

On the other side of the proverbial table, unsolicited advice no matter how well-intended or intentioned is rarely received well. We may legitimately be trying to help, but unasked suggestions usually come across poorly no matter how helpful they may be. This means that if we wish to be an advisor, we need to make sure we understand the question, seeking first to understand before trying to be understood. And, we must know that the person is actually asking for help rather than simply looking for a shoulder to cry on.

This dialogue takes active listening, probing questions and interactive communication on both sides. Once we know the need, we must be certain that we can actually help before giving advice too. Sometimes it's better to send a friend or colleague to an expert rather than trying to weigh in on things we really aren't qualified to assist with.

So, what do martial artists perceive as great advice? Below is a sampling of survey responses on the best single piece of advice that survey respondents have ever received:

Chief Vicky Stormo wrote, "I was told by a veteran Hispanic police officer that I can be myself and didn't need to act or do things to try to fit in. I was a small female in a male-dominated occupation where there were only 22 female officers out of 535 total police officers who were working patrol. When I got out of the police academy, male officers put me to the test to see if I could fit in. I tried to act like many of them, telling jokes, using foul language, and trying to prove I was tough. It was not me. Giving me that advice woke me up. I realized that I had to be me, because that is what works. I couldn't change who I was. It is like learning what your abilities and skills are as a martial artist and utilizing what you were capable of doing."

Mark Hachey wrote, "Always speak the truth. That includes looking at yourself truthfully. My Dad emphasized that during all of my formative years."

Matt Jardine wrote, "When I first started my mobile *shiatsu* clinic (me, a pair of trainers, and a rolled-up futon in the back of my van), I had quite a few private clients in 'swanky' London. One of them, Neville Buch, was a hugely successful businessman. He was incredibly supportive of all my endeavors. One time he asked me how the 'clinic' was going. I told him fine, thank you. He asked me how many clients I had. I said, enough. He asked again. I said I've got more next week. He didn't let me leave his office until I'd written down how many clients I actually had booked in my diary: only four. He taught me to be honest to myself about my 'start line,' no mixers how far back down the track it might seem. 'When you know where you are, you can then make a plan to get where you want to go.'"

> A common theme surrounding the best advice martial artists ever received was knowing themselves and holding true to their values, much as the sage Aristotle advised over 2,300 years ago.

Charles James wrote, "Upon competing and graduating from Marine Boot I ran into one of my Drill Instructors who sat with me and gave me the best piece of advice ever. 'As a Marine, all that you do will always demonstrate your abilities regardless of what other Marines or the Marine Corps says or does.' In short, 'Your accomplishments will depend entirely on you, your attitude, your character and your personality!' Following this advice, I achieved E-6 Staff Sergeant in less than six years of active duty."

Les Bubka wrote, "I was given many great pieces of advice but a quote from Oscar Wilde has stuck with me the most, 'Be yourself; everyone else is already taken'. Following this has changed my life completely."

John Leylegian wrote, "A student (academic, not martial arts) who I knew to be rather tough (veteran, single mom, who got out an abusive relationship) told other students that she thought I was intimidating when she started my class. After expressing my surprise that she would find me that way I told her that I would try to temper my approach with new students. She told me, 'No. Don't change a thing. That little bit of intimidation helps the students realize things are getting real and that you're preparing us for the real world.'"

Chris Agostinelli wrote, "My Father told me: 'The hardest thing to do in life is to look in the mirror and be honest with yourself, but it's something that must always be done throughout your life.'"

Lieutenant Carissa Jenkins wrote, "My brother gave me the best advice, albeit morbid. I was stressed about where I wanted to go to school. I felt immense pressure coming from my parents and mentors to go to an Ivy League institution. I took it all so personally, and I wanted to make everyone proud. My brother told me that, as an adult, you have to own everything you do. It's your life and only you can make the decisions. He told me to live like everyone is going to die someday, because it's true. Everyone will be gone one day, and the only person left on earth who can judge you is you. This is when I started living for myself. I decided to go to West Point on this advice, because it was a decision that I could make and be proud of. It was a decision I made for myself."

Note that responses from these martial artists from all around the world revolve around the theme of knowing yourself, as Aristotle suggested. After all, most believe that knowing ourselves is the first step toward wisdom. By being true to ourselves and our situation, we become empowered to control the direction of our lives, focusing energy on things that move us toward where we want to go.

Chinese philosopher Lao Tzu took this theme a step farther, writing, "Knowing others is intelligence; knowing yourself is true wisdom. Mastering others is strength; mastering yourself is true power." This is not only great advice; it deeply resonates with the martial arts community.

If you had to pick one age to be permanently, which age would you choose

"Age is a very high price to pay for maturity."
Tom Stoppard, Czech playwright and screenwriter.

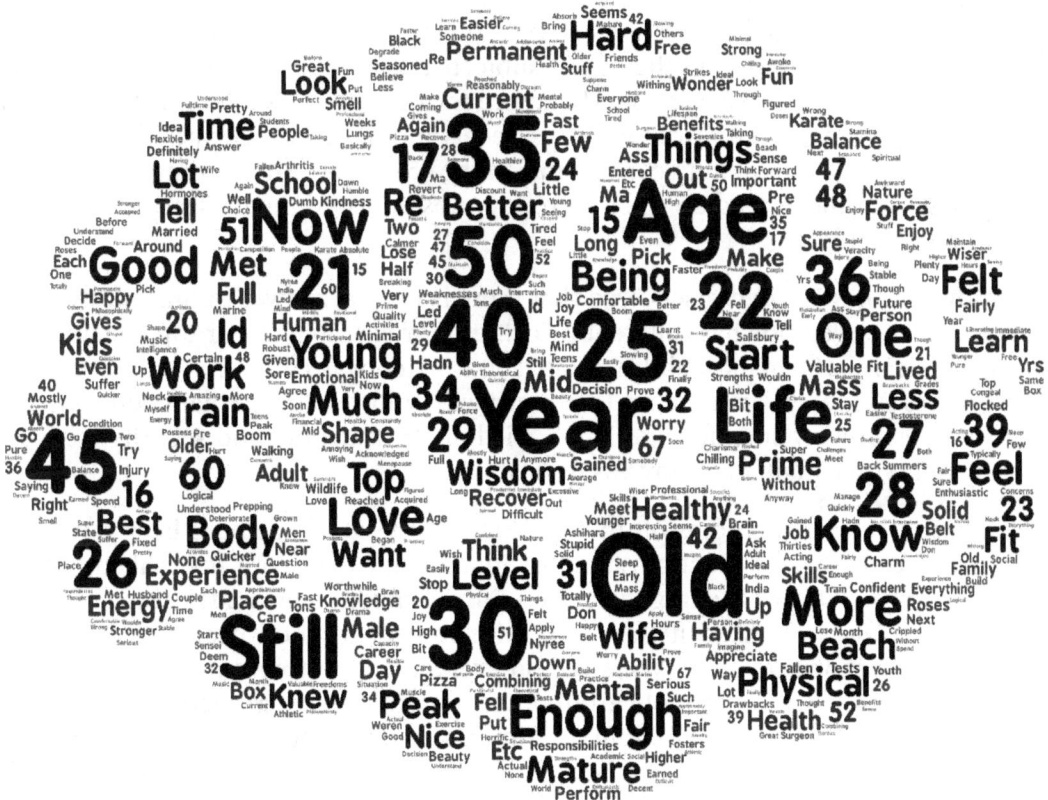

When scientists evaluate the aging process, they find some interesting conclusions. There are strengths and weaknesses that come with every stage in life. For instance, we perform better physically in our youth yet are sharper and more balanced mentally in our seniority. On average, the ideal age to learn a second language is 7 or 8 years old even though our brains reach their peak processing power at age 18 and the ability to remember unfamiliar names peaks at age 22. Maximum muscle strength comes around age 25, yet endurance peaks at 28, and bone mass at 30. Our ability to focus tends to peak around age 43 and our earning capacity is usually at its highest by age 48. Our sense of empathy works best at age 51. Our life satisfaction peaks around age 69, we're happiest with our bodies at age 74, and we experience our highest psychological wellbeing at age 82, assuming we live that long.

This begs the question, what is our ideal age?

In 2018, epidemiologists at the University of Illinois Chicago School of Public Health conducted a study on the aging process, trying to determine the best answer to the question, "If you had a pill that could stop biological aging in its tracks, when would you take it?" Under the assumption that if test subjects reached peak satisfaction with life at a certain age, they might have actionable advice for the rest of us follow, researchers like Dr. Jay Olshansky measured worry and stress levels at different times throughout people's lives. Oddly enough, while study participants in the 65- to 74-year-old range rated among the happiest, and those aged 35 to 54 were the most stressed, hence least satisfied with their situation in life.

That study and others like it discovered that there is no real answer to this question. The challenge is that everyone has different priorities. For example, if our top consideration is peak physical performance, ability to attract a mate, bear children, or have the most opportunities in life, we would tend to answer with a lower age, perhaps somewhere in our 20s to 30s. If we value life experience, wisdom, satisfaction, and security we would likely answer with a higher age, say 50s or 60s.

While dozens of similar studies on this question of the ideal age have been conducted, results are affected by the exact question asked and vary a bit with the makeup of each survey group too. One of the largest of these investigations was a 2013 Harris Poll that found when folks were asked if they could live forever in good health at a particular age, they would choose to be 50-years-old on average. Interestingly, despite the fact that women are deemed most desirable around age 23 while men's attractiveness generally increases with age (within certain limits), women stated that they would choose to be 53, whereas men selected age 47, which is how the average age of 50 was derived from that survey group.

Those aforementioned survey responses were subjective, but let's look at some additional objective information. Data demonstrates that our athletic prime zeniths around age 30, but this actually varies substantially by sport. We find our best speed and explosive performance in our mid-20s, peak strength and physicality in our mid-30s, best endurance in our mid-40s, and greatest tactical proficiency in our mid-50s.

How does this play out in real life? The oldest Olympic boxing champion was a 37-year-old from Great Britain, Richard Kenneth Gunn. Similarly, American wrestler Christopher Campbell earned a bronze medal in Freestyle wrestling a month before his 38th birthday. Contrast this with Sweden's Oscar Swahn who won an Olympic gold medal in shooting when he was 64 years old and followed up that performance with a silver medal at age 72. U.S. Olympian Eliza Pollock earned a gold and two bronze medals in archery at age 63.

So, this begs the question, where does the martial arts community stand on the answer for their perfect age? Like previous studies, their answers varied substantially from person to person. We received just a number from some respondents, and also an explanation from many, which is why we're showing both a word cloud (above) and chart (below) for this one. A majority of respondents looked to a balance of life experience, health, and physical prowess when answering. The average age selected was 33.77 but we'll round up to 34. Oddly enough the lowest answer was 5-years-old and the highest answer was 70-years-old. Here's what these responses looked like graphically:

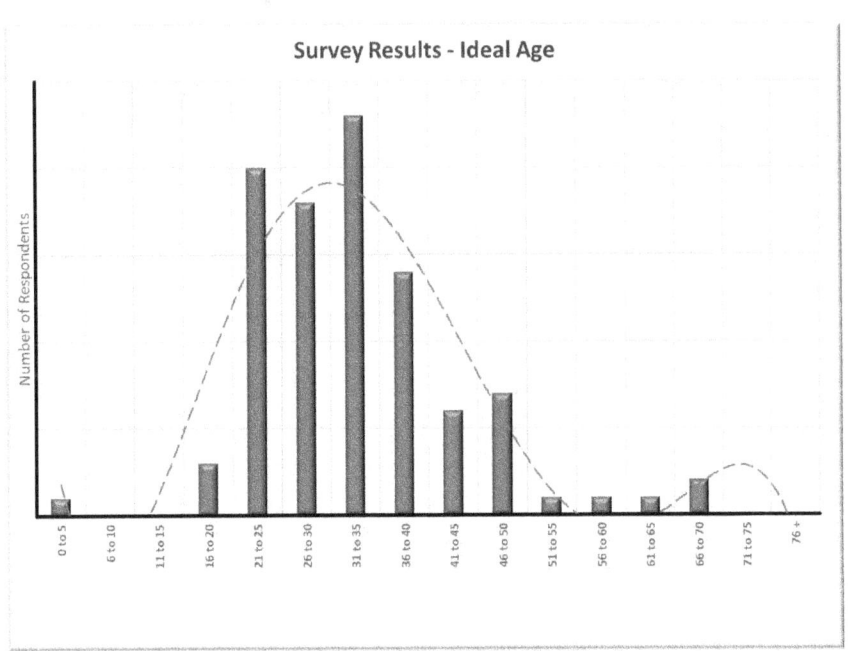

While we might intuit that older folk wish to be younger, or young folks more experienced, our perfect age is really a reflection of our individual goals and values in life. Martial artists focus more on self-development than most, continuously challenging ourselves to improve and grow. We also participate in more rigorous physical activities than the norm. As such, we tend to look toward a lower ideal age than the average person who seeks an easier path through life. This is why martial artists would rather be 34 than 50.

> While the ideal age for the general population who seek comfort and security is 50 years old, martial artists choose 34 years of age, seeking more opportunities to challenge ourselves and grow.

As one respondent, Brian Hassler, put it, that is, "Old enough for the brain to mature but not so old that the body starts to degrade. If I could try it for a couple of weeks, I might decide to go older (like 40) so the hormones weren't so annoying. Being calmer is nice…" This balance of maturity and physicality, wisdom and athleticism, is why most martial artists would love to be age 34 forever if they could.

Martial Artist Profile – Patricia Bolton

Patricia Bolton has been practicing martial arts for over 25 years. She currently holds the rank of 4th dan, is a proud member of Shorin Ryu Karatedo *International (SRKDI), and is certified by Iain Abernethy as an instructor in the practical application of karate. Practicing primary* Matsubayashi Shorin Ryu Karate-do, *she also has training in* Shotokan *karate and* Kyukido. *She lives and teaches karate with an emphasis on self-protection in Southern Wisconsin and is the author of the book* Silhouettes of Abuse. *Her website is* https://www.imokkarate.com/.

For good or ill, what was the biggest impact of your martial arts training on your life?

"When I started martial arts in my mid-20s, I was an emotional mess. I had 3 very young children (the oldest was 3!) and a marriage that was in trouble. My husband at the time had made me quit a job that I loved and he was having an affair. My self-esteem was in the negative numbers and I was beyond hurt and angry. I found a confidence in myself that I never really had. I was able to not only find an outlet for all the hurt and anger inside me, but found strength, discipline and maybe most importantly resilience. What I learned could not be taken from me, it was mine alone. Years later, I was able to share it with others by teaching and helping others to find those qualities within themselves. It has taken me through many hard times. Even when I felt too broken to train, it was still in the back of my mind telling me to get off my butt and train so that I will feel better."

Knowing what you know now, would you do it all over again?

"Yes. To date, I've trained in 3 different styles and I have found value in every one of them. Sometimes I wish I wouldn't have taken any long breaks, but yet those breaks were beneficial to my training one way or another and I think makes me a better teacher because I understand what my students go through. Teaching martial arts is one of my greatest joys in life. Having the ability to do that is priceless."

What is the best compliment you have ever received?

"An assault survivor once told me that she heard me in her head during her assault telling her to fight, to not quit fighting, to not give up. She didn't quit and she was able to escape her attacker and she wanted to let me know how grateful she was. To have someone share that with you and knowing that you helped them through something so horrific is the best compliment I could ever receive."

> "An assault survivor once told me that she heard me in her head during her assault telling her to fight, to not quit fighting, to not give up. She didn't quit and she was able to escape her attacker and she wanted to let me know how grateful she was."

When you were a kid, what did you want to be when you grew up

"So many things! At different times as a kid I wanted to be a singer, an artist, a teacher, a nurse, a truck driver, and a lawyer. I wasn't a good enough singer to ever become a professional. I am an artist, but not in the way I had imagined, just like the teacher. Doing martial arts and teaching it, I wouldn't have imagined that would be possible as a kid because I wasn't really exposed to it. The nurse…I have been in and out of the medical field over the years, although not as a nurse. After being out of high school for several years, I did go back to school to become a medical assistant and I did that for a while, but then life took some weird turns and I wasn't able to continue with that job. I still enjoy the field, but more towards the goal of health and wellness now."

What single event of the past changed the world for the worst?

"Changes to the food industry. The use of glyphosate, farming that is not sustainable and chemically enhanced foods. It's bad for the planet. It's bad for the human body. It's making us fat, addicted to non-nourishing foods, and unhealthy. Poor nutrition also leads to behavior problems. I know it seemed like a good idea at the time, but it's time to realize it was a mistake and fix it."

What's the worst martial arts-related mistake you have ever made?

"When acting as *uke* (person who receives a technique), I tried to look. You should never try to look to see what the other person is demonstrating! I slightly turned right into a choke and managed to get a bruised trachea. One of the most painful injuries I have ever received while practicing martial arts."

If you could go back in time, what advice would you give to your teenage self?

"It takes a very long time to become young."
Pablo Picasso, Spanish painter

We often think of emotional maturity as something that develops at a certain age or with a certain level of experience, but it's really more of a mindset than anything else, hence could happen at virtually any time in life. Some of us are more mature than our years might suggest, while others never seem to grow up.

Psychological research indicates that as folks become more mature, they grow into being more considerate, less self-absorbed, less easily offended, and more forgiving, in many instances as the result of realizing how much they truly don't know. They adopt a longer-term worldview, often passing over instant gratification in favor of enduring benefits. Perhaps counterintuitively, given common stereotypes around older people being set in their ways, they tend to show more flexibility, reasonableness, and openness too. And, they tend to take more reasonability for their circumstances, becoming less apt to blame things on others.

In many ways this can be summarized as having enough experience to be able to see things in context, viscerally knowing what is worth getting worked up about and what is not. We understand that it is okay to fail, know the cost of not trying, and generally make better and more informed decisions.

> Martial artists are much like the rest of humanity when it comes to maturity, though many believe they would have been more willing to follow their older self's advice than the norm had they received it.

While our hypothesis was that we might discover something atypical, as it turns out martial artists are very much like the rest of society when it comes to maturity. Their advice to their younger self wasn't any different than what we find in news articles and blogs on this same subject matter, though many related that they may have been more willing to follow their older self's advice than is the norm.

Simply put, the business of youth is the folly of the youthful. While our younger selves were invariably convinced of their infallibly, believing that they knew everything at that time and place, with life experience came better perspective. In retrospect, survey respondents wish that they had planned better, applied more, tried harder, or thought more before acting. They spoke to taking measured risks, following an easier path instead of learning things the hard way, working harder or at least more efficiently, accomplishing more, or doing less of something later deemed undesirable.

While every narrative related to us through the questionnaire was different, common words and phrases spoke to things like building for the future, not putting on facades, focusing on health, slowing down, enjoying more, relaxing better, asking more questions, and taking good advice. In other words, martial artists understand that they're not perfect. Had they known then what they know now, they believe that they would have made better decisions. This is the same conclusion that any open-minded, mature individual would come to when evaluating the imprudence that more often than not comes from their youth.

Martial Artist Profile – Wallace Smedley

Wallace began training in 1983 to defend against violent bullying. He has trained in boxing, kickboxing, wrestling, Chinese Hung Gar kung fu, Korean taekwondo, and tactical firearms. In 2001, he began teaching full time for Chuck Norris' Kickstart Kids foundation which brings martial arts training to at-risk youth in inner-city schools. This rewarding work has provided the opportunity to have a positive impact on the lives of thousands of kids over the twenty years and counting that he has worked here. His website is www.wallacesmedley.com.

When you were a kid, what did you want to be when you grew up?

"I wanted to be a professional wrestler. I was made fun of a lot for that dream, but I did actually make it happen in the 1990s. I did not stick with it because I could not make a living at it. And it was hammered into my head when I was young that if you can't make a living at it, it is just a hobby."

What is the best single piece of advice you were ever given?

"My father told me once, 'Don't let yesterday ruin today.' Each day needs to be a new day and a new start. Everyone you meet and everyone you know will make mistakes, and you will too. Be the first to forgive, and move on. Don't hold a grudge about what someone said or did yesterday. You can be better than that."

If you could go back in time, what advice would you give to your teenage self?

"Make time for friends. You will always have time for training, but when a friend is gone, they are gone. I gave up all friends and anything resembling a social life in favor of training in martial arts. I regret that now. People around me built and lived their lives while I toiled in the training hall."

What single event of the past changed the world for the worst?

"Social media has brought out so much asinine behavior and has been the point-of-departure for so much violence and destruction that I have to call it the worst change the world has seen so far."

For good or ill, what was the biggest impact of your martial arts training on your life?

"My training opened the door to my job where I get to help kids. Nothing could be more important."

> "I gave up all friends and anything resembling a social life in favor of training in martial arts. I regret that now. People around me built and lived their lives while I toiled in the training hall."

Knowing what you know now, would you do it all over again?

"Yes, because I have changed lives for the better many times over. I cannot sacrifice the benefits to the lives of others which were made through me for some things that could have been better for me personally."

When you were a kid, what did you want to be when you grew up?

"The best part of the journey is the surprise and wonder along the way."
Ken Poirot, American novelist

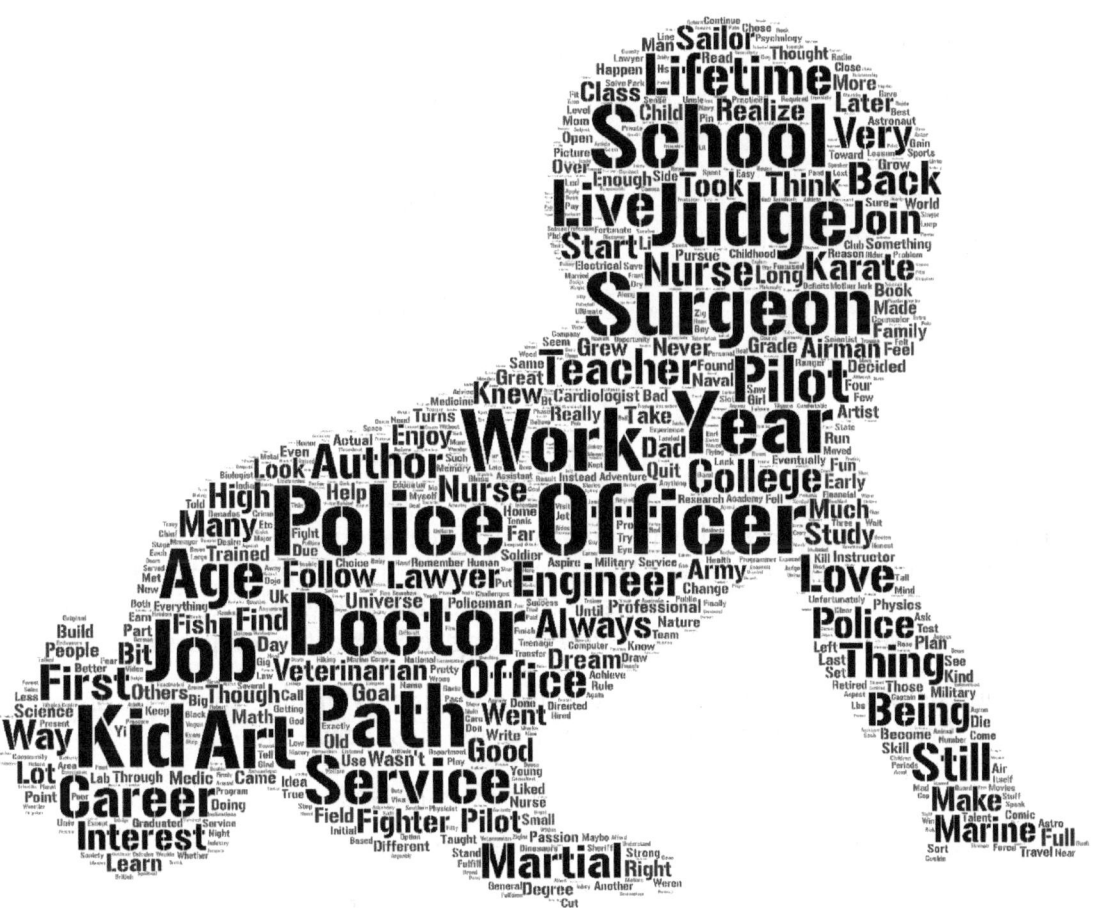

A 2014 study of 4,000 American parents by parenting website Cafemom found that 37 percent of their children wanted to become superheroes when they grew up. Other top career choices were celebrities, prince or princess, President of the United States, and Santa Claus. Apparently martial artists are cut from a different cloth. Responses to our survey question were clustered into a group we classify as service- and process-centric occupations.

In other words, as a community we are attracted to career paths that contribute to the betterment of society, jobs such as:

- Airman
- Army Officer
- Author
- Biologist
- Doctor
- Engineer
- Judge
- Lawyer
- Marine
- Military Service
- Nurse
- Pilot
- Police Officer
- Sailor
- Soldier
- Surgeon
- Teacher
- Veterinarian

Collectively, these roles are all action-oriented, directed toward the benefit of others, often before profiting for ourselves. That certainly does not mean that martial artists are entirely altruistic, but rather that we tend to look outward toward where we can create value through worthwhile endeavors before seeking self-benefit in job pursuits.

The antithesis of career titles selected by our respondents include roles that are more internally directed, self-aggrandizing, or avaricious. This includes jobs like:

- Anarchist
- Computer Scientist
- Entrepreneur
- Diplomat
- Hedge Fund Manager
- Insurance Salesperson
- Journalist
- Pacifist
- Politician
- Real Estate Agent
- Social Media Influencer
- Stockbroker

Let's analyze these results… An aspiration toward careers in law enforcement and the military are overrepresented in our study. These are great examples of putting service to others ahead of one's own welfare. They are low paying, high stress, and largely thankless positions, yet roles that are absolutely necessary for society to function in a civilized manner.

From a Maslow's Hierarchy of Needs perspective, this means that people who perform these kinds of jobs administer to requirements at the bottom of the pyramid, seeing to many of the physiological and safety imperatives that underpin every functioning society. Invented by American psychologist Abraham Maslow (1908–1970) in 1943, this taxonomy (see figure below) helps us understand his theory of human motivation, showing how we must fulfill our deficiency needs at the bottom of the pyramid before being able to move up toward our growth imperatives. That is challenging if not impossible without law enforcement, military, emergency services, and similar roles. People who take these occupations go in knowing full well that they may be called upon to give up their lives, longevity, or wellbeing in service to their community, yet they do so willingly nevertheless. In other words, they realize that it is vital but dangerous work.

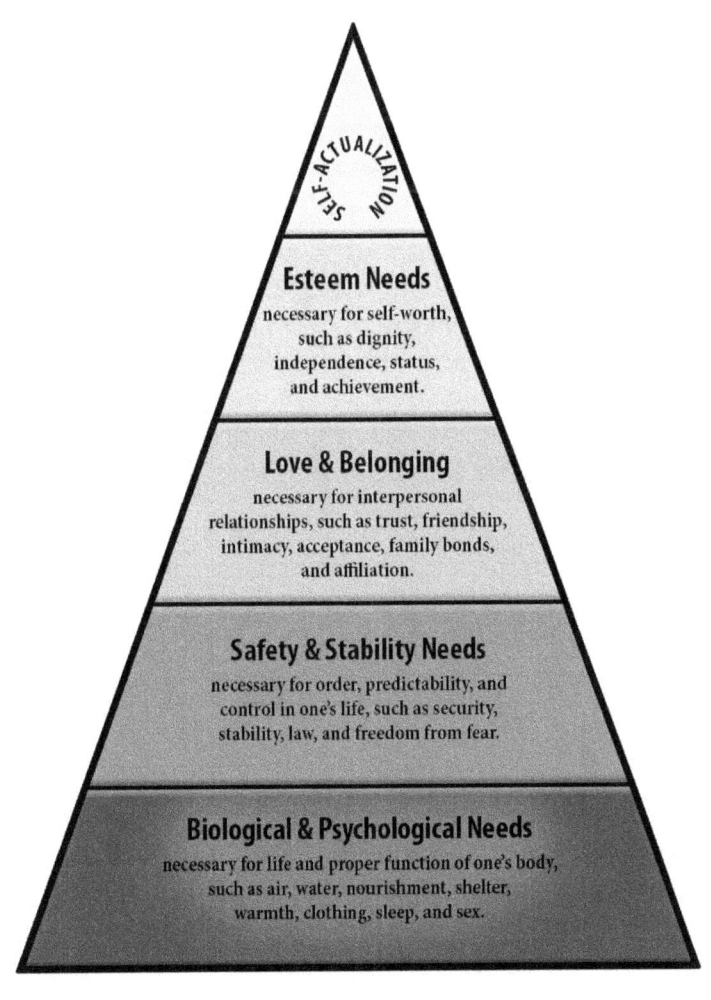

Done right, law enforcement is all about protecting citizens from internal threats against their lives, property, and community. Cops are peacekeepers; they place themselves between ordinary citizens and criminals who wish to prey on them. Their job description is literally to arrest crime. Additional roles and responsibilities include community engagement, patrol, investigation, evidence collection, training, communication, liaison, and a host of other activities. They often work hand-in-glove with other emergency service professionals, performing triage and first aid until firefighters, Emergency Medical Technicians, paramedics, or other specialists can arrive on the scene and take over.

Military careers are somewhat similar, though in most instances they are focused on protecting one's nation against external threats rather than dealing with internal ones. The stronger and better prepared a nation's military, the lower the likelihood that enemy state actors will take kinetic action towards them. Consequently, the job description of most military personnel involves having the knowledge, skill, and ability to kill people, break things, and blow stuff up. Sure, that's a bit sardonic, but it's also accurate. With fourth and fifth generation warfare, where non-state actors are involved (e.g., wars undeclared formally, battlefields anywhere or everywhere, uniforms optional, civilian combatants or targets, psyops, etc.), the job description can get a whole lot more complicated, but we're just summarizing here.

Clearly some law enforcement officers can go their whole careers without ever needing to draw their weapons or take incoming fire, just like some soldiers will never need to step onto a battlefield, but both these occupations are hazardous even in training, and both require sacrifices that most citizens are not prepared to take such as being away from one's family for extended periods of time. They also require strict adherence to process and procedure, honoring codes of conduct, obeying chains of command, following rules of engagement, and enforcing legal orders in the pursuit of their missions.

> Even as children, martial artists are process-focused and drawn toward service, often aspiring to career roles that benefit others in the community.

Judges and nurses fall into the same category of service and process. Judges are the ultimate deciders of disagreements, referees of the courtroom so to speak, and in so doing they help ensure reasonable and just resolution of both criminal and civil disputes. They interpret laws, rules, and regulations using strict processes to adjudicate as fairly and objectively as possible. Without them there is no recourse for injustice and society devolves into anarchy and vigilantism.

Similarly, nurses are all about procedures too, and rightly so. When they do things right, they help save lives, whereas if they make mistakes people can be grievously injured or die. Consequently, they must diligently follow processes for giving care, administering prescriptions, assisting in surgeries, and the like.

Doctors and veterinarians follow along this same theme. They are procedure-oriented, with a heavy dose of deductive work added into the mix. Their environment is one of constant decision-trees, with diagnosis, tests, and reexaminations until the right course of treatment can be identified and implemented for their patients. They work long hours and are often on call for emergency situations. And, many doctors work with older patients or folks suffering from comorbidities whose reaction to treatments are uncertain. Thematically, one could equate these professions with folks who "get shot at for a living" levels of stress. It takes a special kind of person to embrace such things willingly.

It is interesting to note that entrepreneur is not on this list. Although there may be entrepreneurial aspects inherent in many of these professions, they exist in a secondary or tertiary manner, and it was not a career choice specifically stated by our respondents as something they aspired to since childhood. Perhaps this is because most martial artists are strongly pulled toward process and service, and business careers do not clearly fit that mold. After all, the ascendant goal expressed is to make one's mark on the world in a positive manner, one that provides direct feedback as to the success or failure individual actions.

Martial artists can track their achievements through wins and losses, and hold accountability through earned ranks and titles, so their martial journey is reflected in the competencies they master along their path. Even as children, most of us similarly aspired to careers that hold these same values.

Martial Artist Profile – Peter Freedman

Grandmaster Peter Freedman started training under his father in Western-style boxing and bare-knuckle fighting. In 1970 he went into Goju Ryu karate, Ketsugo Jujutsu, and other arts. He began studying arnis in 1985 under Grandmaster George Brewster who passed his system over to him in 2000. Since age 15, Peter began pulling rival gang members and troubled teens and adults off the streets, helping them learn how to read, quit drugs, build up their self-esteem, and become positive role models in their community. In total he has helped transform the lives of over 6,000 teenagers and adults and was honored by the Mayor of Boston, Raymond Leo Flynn, in 1989 for his work. He has taught self-defense and close quarters combat to law enforcement, the CIA, the United States Department of Defense, Special Operations, Mountain Soldiers, Navy Seals, State Troopers, DEA, FBI, Sky Marshals, and Correctional Officers. He also founded and operated Pete's Power Gym where he who taught anatomy, physiology, nutrition, powerlifting, bodybuilding, and posing to men, women, and children and coached and trained over-35 all-natural national bodybuilding champions. He also taught seminars on emotional control and how to properly vent anger, fostering positive emotional healing among thousands of clients. A veteran powerlifter who bench-pressed 505 pounds for 5 reps, military-pressed 350 pounds, and split open heavy bags with a single punch, he was formerly known around Boston as "Mighty Whitey." His website is www.combatscience.com

---

What attributes do you admire most?

"The thing I admire most is compassion. How others treat each other."

If you could go back in time, what advice would you give to your teenage self?

"To learn more how money works and how to invest it. I would also have told my younger self to not hang out with certain people. They are all dead today. I was lucky."

What's the worst martial arts-related mistake you have ever made?

"My martial art is combat. We teach killing, crippling, and controlling lastly. The biggest mistake I ever made was teaching one guy who I should not have taught. I did eventually catch up to him later and had a long hard discussion. It seemed to work."

For good or ill, what was the biggest impact of your martial arts training on your life?

"The first knife fight I ever got into. I realized my training had saved my life... and more than once."

What energizes you outside of work?

I like to help people, all kinds of people. I feel what they feel and in that it guides my lessons they need. I am an empath, and I am a patient person until it is not time to be patient. My strengths are being able to get into people's heads by profiling their actions, facial expressions, moods, body language, voice reading, and then knowing if they're off.

> "The biggest mistake I ever made was teaching one guy who I should not have taught. I did eventually catch up to him later and had a long hard discussion. It seemed to work."

What is the best compliment you have ever received?

"That I have changed someone's life for the better. I get that a lot. Next one is from the troops coming back from overseas that I had taught. They told me thank you Mr. Freedman it all worked out just fine and it saved their lives."

What energizes you outside of work?

"Expressing thankfulness energizes, enhances, and empowers."
Skip Prichard, American business executive

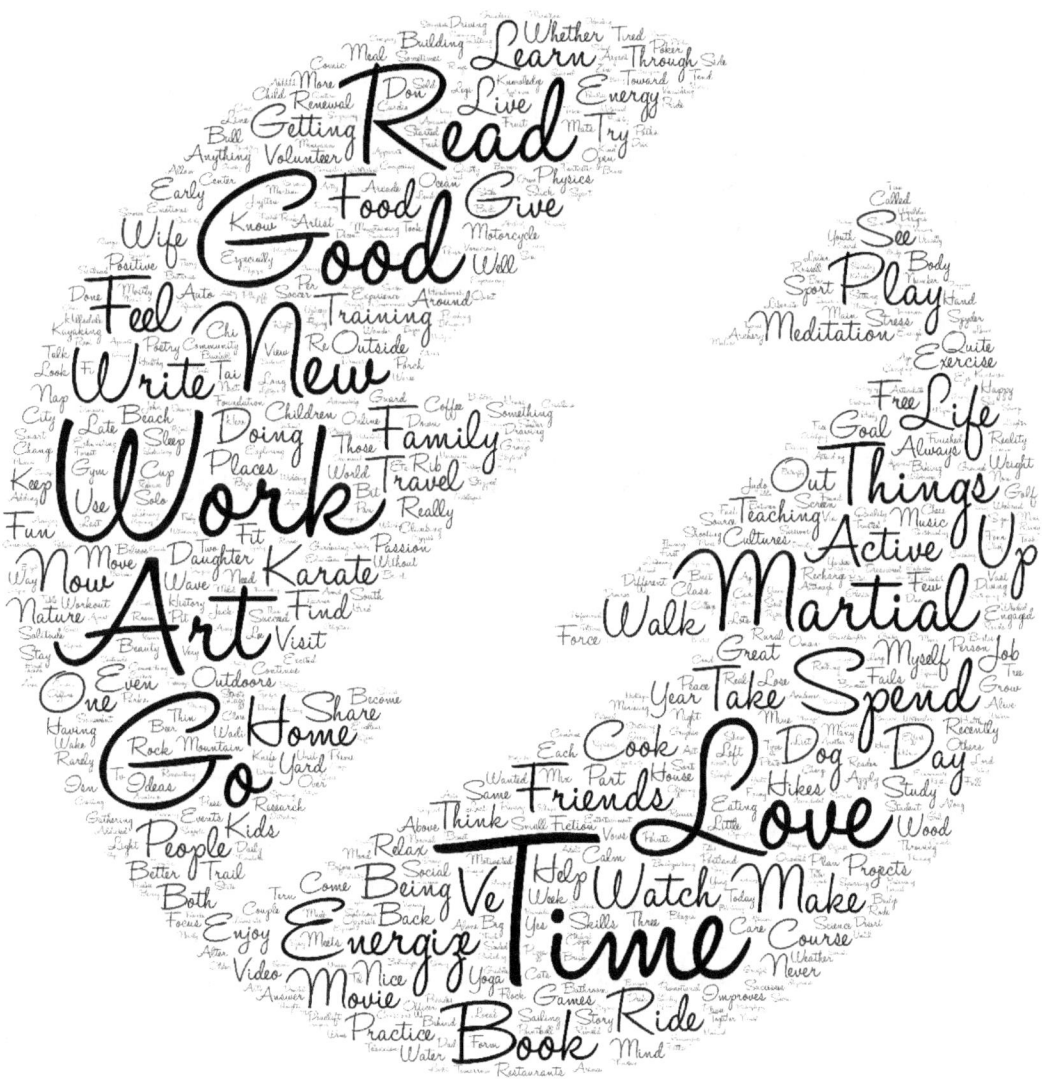

While most of us have work to live, few would voluntarily live for work, yet invariably many find themselves over-rotating in that direction, checking emails, accepting texts or phone calls, and thinking about their job at all hours of the day or night. In today's fully-connected, always-on world, it is common to feel so drained by work that we have minimal if any enthusiasm left to focus on relationships, hobbies, fitness, family, martial arts, or other important activities. Consequently, we must learn to set boundaries, assuring that we both have "off-the-clock" time as well as the energy to enjoy it.

According to a 2012 Gallup business poll, "An alarming 70% of American workers are not showing up to work committed to delivering their best performance, and this has serious implications for the bottom line of individual companies and the U.S. economy as a whole." This was long before the pandemic and work-from-home craze, which likely means that things have gotten substantially worse more recently as evidenced by the so-called "Great Resignation," though to be fair the underpinning reasons behind millions of people quitting or changing jobs are complex and multifold. Nevertheless, we thought it would be interesting to discover what martial artists find energizes them outside of work.

> Martial artists need time off work to relax and recharge in much the same way as anyone else, though we tend to push ourselves more toward personal growth than pure relaxation during our downtime.

Common activities that help people refresh and reenergize include exercise, travel, meditation, spending time with their family, continuing education, and community involvement, and martial artists aren't much different in this regard, though once again we find a propensity to push ourselves more toward personal growth than toward pure relaxation in our off time. For instance, many survey respondents reported being voracious readers who consume books for both entertainment, enlightenment, and academic pursuit.

Others spoke to physical endeavors such as weightlifting, hiking, kayaking, gardening, and, of course, martial arts. As Patricia Bolton wrote, "Being sedentary makes me feel lazy and tired." Some of the more common responses included creative activities such as fiction writing, woodworking, knifemaking, and various forms of community service too.

Below are a few of the more interesting and insightful responses to this question:

Tzviel "BK" Blankchtein wrote, "I get a special kind of energy, motivation, and Zen-like feeling from water. I grew up on the beach in Tel-Aviv, Israel, so water was always a source of calmness and energy. Every morning I would wake up and look at the sea. If there were waves, I'd go surfing, if it was calm, I'd go diving, but either way I would go to the water. Now living in Maryland, I just recently moved south of Annapolis in search of that same connection. I spend my free time kayaking, paddle boarding, and boating. When I cross the bridge over the south river to my little peninsula, I feel my soul settle into a different rhythm that is both serenity and energy. I believe in it so much that I recently named my newborn daughter Gal, which is Hebrew for 'wave'. I hope she encompasses the power and stability of this force of nature."

Dr. Hermann Bayer related, "Until 2005 it used to be sailing and maintaining an antique wooden sailing yacht. Today, tinkering, repairing things, building *kobudo* weapons, maintaining and upgrading our homes gives me great pleasure. My 'work' on the other hand is voluntary and thus energizing too: fulltime karate and authoring publications on karate."

Chief Vicky Stormo wrote, "Giving back to the community, especially through the Behind the Badge Foundation. Finding positives and beauty in life. My goals now are to try to find something beautiful and acknowledge it each day and to try to do something I've never done before each day."

Alain Burrese recounted, "I have always been a voracious reader. I usually read 6 to 8 books at a time, and read a minimum of 101 books a year, often surpassing that number by quite a bit. My family knows that I energize through reading, so they allow me my humongous library and reading time."

Matt Jardine shared, "Writing makes me feel alive, as do walks along the Oman coastline with my wife and Jack Russell terrier. Whether it's a tern diving, a wadi dog come to play, or a flock of flamingo balancing on stick thin legs, the days 'offering from above' never fails to charge us."

Andrea Harkins reported, "I enjoy a couple of good cups of coffee in the morning. I go to the gym and use the elliptical a couple of times per week. I love light weight workouts, yoga, and stretching. I write love poetry (of course, there's a book in the works of love poetry and wedding vows). I spend time with my family. Weekend naps are a must. Hiking in the desert is an amazing experience that energizes me, also. Local sporting events are fun too."

What is your favorite weekend activity?

"Free time was the most precious time, when you should be doing what you loved, or at least slowing down enough to remember what made your life worthwhile and happy."

Amy Tan, American author

The term "working for the weekend" is used to imply that we are only able to get through the rigors of the work week by focusing on the weekend ahead. Despite the fact that many people actually enjoy their vocation, everyone needs time to unwind and decompress from the pressures they face in everyday life and more often than not that's what we do on weekends. A recent poll of nearly 5,000 adults by Surveyon.com listed favorite weekend activities as sleeping in, spending time with family, binge-watching television shows or movies, completing household chores, playing video games, and hanging out with friends.

Martial artists in our study answered this question a bit differently. They either focused on social activities such as spending time with family and friends or looked to the other end of the spectrum with solitary pursuits. External-oriented activities focus on experiences and social interactions whereas internal-oriented activities are more about rest, relaxation, and order. Both types of activities help us set aside the workweek and celebrate our passions even though we experience them somewhat differently. Some of the examples submitted in our survey are listed below:

Internal-oriented activities	**External-oriented activities**
○ Bushcrafting	○ Attending martial arts seminars
○ Crabbing	○ Going shopping
○ Hiking	○ Hanging out with friends
○ Researching	○ Kicking back with my spouse
○ Staying home	○ Knife and axe throwing
○ Watching movies	○ Scuba diving
○ Working on my motorcycle	○ Spending time with my family
○ Writing	○ Taking classes
○ Yardwork	○ Traveling

This dichotomy between internal- and external-oriented pursuits appears to align with an introvert versus extrovert orientation, though there was not a 100% correlation between reported activities and brain type of respondents. In other words, while introverts need more time alone to decompress and extroverts are energized by spending time with others, even highly introverted individuals crave social interaction from time-to-time and even the most extreme extroverts need a little quiet time on occasion.

While activities and interests vary substantially, most folks use weekends to relax, recharge, and ready themselves for the week ahead. It's an opportunity to focus on what we value most, "me time" so to speak. This downtime is important no matter what type of work we do. In fact, a Harvard Business Review study indicated that creativity increases by as much as 33%, happiness 25%, and productivity 13% when employees take a week off work. That's longer than a two- or three-day weekend, of course, yet the benefits of spending one's downtime on something other than work are clear.

Martial artists are no different than anyone else in this regard, although in analyzing survey responses it is evident that as a community we focus more on self-development and less on pure relaxation during our time off than the average citizen. Whether or not this is a healthy thing is open to conjecture, as it can both lead to accomplishing more or burning out easier, though with the mental and physical fitness inherent in martial arts the odds are good that it is a positive phenomenon.

Martial artists focus more on self-development and less on pure relaxation during their weekends than the average citizen.

Martial Artist Profile – Sarah Jackson

Sarah Jackson trains in Goju Ryu *karate and Okinawan* kobudo. *She started her training at age 28 and has enjoyed every minute of it. In the* dojo *is where she met her husband and, 13 years later, her 2 sons have both started their training, as well. She enjoys travel and hopes to combine training and travelling more in the future. She also enjoys helping out in the community and is especially passionate about helping marginalized people. Her belief is that everyone deserves compassion and respect. Her website is* https://niagaramartialarts.com.

For good or ill, what was the biggest impact of your martial arts training on your life?

"I realized how big of an impact the martial arts had on my life after I had my 2nd son. I hadn't been training for over a year and when I was taking my kids for a walk one day, I clued in to the fact that I was using the awareness that I'd developed during training, when I was out. When I saw a few 'ruffian' types, I crossed the street and I thought of what I would do if I needed to act quickly. Same thing when I started running, I'd put some safety measures into place before I ran. During a run I would keep an eye out for other people or even shadows, if it was nighttime. Not to the extent of paranoia, just being aware."

If you could go back in time, what advice would you give to your teenage self?

"That the reason you feel so insecure is because you suffer from anxiety and it's not your fault. I understand that most teenagers feel insecure, but this went much deeper. It was a mental battle for me just to make it to class every day. I've struggled with anxiety all of my life and it's wonderful how much attention mental health gets now, but when I was growing up in the 80s and 90s, the exposure wasn't there. I didn't fully understand what was going on until I was in my mid-20s. By that time, I'd made a lot of bad choices that I probably wouldn't have made if I had had a better understanding of what was going on with myself when I was younger."

What is the best compliment you have ever received??

"Being singled out while training outside of our *dojo* is a huge compliment to me. I have high regard for my *sensei's* opinion of me, but it's always validating to have an outside, respected teacher give special attention. I had the opportunity to train with Chinen *Sensei* on a few occasions, at our *dojo* and at his 40th annual *gasshuku* (training camp). At this *gasshuku*, there were more than 70 people (more people than I've ever trained with, by far). I was shouted-out a couple times during training, not to mention when I was asked to come to the front and say a bit about myself. This was slightly terrifying and unexpected. I had no clue what to say! I was a bit awkward at first but, thankfully after stumbling for words, he took pity on me and told people to ask me questions."

> "I have high regard for my sensei's opinion of me, but it's always validating to have an outside, respected teacher give special attention."

When you were a kid, what did you want to be when you grew up?

"A stay-at-home mom. I'm not sure why, but I assumed this is what I'd do. Just to clarify, gender roles were never talked about one way or another at my house. It's not because 'I'm a girl.' I just thought I'd be like my mom: married at 19, starting her family at 21 (I grew up when a family of 4 could actually live off one income). When I was 19 and had never been in a serious relationship, I realized I needed to get off my butt and do something. So, I travelled, moved across the country and eventually moved back home. At this point going back to school full time wasn't an option, but I realized that I had a decent job and felt comfortable with my situation. I started taking night courses in subjects that interested me, I was able to travel a bit and eventually started taking karate. And I read. A lot!"

What single event of the past changed the world for the worst?

"The advent of reality television. Hear me out: a lot of the shows out there aren't really that bad, but influencers and unreal lifestyles wreak havoc on people's self-esteem. Whether people develop a false sense of superiority because they would 'never demean themselves like that' or it leads to dissatisfaction with their own life. Viewers chase unattainable standards without realizing that people are using photoshop, having surgery or are able to travel and do so much because they're family is wealthy. Or on the flip side, they've accrued so much debt that they are constantly living with that hanging over their head. Sometimes I feel sorry for the influencer types; once they present themselves a certain way, they can't go 'off brand.' They have to put on a front and live like people expect them to."

Knowing what you know now, would you do it all over again?

"Yes! If I could, I'd have started way earlier! I haven't had many negative experiences, but honestly, after the birth of my second child, I wasn't sure if I'd be able to return to the martial arts. Having a family can mean making sacrifices. Fast forward a few years; my husband took over the *dojo* when our *sensei* retired and not only am I back at the *dojo*, but I'm training more than ever. Our whole family is there now! If I had known this earlier, I wouldn't have felt so bad about being away from the *dojo* for a season."

What is your guilty pleasure?

"I adore simple pleasures. They are the last refuge of the complex."
Oscar Wilde, Irish poet and playwright

Guilty pleasures are things we enjoy doing even though they may be embarrassing or shameful to admit in public. This doesn't necessarily mean that they are unproductive or inherently bad for us, though many are, but rather that they are things we'd rather that others do not know about us. Once again, we searched for a good international database on this subject matter and came up empty, hence reverted to the United States for representation. According to a 2018 AP News survey, America's top guilty pleasures included ordering take-out or delivery, eating fast food, falling asleep with the television on, gorging on ice cream, procrastinating, consuming sugary treats, singing in the car, and lounging around in their pajamas all day.

> # Martial artists have many of the same guilty pleasures as most people, but few spoke of enjoying idleness.

Martial artists answered our survey similarly, with the consumption of unhealthy foods or drinks rating high on the list, but interestingly very few spoke of enjoying unproductive or indolent activities like sleeping in, lounging in our pajamas, playing videogames, or procrastinating all day. Oftentimes there was a focus on friends and family in their responses too. The combination of answers could be assembled in this statement, "I like to spend time with friends and family while having good food and drink." A partial list of top indulgences reported by our respondents include:

- Beer (craft beers)
- Buttered popcorn
- Cheesecake
- Cheesy martial arts flix/action movies
- Chocolate
- Cigars
- Fried chicken
- Ice cream
- Potato chips (crisps)
- Reality TV
- Shopping
- Turkish coffee
- Whiskey
- Wine (good)

We asked respondents to be creative in answering this question, and must admit that our favorite, oddly specific response came from Brain Hassler, who wrote, "Drinking Dr. Pepper and biting the heads off of endangered eels." Knowing some of the characters we practice martial arts with, we're not entirely certain how much of his statement was made in jest, though we'll give him the benefit of the doubt on this one. If nothing else, it's an extremely creative answer.

A few additional highlights in response to this question:

Alain Burrese wrote, "My guilty pleasure is to go to movies, especially tough-guy action movies, and indulge in a large bucket of hot buttered popcorn. If nothing good is playing in the theaters, a movie at home (tough-guy action movie still preferred) with chips and salsa or ice cream will suffice."

Lee Taylor shared, "It has to be watching the Cobra Kai series! It's so wrong it's right, so cheesy but unmissable. It must be the nostalgic link to my childhood starting karate and watching the release of *The Karate Kid*, the pull to my past is too strong!"

Michael Millham responded, "My guilty pleasure is enjoying popular craft cocktail recipes pulled from the American Gilded Age—post-civil war—through the interwar years. Manhattans, Sazeracs, Sidecars, the Boulevardier… I'm pretty much a sucker for straight-up rye whiskey cosplay with friends."

In summary, while we are not lazy by nature, the guilty pleasures that martial artists reported were not much different than anyone else, especially when it comes to food and drink. We are, perhaps, drawn to action/adventure movies and television shows a bit more than the average person though.

Would you rather visit the beach or the mountains?

"It's not hard to make decisions when you know what your values are."
Roy Disney, American businessman

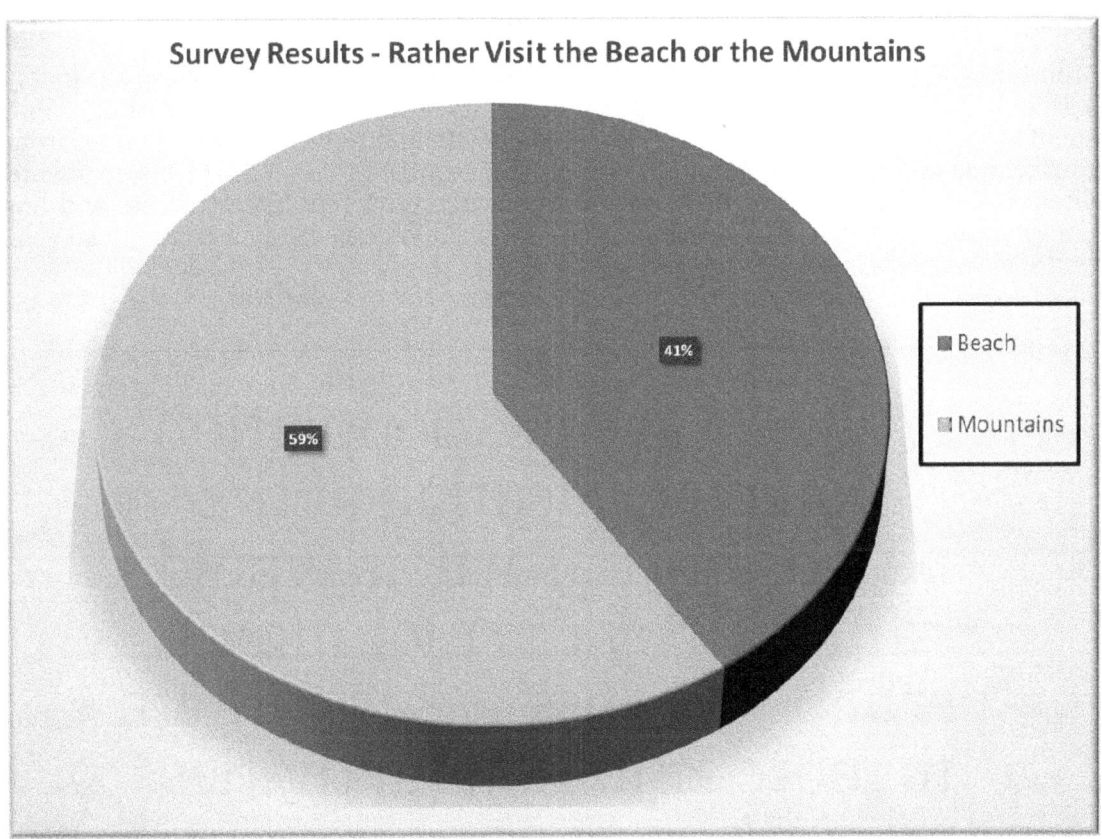

We were unable to find a global survey on this topic, but according to a 2018 Washington Post-ABC News poll, the beach is a top vacation choice for Americans across all racial, ethnic, gender, economic, and partisan lines, with nearly three-quarters of respondents expressing positive views of a summertime trip to the ocean. Surprisingly, older adults are somewhat less likely to have strong positive views of the ocean than younger people, though that study did not elaborate or explain why.

Getting in touch with nature can be a great way to unwind. A beach vacation affords us an opportunity to soak up the sun, and can include enjoyable activities such as boating, surfing, swimming, fishing, dining, or walking. Vitamin D, which is necessary to maintain healthy bones and normal calcium metabolism, is produced endogenously when ultraviolet rays from sunlight strike the skin and trigger synthesis. On the downside, popular beachfront areas can be loud, overcrowded, and expensive to visit during those times of the year when the weather is likely to be at its best for such excursions. And, the beach can be disconcerting for anyone with body image issues.

Mountains, on the other hand, are usually cheaper to visit, representing more outdoorsy activities like hunting, hiking, skiing, canoeing, river-rafting, or snowboarding. Time spent at higher elevations is conducive to good health and reduced mortality rates from cardiovascular disease too. But mountainous climates tend to be colder, wetter, and are oftentimes harder to enjoy than a trip to the beach. With less infrastructure and few tourist destinations beyond ski resorts, you may need to own or rent a recreational vehicle for such trips as well.

> While 73% of the population prefers to vacation at the beach, martial artists would rather enjoy the mountains, perhaps because we are drawn to more ambitious activities.

Based on the Washington Post survey, our hypothesis was that martial artists would similarly have a strong preference for visiting the beach, hence were somewhat surprised to discover that the reverse was true, with a roughly 60/40 preference for mountains. Perhaps this comes from proximity, access, familiarity, or previous experience, or perhaps the global nature of our study is what produced the different results as the Washington Post study was U.S.-centric.

Or, it may be the fact that martial artists like to challenge themselves which is why we are drawn to the mountains. This discrepancy might even be related to the myriad of individual and small group activities that can be done in the mountains where we are able to get away from crowds, at least when compared to popular tourist beaches. Regardless, fresh air, scenery, and elevation are definitely a good thing, one which martial artists appear inclined to enjoy far more than the average citizen.

Martial Artist Profile – Todd Durgan

Like many, Todd's training started at the age of 10 or 11, and later started training with Randy Borden a very large Hawaiian man that move like a gazelle and claimed to be related to 'the' Ed Parker, founder of American Kenpo. He later trained in a hard style Okinawan system through brown belt. He has trained and studied many weapons systems over the years but being ranked was not his priority or purpose. He met Mr. A.C. Rainey in the late 80s and found him to be one of the most gifted kenpoist's he has ever trained with. He still trains with Mr. Rainey and has been his student for over 30 years. Founder Phasic Kombatives Integrated, Todd has been honored to teach many seminars and camps and has published a book and poster sets on facets of the kenpo system and martial arts in general. His website is http://www.kenpoguy.com.

What is the best single piece of advice you were ever given?

"'Go back to school and get some management training and higher education.' This has served me well and was given by an old boss/owner of a company, who ironically should have taken his own advice, I worked for in the early 2000s. It has helped me in all aspects of my life to include my martial arts, particularly since I was better able to write and finish my 1st book as a result of the educational process. I have also since then been better able to organize, articulate, and complete my system of Martial arts Phasic Kombatives Integrated. It was an interesting process and I put it to a peer review with my teacher and several others. I would certainly not have been that confident had it not been for getting my master's degree and other key milestones in education several years prior."

When you were a kid, what did you want to be when you grew up?

"When I was a kid, I was trying to survive and make it to the next day! I had no aspirations to 'be' anything. As a teenager along with my resurgence of love of the martial arts I adopted the desire to be a pilot and went into the Army National Guard as a helicopter crew chief. Sadly, though I was not properly directed or encouraged, or didn't understand the direction and encouragement, as a younger man and did not finish high school due to circumstances of the time and life. I like to think that I followed a good path in the arts as it has helped me get to where I am at in life. Considering the nature of the journey, it has served me well as a contributing member of society."

What's the worst martial arts-related mistake you have ever made?

"Well, I have had two serious injuries in my class one of my own and another was one of my black belts. However, in the grand scheme of things I would consider my last (what I intended to be encouraging) comments to a student of mine who later committed suicide. I never saw him again and received a call one day asking if I would say a few words at his funeral. On arrival I was greeted by his sister and a very somber group of loved ones in attendance and remembered to ask her (the sister) how did he die? Her response took my breath away and changed the intended speech and talk about Don. I remember her telling me about his recent very positive accomplishments and thinking that what I said may have somehow affected him deeply. I will never forget the feeling I had that day."

For good or ill, what was the biggest impact of your martial arts training on your life?

"The martial arts for me have been and likely always will be a sanctuary, a place and thing that I could and can do always without the worry or concern of someone taking it from me or being in control of my art. I have gained so much in the arts, confidence and courage as well as the physical skills and ability that come with the training. Those physical skills and training have translated to many other sports and given me the confidence as well as drive to be better and do better in all things I attempted to do. Humility and respect are the greatest lessons I have gained from the arts through understanding what is possible, and that there is so much that I do not know. On the flip side many injuries now plague me as age starts to affect my art and life."

> "The martial arts for me have been and likely always will be a sanctuary, a place and thing that I could and can do always without the worry or concern of someone taking it from me or being in control of my art."

What single event of the past changed the world for the best?

"The discovery and use or application of the lever and leverage, everything built from then on has been done so with more ease and efficiency. Still to this day, we humans use leverage in most things even though it is a very simple application of physics for mechanical advantage. I challenge you to look and recognize all of the things that use leverage and what type, versus the things that don't use it."

What single event of the past changed the world for the worst?

"The industrial revolution, for several reasons, but mostly that while it certainly got us where we are today as human beings, we have not learned to control our desires and urges for 'greater' things like money or power. Sure, those desires where there already but the industrial revolution created a vehicle through which a person could rise to the top and be so much that is bad in the world, while creating more bad things on a magnified scale of size and destruction of planet and people."

Have you ever spent a night in jail?

"Jails and prisons are the complement of schools; so many less as you have of the latter, so many more must you have of the former."
Horace Mann, American politician

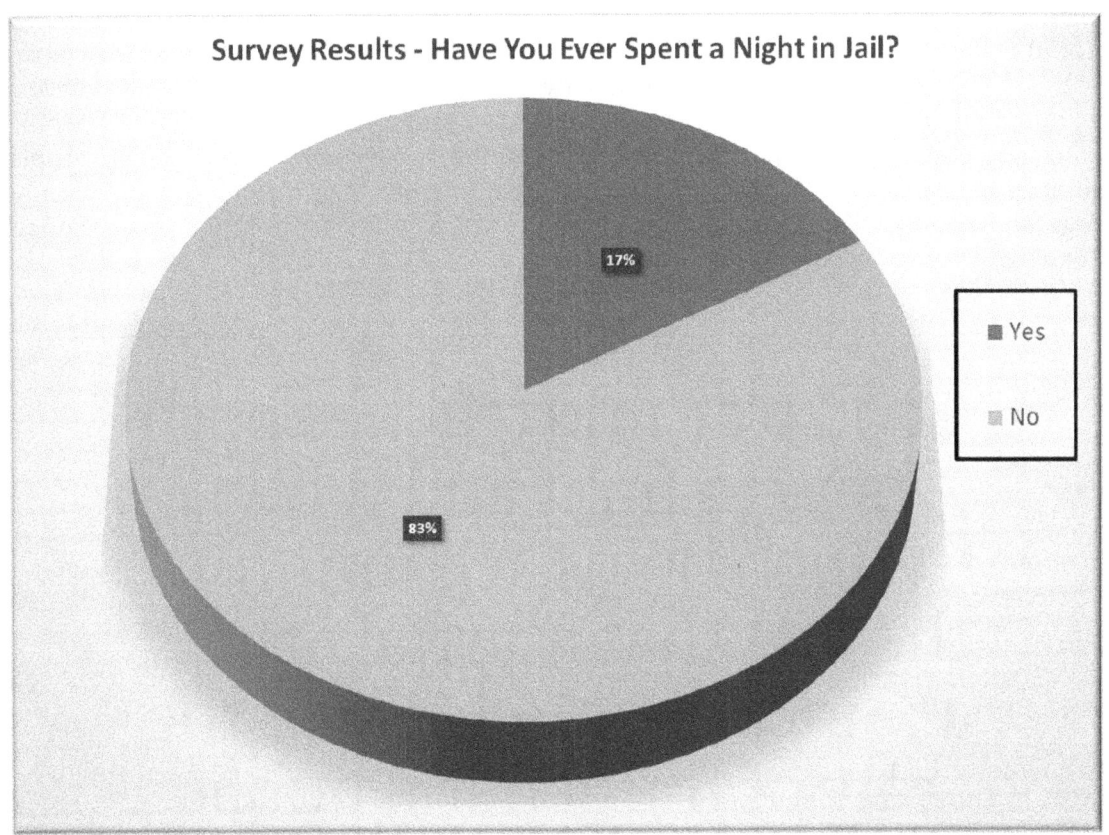

Global crime statistics and arrest records are difficult to study as laws vary from country to country and there is no uniform worldwide reporting that normalizes the data, so we chose to look to the United States to analyze this question. According to the Federal Bureau of Investigation's Unified Crime Reporting (UCR) database, law enforcement officers made 10,085,207 arrests in 2019, the most recent full-year of data available, a rate of 3,011 arrests per 100,000 citizens nationwide. Of those arrests, 495,871 were for violent crimes such as murder, manslaughter, rape, robbery, and aggravated assault, while 1,074,367 were for property crimes such as burglary, larceny-theft, motor vehicle theft, and arson. Of all persons arrested for any type of crime, 72.5% were male and 27.5% female (as of June 28, 2021 the UCR does not designate transgender or non-binary in their reporting), 69.4% were Caucasian, 26.6% were African American, and 4.0% were members of all other races.

About a third (32.8%) of the adult population has spent the night in jail at least once, with U.S. Department of Justice records showing that over 77 million Americans have a criminal record as of 2019. For perspective, that is roughly the same number of people who have earned a bachelor's degree in the country. Collectively, that's enough people to make up the world's 20th largest nation, more numerous than the entire population of Algeria, Argentina, Canada, Colombia, France, Italy, Kenya, South Africa, Spain, Sudan, Thailand, Uganda, or the United Kingdom.

> Good training teaches both how to fight and when, which helps account for the fact that martial artists are incarcerated at half the rate of the general public in the United States.

While the probability of any given individual being arrested by age sixteen is roughly the same today as it was 50 years ago, by the time a person reaches nineteen years old the probabilities begin to significantly rise. As a result, a young adult today is 36% more likely to be arrested than their parents were. Since a past criminal conviction of any sort reduces the likelihood of a person receiving a job offer (where employers are legally allowed to do a background check) by about 50%, there can be significant personal and societal impact from these arrest rates. Only six states, Arizona, California, Illinois, Nevada, New Jersey, and New York offer rehabilitation certifications for potential employees who have a criminal record.

This is where the discipline inherent in martial arts training can have a very large impact. Practitioners learn how to set and achieve challenging goals, develop good character, and use their skills wisely. Taught properly, we not only learn how to fight, but also know when it's appropriate to do so. And, we understand the cost of taking or not taking action far more than ordinary citizens. This accounts for the fact that as a community, martial artists are incarcerated at half the rate of the general public.

In other words, martial artists study violence, but do not become violent from the training. In fact, the reverse is true. So, if you're a parent or guardian who is concerned about your child's welfare, and who isn't, one proven way of protecting them from a diminished future it to get them started in martial arts before the age of sixteen.

Since a children's personality stabilizes from late adolescence into adulthood, and cognitive, social, emotional, and physical development are greatest during their formative years, it is actually best to introduce them to the martial arts somewhere between the ages of 8 and 11. In this fashion their character development will be accelerated well before they become teenagers when the risks of getting sideways with the law markedly increase.

All sports can be beneficial for youth, yet martial arts have a greater emphasis on individual growth and development than on team competition which is especially important for those who are less physically gifted than their peers. Among a myriad of other benefits, they are competency-based, teaching students how to achieve ambitious goals by chunking complex tasks into digestible components, setting goals, tracking progress, and leveraging incremental achievements to remain motivated and on track.

Martial arts provide structure, require discipline, and emphasize self-control. Data shows that parents and guardians discover that their children perform better in school as well as in life when they find a talented martial arts instructor to help guide their development. For best outcomes, find a good school and get your child(ren) started before the age of 12.

What three words would your friends use to describe you?

"Character cannot be developed in ease and quiet. Only through experience of trial and suffering can the soul be strengthened, vision cleared, ambition inspired, and success achieved."

Helen Keller, American author

Police Detective: "Can you describe the person who robbed your store?"

Clerk: "Yeah. He was sarcastic, smart and loyal."

The idea of the conversation above actually taking place is ludicrous. Clearly the salesclerk's description of the perpetrator would be completely useless to the responding officer, yet when asked what three words a martial artists' friends would use to describe them, physical descriptions appeared so few times they could be counted on one hand with a finger or two left over. Interestingly, these self-selected descriptions all conveyed positive attributes.

Words like loyal, smart, caring, kind, funny, honest, trustworthy, giving, and reliable were some of the top terms used to answer this question. One position would be that since this was a self-selected list, these positive attributes are qualities the respondents believed they have. It is possible, however, that others could see things differently. A case could even be made that these positive qualities are ones the martial artists listing them aspire to, or that they are characteristics these practitioners have, but at a lower level than they realize.

In other words, these descriptions could be an overestimation similar to the Dunning-Kruger effect. Coined in 1999 by Cornell psychologists David Dunning and Justin Kruger, the Dunning-Kruger Effect is a cognitive bias where people who are incompetent at something are unable to recognize their own shortcomings. Ironically, not only do folks fail to recognize their incompetence, but they are also likely to feel absolutely certain that they actually know what they're talking about. This means that a lack of self-awareness may have prevented survey respondents from realistically assessing their own attributes.

> While martial artists all portrayed themselves in a positive light, these results are sufficiently consistent with the rest of our analysis to make them believable.

However, results of the Meyers-Briggs personality type assessment we described earlier seem to indicate that is not the case. The majority of the martial artists completing our survey listed themselves as Advocates, Protagonists, Architects, Logisticians, and Defenders in descending order. These roles are ones of responsibility, brain types that necessitate an aptitude for realistic self-reflection and appraisal. Few would argue that in order to earn a black belt or pursue higher rank requires this aptitude, so we believe that it is a safe bet that these characteristics, while self-reported, were portrayed accurately.

While we stated that the respondents were all positive, not every word used comes across that way at first blush. Even so, it is hard to designate words like nuts, sarcastic, weird, blunt, odd, or crazy as wholly negative. Let's face it, genius and insanity run hand-in-glove. For example, some of the greatest minds in history were eccentric to say the least… Michelangelo (1475–1564) was peculiar, Charlie Chaplin (1889–1977) was outlandish, Albert Einstein (1879–1955) was odd, Winston Churchill (1874–1965) was notoriously sarcastic, and Nikola Tesla (1856–1943) was seen as crazy, especially in his later years. Indian Prime Minister Morarji Desai (1896–1995) was a genius, yet he famously drank his own urine every day without fail. That habit is eccentric to say the least…

American actor, singer, musician, and producer Alfred Matthew "Weird Al" Yankovic made an entire career out of being… well, weird… with cult movie appearances in shows like *UHF*, *The Naked Gun*, *The Naked Gun 2 ½*, and *The Naked Gun 33 $1/_3$*, hit songs like *White & Nerdy, Amish Paradise, Smells like Nirvana, Eat It, Like a Surgeon,* and *Pretty Fly for a Rabbi,* and over 1,000 television appearances. His works have earned him three Grammy Awards, four gold records, and six platinum records, among other honors. From Al's example, we must say that weirdness works, at least in certain professions.

The truth of this question is a case of perspective, the internal viewpoint and the external estimation. Clearly, we only have half of that equation here. Nevertheless, we are convinced that these self-assessments can be taken at face value. They are consistent with other results in our analysis, such as the MBTI analysis we mentioned earlier in this chapter as well as the prior chapter about most admired attributes where integrity, honesty, perseverance, humility courage, patience, compassion, empathy, loyalty, and dedication topped the list. Simply put, when martial artists say that they can be described with positive attributes, we believe them.

Martial Artist Profile – Shandra Stevenson

Shandra's martial arts journey began in 1981 at the age of nine, at a judo class at the Effingham YMCA, in downtown Portsmouth, Virginia, the initial home of Authentic Judo Club, headed by Sensei Charles Neal (dec). *She attained junior green belt rank before his passing in 1988. After relocating to Appleton, Wisconsin, she began studying again in the fall of 1999 at the Neenah-Menasha YMCA under* Sensei Mehdi Mohammadian *of Fox Valley Judo and Jujitsu of Wisconsin. Since that time, she has attained the rank of* nidan, *or second-degree black belt, and is currently an assistant instructor and coach for her club. She also still actively trains for, and competes in, National and International Masters Judo competitions. She has earned 13 Gold, 13 Silver, and 12 Bronze medals; one of these was the Gold Medal in her division at the World Masters Judo Championship in Montreal, Quebec in 2010.*

What is the best compliment you have ever received?

"Whether as a parent, friend, teacher, coach or other mentor, you don't often know if what you have imparted to others ever truly makes a difference in their lives. Last November, I received a message from an unknown contact via Instagram. The message read that the person was hoping to find Shandra Smith (my name then), her *sensei* from when she was 12 in Appleton. 'She always told me to trust in myself. I am looking for her because I want that again.' That woman was just a young a girl when I taught classes at the Appleton Rec Department for my *sensei* (2000 to 2004). I was blown away by her remembrance of me and that it had made such an impact that she would reach out many years later. These are the moments that make up the good stuff in a martial arts person's life."

When you were a kid, what did you want to be when you grew up?

"I wanted to be a teacher, specifically a history teacher. Unfortunately, I did not follow that path. I left home at 17 because my family was being transferred to another state, and I didn't want to go. I got married and had 3 children over the course of a 16 ½ year marriage. I worked in the clerical/administrative field throughout, and never had the time or ability to go to college. When I did, in my late-20's, my former spouse made me quit after the 1st semester. It wasn't until I was 42, after life had changed for me quite a bit, that I finally earned an Associate's Degree. Being an assistant judo instructor, however, has helped me fill the yearning to teach that I always had, and it is one of the most rewarding things in my life."

What energizes you outside of work?

"I honestly love being on the judo *tatami* (mats), whether it is teaching, training or competing; Judo is an integral part of my life. I also enjoy simply sitting in the sun, listening to the nature around me, it is quite calming and peaceful."

For good or ill, what was the biggest impact of your martial arts training on your life?

"The biggest impact my martial arts training has had on my life has been the ability to share the judo I've learned over the years with others who are just as passionate about the art and sport as I am. I've been fortunate to travel the country and world for competition and have been mentored by some wonderful people, I am honored to be able to impart that knowledge to others. To watch students of all ages practice, practice and practice more, then see the 'ah-ha' light come on as they finally get it, those are moments that I feel joy for, the accomplishments of others. My *sensei* has been teaching for 55+ years, providing judo instruction to generations of families, I can only hope that I can come close to that amazing milestone."

What single event of the past changed the world for the best?

"I feel that the invention of the printing press (Gutenberg) was a turning point in history. The press brought increased literacy, education, and communication to the everyday masses, and provided the ability to share in, and understand, information and knowledge across a broad range of peoples, languages, and cultures."

> "My sensei has been teaching for 55+ years, providing judo instruction to generations of families, I can only hope that I can come close to that amazing milestone."

What single event of the past changed the world for the worst?

"Genocide, created by war, has been an atrocity in every era and century since 'civilization' began. I feel very strongly that the attempted extermination of a people solely because they exist, whatever the reason, is an absolute evil. In terms of the 20th century, the heinous acts committed by the Nazis on the Jews, Catholics, Disabled, Homosexuals, Romani and so many others, for me is a black mark of the cruelty that man can visit upon another. Can one even imagine the outcomes of those nearly 17 million lives that were taken, simply because they were considered 'inferior' to the group in charge? What contributions might have they made to the world? What families might have prospered? What business owner might have been the next titan of industry? Who may have been our next Einstein? We will never know, and that is the world's loss."

What is one thing, big or small, that you are truly bad at?

"Failure is the condiment that gives success its flavor."
Truman Capote, American novelist, screenwriter, playwright, and actor

American author, actor, and screenwriter Neale Donald Walsch once wrote, "Life begins at the end of your comfort zone." This means that failure isn't the opposite of success, it's part and parcel to it. After all, it's impossible to become good at something without struggling along the way. For example, when we begin training in the martial arts, we have to relearn fundamental things we thought we had already mastered like breathing, moving, postural control, and body alignment.

Proper breathing is instrumental to any physical endeavor. Consider *ibuki* (quick energy breath) techniques found in traditional karate. *Ibuki* is a form of breath control typified by audible inhalation and exhalation, which more-or-less exaggerates the type of breathing that karate practitioners should be doing automatically. It is taught because proper breathing has a calming effect on the mind and body which can be used to overcome fear and anxiety during a violent confrontation.

Ibuki is similar to the 4-count "combat breathing" technique that is taught to elite military personal to help them control adrenal stress. Psychologists often use comparable breath control techniques to help their patients relax during therapy too. So, we think we know how to breath, it's subconscious after all, but after we take up martial arts, we find that it takes a heck of a lot of practice to do it properly. That is but one of many areas in our training where we all start with failure, struggle, overcome, and eventually take steps toward mastery.

> Martial artists have a healthy, often humorous view of the things we are bad at. As a community, we understand that failure is not the opposite of success, it is indispensable to it.

Most martial artists who participated in this study had a healthy, almost humorous view of their inabilities. Some of the truly bad items they selected were physical, such as working with their hands, do-it-yourself home renovations, or handywork. Others reported that they were not good at certain social interactions such as being poor at small-talk or having difficulty forgiving transgressions. Many spoken to poor time management, particularly around estimations of time needed for complete tasks, as well.

The following list is a fun example of the diversity of things that martial artists consider themselves truly bad at.

- ○ Admitting I am wrong
- ○ Basketball
- ○ Billiards
- ○ Completing projects
- ○ Cooking
- ○ Drawing
- ○ Golf
- ○ Handwriting
- ○ Math
- ○ Music
- ○ Odd jobs around the house
- ○ Organization
- ○ Racket Sports
- ○ Singing
- ○ Small talk
- ○ Starting a conversation
- ○ Time management
- ○ Unicycle riding

Knowing our weaknesses is the first step toward growth. There's no imperative to shore up anything or everything that we're bad at, of course, but there is value in trying. For instance, scientific studies have demonstrated that when a right-handed people incorporate their left hand more often everyday tasks, it increases their brain activity and function. This is because when we use our dominant hand only one hemisphere of our brain becomes active, whereas both hemispheres are activated when we use our non-dominant hand. If we never fail, we can never truly succeed.

Martial Artist Profile – Randy Haskins

Randy's story is much like the story the comic books are made of. He endeavored to study the martial arts as a youth and sought to find the system that best fit his needs. After experiencing a few other dojos, *he settled into the* Kudo Kai, *an umbrella organization which housed a couple different expressions of karate, a method of* aiki-jutsu, *a method of judo, and the art of* kobudo *under one roof. He chose karate because of the power he witnessed karate practitioners to have, and studied under William Mark Whitley in his family art of* Taikido *karate. There was always this burning question floating around the* Kudo Kai, *"What would happen if we took one person and trained him in everything?" Randy became that experiment. He now holds ranks in two methods of karate, in judo, in* aiki-jutsu, *and a purple belt in 10th Planet Jiu-Jitsu. His website is* http://www.undergroundalliancehombu.com.

What energizes you outside of work?

"Writing, martial arts training, martial arts research, exercising, and witnessing my daughter and grandson grow and succeed in life."

What's the worst martial arts-related mistake you have ever made?

"During a martial science research session, I neglected to observe the principles of leverage and grabbed my own foot in an attempt to secure a leverage-based ankle lock on my training partner while he was on my back in a seatbelt mounted position. I ended up breaking my own knee attempting to crush his crossed ankles with a figure-4 lock."

If you could go back in time, what advice would you give to your teenage self?

"I would tell my younger self to stay in the military and complete 20 years as opposed to the 8 years I did, and to try to be more patient, tolerable and understanding of the differences in men and woman mindsets in reference to relationships."

For good or ill, what was the biggest impact of your martial arts training on your life?

"I met individuals I would have never come across, became a published author, traveled and trained in many places across world, and with confidence successfully and safely navigated a career in law enforcement working in the most violent isolated society in the world, the United States penal system, all as a direct result of my martial arts education."

What is one thing, big or small, that you are truly bad at?

"I'm extremely bad at tolerating others unrealistic expectations and disrespectful behaviors."

> "I successfully and safely navigated a career in law enforcement, working in the most violent isolated society in the world, the United States penal system, as a direct result of my martial arts education."

When you were a kid, what did you want to be when you grew up?

"I wanted to be in law enforcement and I did follow that dream. I was a Military Police (MP) officer for my last four years in the military then I worked 22 years as a Hampden County Sheriff, doing double duty as a Massachusetts Sheriff's Association Defensive Tactics Instructor Trainer (Retired 2/20/21)."

What is one thing you are currently trying to make a habit?

"A man who can't bear to share his habits is a man who needs to quit them."
Stephen King, American author

As a general rule, humans abhor change. When things change, we feel fear, anxiety, uncertainty, and loss of control, any of which can overcome our desire to embrace something different no matter how beneficial it might be. In fact, this dynamic is so hardwired that our fear of change can be expressed mathematically.

In the 1960s David Gleicher created a formula, **D** x **V** x **F** > **R**, or **D**issatisfaction x **V**ision x **F**irst steps > **R**esistance. In English, this means that in order to overcome resistance to change and actually alter our behavior, our level of dissatisfaction with our current state, multiplied by our positive vision for a better future state, multiplied by our first concrete steps toward achieving that vision must be greater than our inherent resistance to change or nothing lasting will happen.

Here are three examples of humans disliking change that most folks can relate to:

- **Toddlers:** If you are the parent of a small child or have spent much time around one you know that when you take a toddler out of their daily routine you will pay a price. Typically, this price is an emotional meltdown, hence the term "Terrible Twos." Fighting, biting, pouting, and screaming are commonplace.

- **Teens:** If you think that tantrums are unique to toddlers, you're wrong, though the composition of such outbursts does change over time. Go to a high school cafeteria on "Taco Tuesday" and change the meal plan and you'll see what we mean. You could offer up a juicy, tender USDA Prime 14-day dry-aged bone-in ribeye American Wagyu steak or a mouthwatering Alaskan Copper River salmon filet fresh off the boat and the response will be, "Where's the tacos, it's Taco Tuesday?!"

- **Adults:** Grownups suffer from this dynamic too. Sadly, a fear of change is why it's so hard for folks to leave dysfunctional relationships or make needed lifestyle changes, even they know such things could save their lives. The weight loss industry rakes in more than $295.3 billion a year in large part because even though adults understand the importance of healthy eating and exercise, they lack the emotional fortitude to do the right things and look for an easy way out.

It is inescapable fact, humans do not like change. We may say that we do, but in reality, we don't. We all have habits. These habits are grooves in the proverbial road of life; for good or ill they keep us stuck in the rut, making it hard to change lanes. The more they're reinforced, the deeper the grooves our routines cut.

Because of these ingrained conventions, new behavior patterns are challenging to create, taking far more energy to get started than is required to maintain them after they are habituated. The grander the goal, the bigger the change, the more energy it takes to get started. This circles back to Gleicher's formula; we must not only overcome our inherent resistance to change but also take concrete, positive steps in the right direction before things begin to get easier.

Once the process of entrainment (cutting a new groove) has started then we can begin to build a self-referring loop of gratification, after which things become less demanding. Nevertheless, even once that feedback loop has been established it must be fed energy to maintain. We might imagine habits akin to a commercial airplane's autopilot system, but no matter how good the computer, it's wise to have a human pilot on hand to take over should something go awry. In other words, when we run into headwinds it's easy to backslide unless we consciously and conscientiously forge ahead along our desired path.

Here's our general rule: You know that you have established a habit when others recognize it. For example, when an acquaintance wonders aloud why you're not responding to their text your friends would say, "Oh, you can't get ahold of her right now, she's at kickboxing class." It's Tuesday, and it is 6 o'clock, so of course you're at class. That's what you do on Tuesday and Thursday nights at this time. This is your routine. When a repetitive behavior can be predicted from an external observer, you have successfully embraced a habit. From there you need only reinforce it.

> Despite the fact humans tend to fear change, martial artists are more introspective, with 100% of survey respondents seeking to habituate one or more ways of improving themselves.

Our survey respondents had a wide variety of things they were striving to habituate, but each and every respondent was working on something, a fact which sets them far above most folks in society. Additionally, they all had a multipoint plan to address their mind, body, and spirit in making the desired change(s). Emphasis varied by individual, of course, but a stress on words like "daily" and "day" points to frequency in positive reinforcement. Whether the goal is to meditate, eat better, rise earlier, perform more physical activity, perfect a golf swing, or habituate anything else, the plan has a far better chance of coming to fruition when it's reinforced every single day.

It is interesting to note that the changes respondents wished to habitualize were all self-focused. For instance, nobody suggested that the habit they were trying to create was to go to every single homeowner's association meeting to ensure that their neighbors were not exceeding the proper residential fence height for their community. These self-focused goals can be broken down into two categories, (1) mental habits and (2) physical habits. Clearly some goals can cross categories, such as eliminating stress eating, a physical act that is mental in origin, but the root cause of that goal would push it into the mental habit bucket.

Every habit selected by our respondents was designed to make them a better person. In some instances, they spoke to adopting a positive tendency and in others removing a negative inclination, but in every instance the goal was shaped toward personal growth and development. This is not only remarkable, but something that sets martial artists far above the norm.

Mental habits examples:
- Anger management
- Continuous learning
- Meditation
- Mindfulness
- Stop gratuitous shopping
- Thankfulness and appreciation
- Time management

Physical habits examples:
- Eat healthier foods
- Intermittent fasting
- Lose weight
- Rise earlier
- Stretching and flexibility
- Walk more
- Weightlifting

It is important to note that most of the choices respondents made regarding their habits fell into the realm of lifestyle choices, not martial arts. It was rare for a responded to say something along the lines of, "I will practice my *kata* (forms) 6 times a day."

Humans may not like change, but martial artists act differently. We are self-reflective as a group, appraising our strengths and weaknesses, and taking personal responsibility for our behaviors and attitudes. Whenever we perceive the need for change, we are inclined to act. Near universally, we struggle to improve ourselves mentally, physically, and/or spiritually. In this fashion we can address old conventions, build new routines, reinforce desired outcomes, and do our best to remediate deficiencies.

We are by no means perfect, but unlike many we are willing to admit it and actually able to take concrete steps in our drive toward perfection.

Martial Artist Profile – Alain Burrese, J.D.

Alain Burrese, J.D. is a 5th degree black belt in hapkido, *a former Army paratrooper and sniper instructor, a licensed attorney, the author of nine books and eleven instructional DVDs, including the highly acclaimed book* Survive a Shooting: Strategies to Survive Active Shooters and Terrorist Attacks *and the video program* Hapkido Cane. *Alain's primary martial art is the Korean self-defense art of* hapkido. *He lived and trained in South Korea and continues to go back to Korea to train with his instructors there. Alain is currently the Director of Active Defense Training for Reflex Protect, where he conducts trainings for institutions on effective communication for conflict and dealing with angry people, active threat response, and the use of Reflex Protect's revolutionary non-lethal defensive spray. When not working for Reflex Protect, Alain enjoys hikes with his dog, traveling with his family, and working on new books and educational programs. His website is* www.yourwarriorsedge.com.

What is the best compliment you have ever received?

"One of the most memorable was given to me over 30 years ago while I was stationed at Camp Hovey, South Korea. I was designated as our platoon's sniper when I wasn't working special duty as an assistant instructor at the 2nd Infantry Division Scout Sniper School. My Platoon Sergeant told me one day, 'Burrese, out of everyone I've ever served with, there's no one I rather have with me if we go to war.' That meant a lot to me, because I took being a soldier, and especially a sniper, seriously. I kept myself in top physical condition and trained so that I excelled in all the skills needed to kill the enemy and keep myself and my fellow soldiers alive. I continuously trained for battle. Later, the same determination and self-discipline helped me excel outside of the military too."

What's the worst martial arts-related mistake you have ever made?

"I've made many, but one humorous one was while sparring a yellow belt who was taking karate classes with his son. I was a black belt, and a bit overconfident and not protecting myself as I should. The guy knew one kick, which was basically a front rising kick, and he had one speed, full-bore. As I danced and threw up a roundhouse kick, stopping an inch from his head, he brought that front rising kick straight up into my groin. It picked me off the floor and when I landed, I crumpled into the fetal position wishing I'd worn a cup or hadn't been so careless. The guy who kicked me stood there apologizing, while my instructor walked over and looked down at me and smiled. As I tried to take it like a black belt, my instructor laughed and said, 'Yellow belts, get you every time.'"

> "If I hadn't gone to Korea to pursue my hapkido training, I wouldn't have met my wife... I consider myself a martial artist. I always have been, and always will be, and wouldn't have it any other way."

What is the best single piece of advice you were ever given?

In the mid-1990s, I forwarded a joke I'd received to different friends through email. I don't remember the joke, only that it depicted unnecessary violence in the punch line. A friend and mentor, John Madden, former Dean of the Davidson Honors College at The University of Montana replied. He asked if the joke represented who I was, and what I endorsed. Knowing that I am a fan of the *Karate Kid* movies, he also asked if Mr. Miyagi would agree with such a joke. I've never forgotten that e-mail, and I am more aware of what I share through email and social media because of it. I try to ensure everything I send, post, or share, represents my beliefs and virtues, and I don't post or share things that may hurt my reputation or tarnish my character on different social media platforms."

Knowing what you know now, would you do it all over again?

"Yes, I would do it all over again. Martial arts have always just been a part of me. From those first days of trying to learn from library books to today, martial arts have been a part of my life. Even during "breaks" of formal training due to moving locations, I trained and studied on my own. Martial arts have introduced me to many friends and have assisted me in different jobs throughout the years. If I hadn't gone to Korea to pursue my *hapkido* training, I wouldn't have met my wife. While there may be a few things I'd change if I could do it all over again, the study of martial arts wouldn't be one of them. I consider myself a martial artist. I always have been, and always will be, and wouldn't have it any other way."

If you could go back in time, what advice would you give to your teenage self?

"The advice I'd give my teenage self would probably not be listened to, but if I could, I'd try to convince my younger self to get better control over the short fuse and quick temper that I seem to have been born with. My explosive temper was scary to others, destructive, and something I once believed to be uncontrollable. The tendency to anger easily has cost me on numerous occasions, especially when younger. Realizing that I needed to control this, and that I actually could control my temper, and working to control it, earlier than I finally did, would have saved me from much trouble, grief, and hardships. So, I would give the advice that you can control your emotions and temper, and you must control them if you want to avoid a lot of negative consequences in your life."

For good or ill, what was the biggest impact of your martial arts training on your life?

"The biggest impact martial arts have had on my life are the relationships I have developed because of my study, training, and teaching of martial arts. I moved to South Korea to further my study of *hapkido*, and taught English to pay the bills. Besides the relationship with my instructors, I met my wife who was also a teacher at the school where I was teaching English. While my wife is the most significant relationship that came from my pursuit of martial art training, I also have a network of friends around the world, some being very good friends, that have all been a result of my martial art training and teaching. My wife and these friends are definitely the greatest things to come from my years of martial art study, training, and teaching."

Who is/was the greatest athlete of all time?

"Fame is an accident; merit a thing absolute."
Herman Melville, American novelist

Societally 39 percent of men and 12 percent of women in the United States consider themselves avid sports fans according to Statista, a leading market research portal, with more than half the population watching a game from time to time. Many martial artists do not spend their time watching other sports, but for those who do their only qualifying metric for answering this question was the athlete's record, their accomplishments on the field, in the ring, or wherever it is that they compete. In a world of soft measurement and participation trophies, modern society seems to applaud effort alone, yet martial artists as a group tend to value things differently. We care about what folks have actually done.

In traditional martial arts, for example, rank tests require application of certain techniques in front of a jury of senior practitioners and instructors who determine whether or not sufficient competency has been demonstrated to warrant a promotion. Outcome matters; the aspirant either completes the assignment, breaks the board, performs the *kata* (form), defeats the opponent, or whatever is required, or she does not. He withstands the rigors of a 25-man *kumite* (sparring) or he fails. As the little green guy in that galaxy far, far away once proclaimed, "Do or do not, there is no try!"

Votes for the greatest athlete of all time were open-ended. In other words, martial artists from across the globe were given free rein to nominate whoever they perceived as the world's greatest athlete, pulling from any nation, any time period, and any athletic endeavor. The choices they made crossed race, gender, and religion; such things are irrelevant when it comes to sports achievements. Participants voted their selections based entirely on merit. Did the nominee earn their position or did they not?

This creates an interesting dichotomy from mainstream society. And, it begs the question, "Does the structure of martial arts serve as a furnace where these attitudes of merit are forged?" In other words, are people learning to judge others solely by their actions and accomplishments because of the environment inherent in martial arts training? One hypothesis is that it is the hierarchical belt/rank structure utilized by most martial systems that creates this attitude. That thought warrants exploration…

It is certainly plausible that the rank system with its public display of competency creates this predisposition toward accomplishment. However, we must simultaneously wonder whether or not martial arts attract people who are instinctively inclined toward earning reward through effort in the first place. A third possibility is that the true answer is a blend of both the martial artists and their environment.

You see, martial arts attract certain types of personalities (as we discussed earlier in the Myers-Briggs personality type assessment), and those who excel in the arts do so in an environment that is conducive to people who orient themselves toward merit. Makes sense, right? Unfortunately, while we may speculate, we do not have a definitive answer. We can, however, state with certainty that martial arts are an individual pursuit set in a group atmosphere and that makes an impact on practitioners. Like the old "nature versus nurture" argument, this is likely something that is determined on a case-by-case basis, but we did not have a good way of measuring the effect of the group atmosphere on the individuals who participated in our survey.

> **Martial arts are competency-based, with practitioners venerating merit grounded in athletic achievement in both themselves and others. Society seems to applaud effort alone, yet martial artists care about what folks have actually done.**

The clear measure of the world's greatest athlete question, as expressed by our participants, was one based on achievement. This dynamic is why "household names" like Muhammad Ali (Olympic gold medalist and 3-time world heavyweight boxing champion), Tom Brady (7-time Super Bowl champion quarterback), Michael Jordan (6-time NBA champion shooting guard), Jim Thorpe (Olympic gold medalist, and professional baseball, basketball, and American football player), and Bruce Lee (founder of *Jeet Kune Do*) rose to the top of the list. Is your choice listed here?

Although men tend to be better biologically suited to physical endeavors than women, there are numerous gifted female athletes, yet none of them earned a top spot on this list. It is interesting to note that men's sports generate far larger audiences than comparable women's sports, with a whopping 95% of coverage across all media is focused on male sports according to NiemanLab, an institute dedicated to bringing journalism into the internet age.

For example, the WNBA averages roughly 231,000 viewers a game compared to more than 15,140,000 who watch the NBA, a 66:1 ratio. This may help explain why lesser-known, elite athletes like Susan Butcher (4-time Iditarod champion), Simone Biles (tied as the most decorated gymnast of all time), and Kathy Long (5-time world kickboxing champion) all earned votes, but did not top the list of world's greatest athletes.

What single event of the past changed the world for the best?

"Innovation comes from conflict."
Jeff "Skunk" Baxter, American guitarist and cybersecurity technologist

In the quote above Jeff Baxter succinctly points to the fact that there are at least two sides to most issues, acts, and inventions. When asked about the best (discussed here) and worst (covered in our next chapter) event in world history, many of our respondents answered with the same result for both questions. Examples include information technology, the internet, social media, and splitting of the atom/creation of the nuclear age.

Think of it this way, ammonium nitrate is a common fertilizer that is used worldwide. In fact, 21.6 million tons of it were consumed in 2017 alone because it is highly effective at providing nitrogen that plants need for rapid, strong growth. Ammonium nitrate is manufactured using a version of the Haber Process, a method named after its creator, German inventor Fritz Haber (1868–1934).

Sounds pretty harmless, right, yet the Haber system was first used to create chemical weapons during the World War I as a response to the Allied Powers blockade of elements necessary for Germany and its Central Powers partners to build explosives. So, while this process began as an implement of horrific warfare, one so bad that it was outright banned by the international community with a chemical and biological weapons prohibition (e.g., United Nations Biological and Toxin Weapons Convention, Geneva Protocol), it was ultimately repurposed to help solve world hunger.

In the 1940s the Germans created something else, a new soft drink. This fruit-flavored soda was invented by necessity, because… wait for it… because of another American trade embargo. You see, before the American troops became embroiled in World War II, their country cut off a variety of exports to Germany, including Coca-Cola syrup and sugar. This inspired Max Keith (1903–1945), who once ran Coke Germany, to develop a soda that they could brew with ingredients found solely inside the country, using byproducts like whey from cheese-making and apple pulp. Once again, innovation comes from conflict.

What has changed the world for the best? What has changed the world for the worst? Sometimes we get answers that appear to contradict…

Would you rather be rich or famous? Why not both? This is an answer, but it doesn't provide useful information. By saying, "I'll have both!" we mix content and context. This answer in essence states, "I want a new ride that has all the luxury of a Rolls-Royce Ghost, but I simultaneously want the performance of an F1™ Formula 1 racing car too." Unfortunately, no matter how much we might desire such a combination, it does not exist in the real world. Luxury and performance at those extreme ends of the spectrum are mutually exclusive with current technology.

This automobile analogy appears to break the paradigm with "outside-the-box" thinking, but it really doesn't. Such responses from martial artists are consistent, with valid answers that might change due to differences in context. For example, think of the simple spoon. One might argue that spoons create obesity and as such need to be outlawed. This conclusion fails to take context into account—it is the amount of food delivered that can become problematic, not the spoon (or fork or person's hand) that delivers it.

In this same vein, banning the automobile because of highway deaths would save 38,680 lives per year based on 2020 statistics from the United States Department of Transportation. If some foreign country killed 38,000 Americans by dropping a bomb, we would be at war in a heartbeat.

Much as we might wish to avoid unnecessary death and destruction while simultaneously reducing harmful greenhouse gas emissions, we would be foolish to ban automobiles because, among other things, 70% of goods in the United States are transported by truck. That means that city folk who do not have proximate access to farms would starve to death, $52.7 billion dollars of revenue would be wiped out of the economy each and every day, unemployment would skyrocket, housing prices would tank, and civil unrest would jump off the charts leading to murder, mayhem, and mass destruction. Clearly that is a trade-off that most of us are not willing to accept.

> Martial artists tend to view the world holistically, making judgements based on both content and context.

Fertilizer isn't inherently bad. Spoons aren't harmful. And, cars and trucks are not evil. Consider this in context with our training. Martial artists learn how to fight. We know a variety of ways to use our bodies to disable and dispatch others. Oftentimes we practice with implements of destruction, learning how to use swords, knives, bludgeons, arrows, or firearms too. When one studies how to damage other human beings, they viscerally become aware of the risks and responsibilities that come with those skills. This is likely why we received the inputs we did from our respondents.

As humans, are we monkeys with a flamethrower? Or, are we in control of the transformational element of flame?

It appears that martial artists choose to control, responding rather than reacting, and as such make distinctions about both content and context. For instance, we see that the internet makes the world smaller, uniting humanity in many ways, yet the concurrent evolution of social media often conspires to separate us into like-minded tribes, "other" folks who don't think like us, and ultimately tear us apart. Similarly, conflict and war cause destruction on an epic scale, yet simultaneously create advances in medicine, healthcare, and human longevity. It's enough to make your brain hurt…

We'll end with a quote from one of our respondents, Dr. Wendell Goins, who wrote in response to this question:

"Due to the universal laws of cause and effect, there can be negative consequences to even the best of events. For example, Christianity resulted in the Spanish Inquisition and the St. Bartholomew Massacre among many other atrocities. However, I would venture to say that the most important event that changed our world was the founding of the United States of America. Before 1776, revolution against a world power was unthinkable. The Declaration of Independence (and later the Constitution) expanded the rights of the common man (although initially some were excluded) which was unthinkable before. Due to the abundance of natural resources and the individual freedom to create one's own life, the U.S.A. quickly became a world power and influenced the rest of the world to mimic our form of government. Technology and the standard of living rapidly advanced and we went from horse-and-buggy to landing on the moon in a short 70 years."

Martial Artist Profile – Dan Anderson

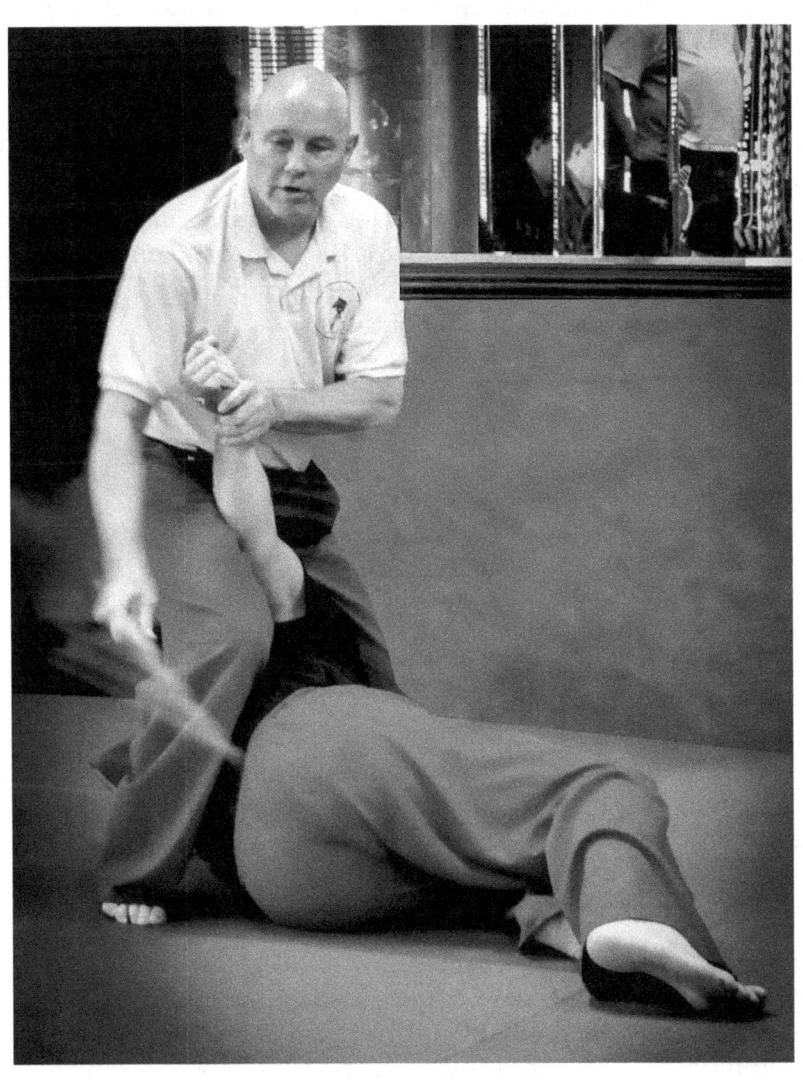

Grandmaster Dan Anderson's martial arts career began at the age of 14 under the tutelage of martial arts Masters Hall of Fame member Loren Christensen in Vancouver, Washington. Dan achieved his 1st degree black belt on January 7, 1970 at the age of 17. For the next 10 years Anderson committed himself to becoming a karate tournament champion, eventually becoming rated in the national top 10 ratings four years in a row. He began his writing career with the book American Freestyle Karate: A Guide to Sparring, *first published in 1981. He has since authored 20 books on karate and Filipino Martial Arts (FMA) as well as producing 25 DVDs on the subjects. In 1980, Dan began training in the second martial art that would shape his research and career from that time forward, Modern Arnis, under Remy A. Presas. Since then, Dan has been personally accepted as a student of Manong Ted Buot, a student Balintawak Eskrima's founder, Anciong Bacon. In 2006, Dan traveled to the Philippines to teach at both the 3rd World Filipino Martial Arts Festival and the 1st Remy A. Presas memorial Training Camp, one of a handful of westerners to teach at these events. It was during this trip where he became a founding member of the Worldwide Family of Modern Arnis. His branch of Modern Arnis, the MA80 System Arnis/Eskrima was also recognized by the International Modern Arnis Federation Philippines as a valid branch of the Remy Presas' art. In 2008, Dan Anderson received the Gat Andres Bonafacio award from the Philippine Classical Arnis society. In 2012 Dan Anderson tested for and passed the examination for 9th dan in karate by the American Karate Black Belt Association. Dan Anderson currently teaches karate and Filipino Martial Arts at the Dan Anderson Karate School in Gresham, Oregon. He is aided by his wife, Marie, and his daughter Amanda. His website is* https://superdanonlinelibrary.com.

What's the worst martial arts-related mistake you have ever made?

"I was sparring with a friend of mine, Doug, who was 230 pounds and a street fighter. We were banging away on each other and at one point he pulled back and said, 'Dan, do you have to hit so damned hard?!' It finally dawned on me that I was using how it felt to me as opposed to observing the reaction on my partner. For years I wondered why sparring partners would ramp up on me and begin to try to take my head off. I just figured they were being a butt so I would beat on them to teach them not to hit me so hard. It never occurred to me that I was the one who was hitting too hard in the first place. I watched my partner's reactions after that and what do you know, everybody stopped trying to beat on me. Imagine that!"

If you could go back in time, what advice would you give to your teenage self?

"'You are not the white Muhammad Ali!' Show respect. Back in my competition days, Super Dan (my nickname at the time) was quite something. I was a rebel. I was cocky. I got away with it because I won far more often than I lost. Then I stepped out of competition for about seven months. I was grousing about poor judging or something like that. It was quite some time ago. I started hearing Super Dan stories… and they weren't good ones. Finally, it occurred to me that the image I had of myself was not the image I was projecting. Wait a minute. Super Dan is fun lovin' and very funny guy! He's like his idol Muhammad Ali! That is not the Super Dan they were talking about. The 'bad' Super Dan was cocky and borderline disrespectful. That's when it hit me, the image I was projecting was not the one in my mind. It took me five years to work off the bad image I created for myself."

What's the best compliment you have ever received?

"It was after a seminar when I received this one. Barry and I were coming back from a seminar I taught at. It was about 11:30 PM and I was hungry. I asked him if it wasn't too much trouble, if we could stop and get a burger. He looked at me and said, 'Professor, you are the lowest maintenance Grandmaster I've ever met.' Jackie Bradbury once said that I was the most approachable Grandmaster she'd ever met. These compliments reflect how I want to treat others. My seniors like Ed Parker, Jeff Smith, Bill Wallace, and others treated me with respect for an upcoming black belt. This is my way of paying if forward."

> "He said, 'Professor, you are the lowest maintenance Grand-master I've ever met.' …My seniors like Ed Parker, Jeff Smith, Bill Wallace, and others treated me with respect for an upcoming black belt. This is my way of paying if forward."

When you were a kid, what did you want to be when you grew up?

"I wanted to be a cartoonist when I was a kid. I loved comics, especially comic books. I remember back in the 7th grade how Guy and I drew our own comic strip, Captain Avenger, in the back rows during math class. In retrospect, that's probably why my math skills are pretty poor to this day. Anyway, I kept drawing and drawing all through grade school and junior high. Then something funny happened… I took my first karate lesson. That night, karate bit me like a mad dog and I dropped everything else to be a karate maniac. 55 years later I've decided that wasn't such a bad thing."

What energizes you outside of work?

"Outside of work, I love to go riding on my Spyder. A Spyder is a three-wheeled motorcycle. When I am on 'the beast' I am nearly flying. I love riding in all environments; back roads, city streets, freeways—it's all the same to me. I've always wanted to ride a motorcycle but I never trusted the weather in the Pacific Northwest, too rainy, so when I found out about the Can-Am Spyder I wanted one. The first time I rode on one, I was sold big time, but my wife wasn't. It took me about a year to get her to sign on to me having one, and then she actually surprised me by getting me one for my birthday in 2019. Ahh, I think it's time for another ride."

Why did you start training?

"I began training in karate in November 1966. My older brother just got sent up to reform school so I no longer had a protector. I also thought taking karate would transform me from being a goon to being cool. The jury is still out on that one."

What single event of the past changed the world for the worst?

"You have to know the past to understand the present."
Carl Sagan, American astronomer and astrophysicist

Many choices were presented in response to this question. Obvious selections that make it into the top ten of most everybody's list are present, things like the Holocaust (in which 11 million people were systematically murdered), the atomic bombings of Hiroshima and Nagasaki (which caused 199,000 human beings to burn to death), World War I (which produced about 15 million casualties), World War II (in which roughly 3% of the world's population was wiped out), the African slave trade, publication of *The Communist Manifesto* by Karl Marx (according to *The Wall Street Journal*, Communism is directly responsible for 100 million deaths worldwide over the last century), the Crusades (which took about 6 million lives), The Holomodor (murder by starvation of approximately 7 million Soviet Ukrainians between 1932 and 1933), the Armenian Genocide (which killed about 1.2 million people), and the Chernobyl nuclear disaster (which "only" killed 31 people, but caused irreparable environmental destruction). As horrific as these events are, we must note that they are all manmade.

While various governments' handling of SARS-CoV-2 (Covid-19) was mentioned by a couple of respondents, cholera, HIV/AIDS, various Flu pandemics, the Antonine plague, and even the Black Death (bubonic plague) did not make our respondents' list. Other infamous natural disasters which were left unmentioned include the 1138 Aleppo Earthquake in Syria (which left 230,000 people dead), the 2004 Indian Ocean Tsunami (which killed 230,000 people), the 1920 Haiyun Earthquake in China (that caused 240,000 casualties), the 1976 Tangshan Earthquake in China (which killed 242,000 people), the 526 Antioch Earthquake in Syria and Turkey (that left 250,000 dead), the 1839 India Cyclone (which caused 300,000 casualties), the 1556 Shaanxi Earthquake in China (which killed 830,000 people), the 1970 Bhola Cyclone in Bangladesh (that caused a million casualties), the 1887 Yellow River Flood in China (responsible for 3 million deaths), or the 1931 Yellow River Flood in China (in which 4 million people died).

For perspective, one would imagine that we would all react negatively to the idea of an asteroid destroying life on the earth as we know it. That actually happened historically and could conceivably occur again in the future... No single event brought more pain, suffering, and death than the Chicxulub Impactor, which scientists believe wiped out the dinosaurs some 66 million years ago. That asteroid strike left a crater off the coast of Mexico that spanned 93 miles wide by 12 miles deep. It also ended about three-quarters of all plant species on our planet, a catastrophe that forever changed the course of history. And, it resulted in a complete shift in biological platform dominance, one that killed off reptiles while giving way to the rise of mammals. So, as with the best event in human history, both content and context matter in our respondents' answers to the single event of the past changed the world for the worst.

In selecting human-caused catastrophes over natural disasters, the martial artists who responded to our survey demonstrate a penchant for taking personal responsibility. That is not to say that a German citizen born in 1970 holds themselves accountable for the rise of Nazism in the 1920s, but it does point to the idea of choices and consequences thereof. We make determinations as human beings about the use of tools, ideas, and actions, deploying them for purposes good or ill. In doing so, it is the individual who wields the mechanism who becomes responsible for the outcome of his or her choice(s).

Further, the selections made by these martial artists are in temporal proximity to their current state and time. For instance, the Gutenberg Press with its movable type revolutionized access to the written word and by extension to information for the masses. Before this invention only a select few were able to access information, let alone read or interpret it. We can recall creation of a printing press in 1440 yet fail to recall extinction of a species that dominated our planet for multiple millions of years. Perhaps this relates to what's urgent and imperative in our everyday lives, but more likely it is simply a matter of proximity that makes these events salient. Psychologists know that humans have an inherent cognitive bias that favors recent events over historic ones.

> Like Buddhism, Taoism, and many Native-American traditions, the martial arts ethos breeds mindfulness through practice, resulting in practitioners becoming happier, more secure, and (oftentimes) more successful in all aspects of their lives.

It is reasonable to conclude from evaluating responses to this question that martial artists as a community tend to focus on things that we can influence or control. Likely this stems from the importance of mindfulness in martial arts training. Mindfulness is the ability to be fully present in the moment, aware of where we are and what we are doing, yet not overly reactive or overwhelmed by what is going on around us.

吐く息にも生命が宿り

英利

The Japanese expression, "hakuiki hitotsu ni mo seimei ga yadori," as depicted in the image here which was provided courtesy of Master Japanese Calligrapher Eri Takase (www.takase.com), translates as "life in every breath." Popularized in the 2003 movie *The Last Samurai*, this perspective means living in the moment fully, consciously, and intentionally. In such a state, moments linger longer. There is a fullness to even the most mundane experience, say gazing upon a cherry blossom in full bloom, where each and every action we take feels perfectly complete no matter how mundane it may be.

Much of the warrior ethos centers around this concept of living in the moment. Mindfulness is at the root of Buddhism, Taoism, and many Native-American traditions, often applied through meditation and/or breathing exercises.

Life can be stressful enough without compounding it by contemplating everything that can or could go wrong. Negative self-talk and dwelling on the past should have no place in a martial artist's world. When we focus on the life in every breath our tribulations become more manageable, our goals more achievable. So, while martial artists acknowledge the worst events in human history, they are not disquieted by them.

Scientific studies demonstrate that mindful people are able to set aside things that are beyond their control. They have higher self-esteem that the average citizen even while accepting their own shortcomings, and as a result are happier, more secure, and more successful. That pretty much sums up our research group.

Who is your favorite musician or band?

"After silence, that which comes nearest to expressing the inexpressible is music."
Aldous Huxley, English writer and philosopher

Our taste in music reflects our personality. According to a study by University of Cambridge psychologist David Greenberg, people who are systemic prefer different types of music than people who rate high on the empathy scale. Neuroimaging scans demonstrate that systemizers' brains tend to be larger and more active in regions responsible for pattern recognition, whereas empathizers are more tuned toward their ability to understand the thoughts and feelings of others. This is why systemizers prefer energetic music like that produced by *AC/DC, Aerosmith, Guns n' Roses, Judas Priest, Led Zeppelin, Metallica,* or *Powerwolf,* whereas empathizers prefer the mellow tones of Adele, Billy Joel, Carole King, Elton John, Joni Mitchell, Ray Charles, or Stevie Nicks.

This plays out in an interesting way. When listening to mellow music that make can us feel sad, our brains naturally begin to release hormones that soften the mood. Since empathizers get a bigger dose due to greater development in the region of their brain that is responsible for regulating the chemical's release, they tend to prefer music that evokes deep emotion. Systemizers, on the other hand, are more attracted to complex, harder-hitting sounds because of their brain chemistry.

While martial artists are attracted to a wide variety of music, most of our choices run toward the classics, not older music necessarily, but rather musicians and bands whose creative works have withstood the test of time. The artists we like are leaders not followers. They are unique, with a distinctive voice or sound that makes them stand out from the crowd.

> Good patterns repeated well are valued by martial artists. This is reflected not only through the practice of the arts but also in our tastes in music.

To paraphrase Ted Templeman, the American record mogul who worked with award-winning talent like Bette Midler, Carly Simon, David Lee Roth, Edgar Winter, Joan Jett, and Sammy Hagar, and produced popular albums for bands like *Cheap Trick, The Doobie Brothers, Van Halen,* and *Van Morrison,* good music must catch listeners' attention instantly. And, they should know who the band is within the first few notes. Note that all the bands on this short list have been inducted into the Rock and Roll Hall of Fame, so clearly Templeman was on to something with his statement. Truly, these are the marks of originality and longevity, factors that separate imitators from trailblazers.

This exploration leads to the idea that martial artists like strong clear messages in their music. No matter the genre, it must be good, be recognizable, and be unique. *Pink Floyd* obviously doesn't sound like *Nirvana,* and *Nirvana* sounds nothing like Bach, but all are distinctive on their own merits. The majority of bands and musicians selected by our respondents were trendsetters, reflecting the edge of their industry. They are exceptional at what they do, speaking with a voice like no others.

When we return to our favorite band or musician and listen to their songs over and over again, we demonstrate that we find satisfaction from known, high quality, creative work that is repeated over and over. Likely this means that, in general, good patterns repeated well are of high value to martial artists as a community.

Perhaps this conclusion is a bit of a stretch, yet *kata* (forms) do much the same thing for those who practice traditional martial arts. *Kata* are not found in every system, but fighting sports, military, law enforcement, and RBSD practitioners all use repetitive drills. There is nuanced difference among systems, but all forms of training do much the same thing. Where present, repeated patterns within our training can represent the unique and recognizable perspectives of our martial system while simultaneously helping practitioners grasp the strategy and use the tactics and applications more adroitly.

Martial Artist Profile – Dana Abbott

Shihan *Dana Abbott is an expert in* kenjutsu, iaido, batto-do, *and* tameshigiri *Japanese Swordsmanship. Martial arts industry association* MASuccess *magazine wrote, "Dana Abbott's story could be the plot of a martial arts action movie: a young man from Arizona dreams of learning swordsmanship, sets off for Japan to follow the same path as the samurai warriors from centuries past, and studies under one of the world's premier masters to emerge decades later as a master in his own right. Although it would make a cool movie, this story isn't from a film and it isn't even fiction. Shihan Dana Abbott, 7th-degree black, and Black Belt Magazine Hall of Famer' recently recounted the story of how he came to join the ranks of top-echelon martial artists." His website is* www.learnthesword.com.

What's the worst martial arts-related mistake you have ever made?

"Diligent training with the world's best swordsmen was a killer! If I did not urinate brown or blood at least a few times a month I was not putting forth enough effort. A very spartan existence practiced at a young age creates arthritic consequences later in life."

For good or ill, what was the biggest impact of your martial arts training on your life?

"I have learned over the past 40 years that being consistent has the most value. Being consistent creates a healthy lifestyle."

Knowing what you know now, would you do it all over again?

"Yes, as I am right on target with my life and family. I have been very lucky to get the stuffing beat out of me by some of the greatest swordsmen in Japan and many other master martial artists from around the world. I have lived and trained the way of the *samurai* being accomplished in Japanese swordsmanship just like in an old Chuck Norris movie."

Why did you start training?

"It was September 1978 when I began my first punch and kick at the old armory in Prescott, Arizona. The town where Billy Jack kicked butt. Needed to harness the excessive energy my hyperactive body would produce. I was hooked with my first kick."

What single event of the past changed the world for the best?

"When Rome decided to standardize the width/length of the wheel base for their legion's chariots, which the width is still used today throughout the world's train tracks and roadways."

> "I have been very lucky to get the stuffing beat out of me by some of the greatest swordsmen in Japan and many other master martial artists from around the world."

What single event of the past changed the world for the worst?

"The internet… 'nuff said!"

What is the best single piece of advice you were ever given?

"I have been a 'lone wolf' my whole life. I honestly cannot think of any serious advice or tips that changed my life. Instead, I view the world with open eyes and ears thus creating my own guidelines."

What terrifies you?

"I am all in a sea of wonders. I doubt; I fear; I think strange things, which I dare not confess to my own soul."
Bram Stoker, Irish novelist

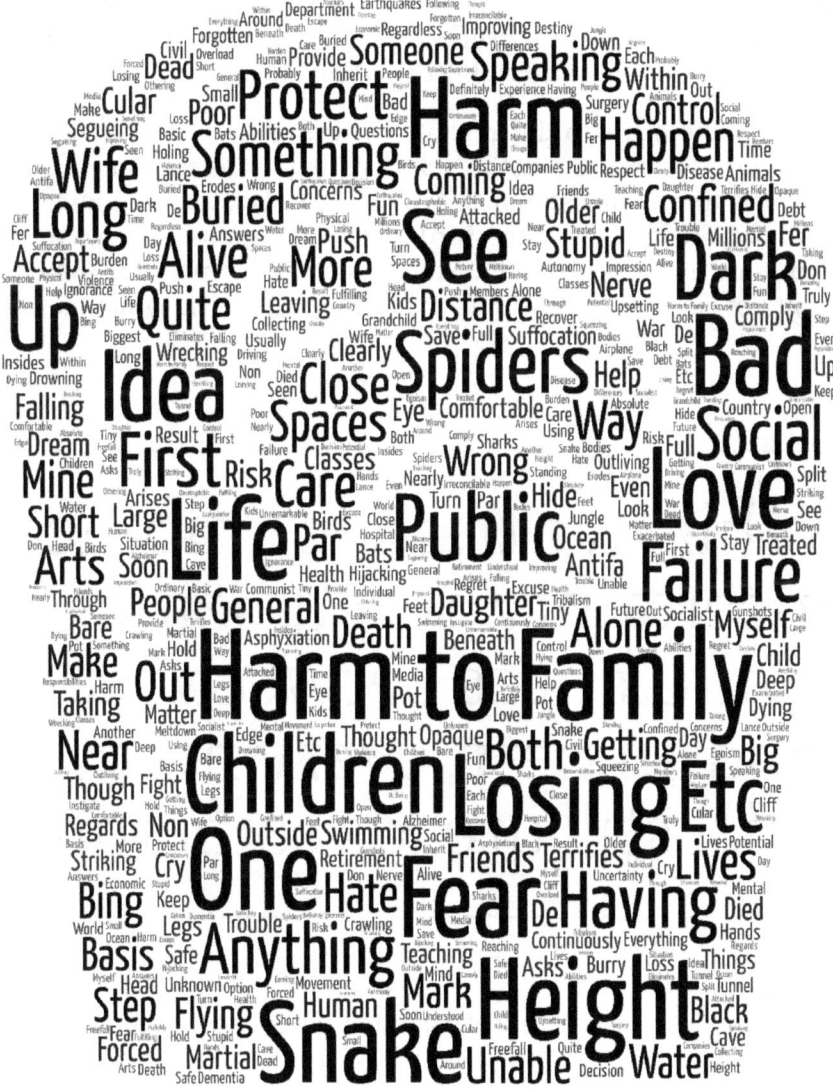

Scientists have been able to specify the sets of stimuli that normally elicit fear in humans, along with individual behavioral, autonomic, endocrine, and cognitive responses caused by that state of terror. According to psychological research, prototypical fear scenarios include things like (1) dangerousness, (2) inescapability, (3) distance, and (4) identifiability, with common responses that include such things as attacking, running away, freezing, assessing risks, screaming, or hiding. In any particular situation, one or more of these actions may prove more beneficial than others, so martial artists train to perform better than average in high stress situations such as physical combat, using breathing exercises, meditation, visualization, and various skill drills to hone their responses.

It is critical for practitioners to differentiate between fear and anxiety. Fear is usually conceptualized by psychologists as an adaptive but transient state elicited through confrontation with threatening stimulus, whereas anxiety is a more tonic state related to prediction and preparedness. In other words, fear is a response to what we actually face in the moment, such as physical danger, while anxiety is a response to something that we might or might not be confronted with in the future. It is our imagination reacting to the unknown.

> While we train to embrace uncertainty, recognizing the differences between fear and anxiety, every martial artist still dreads something.

Physically, people in a short-term state of fear often experience dry mouths, tense muscles, hot or cold sweats, churning stomachs, loose bowels, weakness, fast breathing, difficulty concentrating, and increased heartrates. Consider what it might feel like to suddenly be confronted by a hungry lion in the wild and you'll have a pretty good idea of what we mean. Practitioners often talk about fight, flight, or freeze in such situations, but in certain circumstances people may flinch, inexplicably laugh, or simply feel an intense sense of dread followed by powerful relief after the threat is extinguished.

People experiencing long term anxiety, on the other hand, often become irritable, have trouble sleeping, develop headaches, have trouble planning for the future, experience sexual disfunction, loss of confidence, and diminished self-esteem. A challenge is that our brains use sensory input to predict what will happen next in any given situation and then generate a physical response that is unwarranted to the reality of the situation. Consider public speaking, a common phobia, by way of example. There is no immediate physical threat, yet our bodies react as if there was.

Common fears of our respondents included terrible things like outliving their children, being unable to prevent harm to their families, and losing loved ones. Interestingly enough, while death itself did not top the list, certain methods of dying such as being buried alive did. Snakes, spiders, confined spaces, and, surprisingly, public speaking also topped the list. Think about it, this means at least some folks who feel more comfortable than the average citizen in dealing with physical violence that could cripple or kill them still dread standing in front of a crowd and talking about stuff. Go figure…

One especially notable input came from respondents who were deeply concerned about the effects of social media, tribalism, and isolation caused by the pandemic on the future of society. This is very much in line with Pew Research studies which also pointed to diminished levels of trust in government, negative impacts on personal relationships, and various other adverse societal, political, and safety impacts.

Thematically the fears expressed by our participants included things like loss of control, the inability to protect or rescue loved ones from harm, and the unknown. Psychologists relate that people can develop post-traumatic stress disorder (PTSD) after witnessing or experiencing traumatic events such as murder, torture, domestic abuse, serious accidents, death of their child(ren), sexual assaults, and severe health problems (such as cancer), even after they're cured. While the reasons that some people are afflicted by PTSD while others are not is still being investigated, a key indicator appears to be the person's level of control during the critical incident they underwent. Consequently, our respondents may be on to something profound with their inputs on this topic.

Proven ways of coping with fear and anxiety including noting how and when physical cues manifest, owning the emotions, and controlling one's breathing. Keeping on top of our biological needs for exercise, nutrition, and rest help significantly, as does taking our negative thoughts to trial by examining if perceived threats are actually real or imagined. Most practitioners already know this, yet every one of them responded to this question on our survey with something they were terrified of nonetheless.

Do you regularly carry a weapon?

"It is well-settled fact of American law that the police have no legal duty to protect any individual citizen from crime, even if the citizen has received death threats and the police have negligently failed to provide protection."

United States Supreme Court,
Castle Rock vs. Gonzales, June 27, 2005

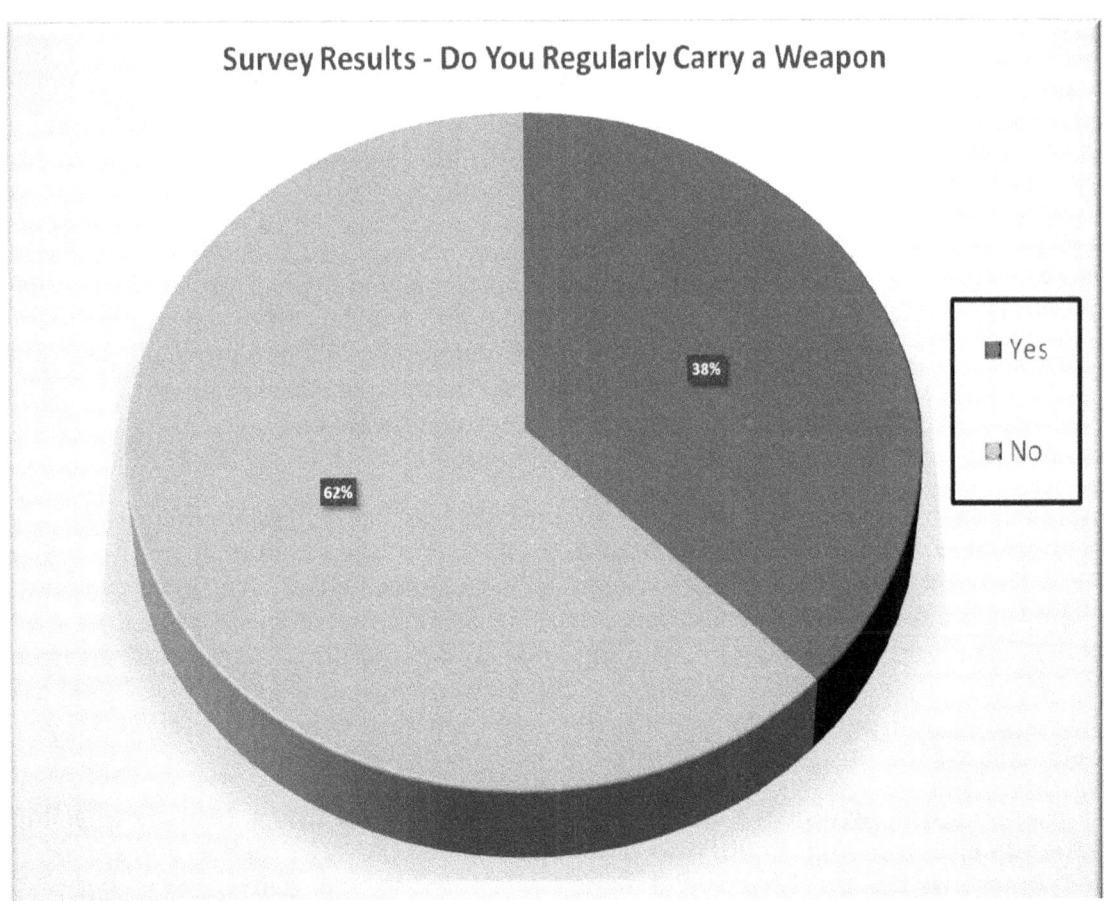

In the United States Supreme Court case cited in the quote above, the high court determined in a 7-2 decision that the plaintiff Jessica Gonzales could not sue her local police department for failing to enforce a restraining order against her estranged husband. The victim of domestic violence and spousal abuse, Gonzalez had obtained a legal order requiring that he to stay away from her and their three daughters. This court order included a directive to law enforcement officials mandating that they, "Shall use every reasonable means to enforce this restraining order."

When her ex-husband took their children without permission despite the restraining order, the plaintiff contacted the Castle Rock, Colorado Police Department several times throughout the night, seeking her estranged husband's arrest and the safe return of her children. When law enforcement officers failed to take any action during these frantic phone calls, she went to the police station in person and filed an incident report.

Regrettably, while the plaintiff was still pleading unsuccessfully with the police for help, her ex-husband murdered all three of her children. At 3:20 AM he showed up at the police station too, and began firing at officers with a semiautomatic pistol where he was killed by return gunfire. The plaintiff subsequently sued the city and the police department for violating the Due Process Clause of the U.S. Constitution by depriving her of the rights granted by the restraining order without due process.

In their ruling, the U.S. Supreme court made it clear that despite their public safety mission, it is not the job of law enforcement agencies to protect any individual citizen from crime, even if that person has already suffered from domestic violence, received death threats, obtained a legal restraining order, and the police negligently failed to provide protection afterward. Self-defense laws vary from country to country, and U.S. law is not necessarily representative of the situation worldwide, but for all intents and purposes this ruling means that when it comes to personal safety, we're pretty much on our own.

While we cannot count on the authorities to safeguard our safety, it seems that citizens are surprisingly good at protecting themselves. According to the London Center for Policy Research, armed citizens stop more crime than law enforcement officers do every year in the United States. Data strongly suggests that they prevent more than 7,000 murders and 60,000 rapes each year, though depending on what data we draw our conclusions from these numbers could actually be as high as 20,000 murders and 175,000 rapes. Those are pretty impressive numbers. Whether or not any individual chooses to carry a weapon, data indicates that an armed population is in fact a safer population.

When asking this question in our survey, we knew that laws regarding weapon ownership vary significantly from country to country. Consequently, we defined weapons as instruments or devices specifically designed for use in attack or defense such as pepper sprays, stun guns, knives, kubatons, brass knuckles, or firearms. We did not include makeshift implements that could be used as weapons but are not designed as such, like car keys, belts, water bottles, or boots. And, we intentionally did not specify what kind of weapon people carried, just asked whether or not they regularly bear one.

In some countries we know that firearm ownership, for example, is not a legal option for civilians (e.g., Japan) whereas in others gun ownership is considered a patriotic duty to protect the homeland (e.g., Switzerland). Some countries heavily restrict knife ownership too (e.g., United Kingdom) while others (e.g., South Africa) do not. And, some devices, such as canes or walking sticks, could be perceived as mobility aids or as tools for self-defense depending on one's perspective (several martial arts such as *hapkido* teach cane techniques in their weapons curriculum), so we left it up to individual respondents to interpret how to answer this question.

Regardless of what we may or may not legally own in any given jurisdiction, or how any given individual interprets the word "weapon," we know that martial artists as a community are more keenly aware of violence dynamics, how criminals think, and ways of keeping themselves from becoming victims than the general population. And, we know that nearly 70% of survey respondents found themselves needing to use their skills outside the training hall, so in light of these facts responses to this question were fascinating, with roughly a third of respondents reporting that they carry a weapon regularly.

The type of martial art studied is, surprisingly, not directly correlated with a person's inclination to regularly carry a knife, gun, or other weapon or to forgo that practice altogether. For example, we had retired law enforcement officers report in our survey that they are not routinely armed (which was not even an option while they were on the force and required to carry a firearm at all times both on- and off-duty) and folks who study traditional martial arts who never leave home unarmed. This leads us to the conclusion that carrying a weapon is a deeply personal choice, one that martial artists make knowing the both the risks and responsibilities inherent in their decision.

Data indicates that most violence can be staved off without resorting to the highest levels of force which might necessitate using a weapon, yet in certain circumstances the only way we can reasonably extricate ourselves from danger with any rational chance of survival is with a gun. In other words, the judicious use of countervailing force is a giant "it depends" situation. Sometimes our life is on the line, while other times it's just our ego. We might be able to choose whether or not to get involved, or we may find ourselves with no option but to fight. The perfect response to one situation could easily prove disastrous in another.

> Carrying a weapon is a deeply personal choice, a decision martial artists make knowing the risks and responsibilities inherent in their selection.

You see, some violence can be staved off simply by presence, that is by looking and acting like we're more trouble than we're worth so that those with nefarious intent move on to easier targets. We can use words to defuse many situations, or apply calming or directive touch to reach resolution without injury. But not always. Sometimes empty-hand restraint is required, particularly if we need to control a situation without seriously hurting anyone. Other times, less-lethal or even lethal force is necessary to save our lives or the lives of our loved ones. While not a rigid scale, these choices form a continuum:

- **Presence**—use of techniques designed to stave off violence via posture or body language that warns adversaries of our readiness and ability to act or that poses no threat to another's ego.
- **Voice**—use of techniques designed to verbally de-escalate conflict before physical methods become necessary.
- **Touch**—use of techniques designed to defuse impending violence or gain compliance via calming or directive touch.
- **Empty-hand restraint**—use of techniques designed to control an aggressor through pain, or force compliance through leverage.
- **Less-lethal force**—use of techniques or implements designed to incapacitate an aggressor while minimizing the likelihood of fatality or serious injury.
- **Lethal force**—use of techniques or implements likely to cause death or permanent injury.

It's vital that we enter this force scale at the right level. If we use too much or too little force, we are in for a world of hurt. Consequently, it is imperative to understand the various options, knowing how and when to apply them judiciously. Knowing this, most martial artists weigh their options and logically determine whether a weapon is necessary or desired, and if carrying one fits into their lifestyle.

Many states in the United States, including Alaska, Arizona, Arkansas, Idaho, Iowa, Kansas, Kentucky, Maine, Mississippi, Missouri, Montana, New Hampshire, North Dakota, Oklahoma, South Dakota, Tennessee, Texas, Utah, Vermont, West Virginia, and Wyoming have adopted "Constitutional Carry" laws which allow for law-abiding citizens to own firearms without requiring any permit to carry them. In the remaining 29 states, there were over 18.66 million adults, approximately 8.3% of the population, who owned a legal concealed carry permit as of 2020 according to national security think tank 19FortyFive. Collectively, these individuals tend to be extremely law-abiding, going through rigorous background checks before purchasing their weapon and taking training afterward to know how and when to use it.

While this was a yes or no question, our curiosity got the better of us and we delved a little deeper in conversations with a representative sampling of survey respondents to find out more. For some, weapon ownership was simply not an option for a variety of reasons, whereas for others it was the word "regularly" in the question that determined their answer. Many stated that while they owned one or more weapons, they chose not carry one most of the time. Regardless, they all spoke to a balance of risk and responsibility in making their determination and we captured some of their thoughts and counsel below…

Those considering purchasing a weapon for the first time must be both mentally and physically prepared to do so responsibly. That decision warrants deep thought and consideration. Here are a few things to ponder that can help you make a wise choice:

- Are you capable of remaining level-headed in stressful circumstances and confrontational situations?
- Do you have any moral or religious beliefs that prevent you from protecting yourself or your loved ones by any means necessary?
- Are you capable of taking another person's life if necessary to defend yourself or your loved ones?
- Do you fully understand laws regulating weapon ownership and self-defense in areas where you live, work, and travel?
- Are you committed to learning how handle the weapon(s) properly, proficiently, and responsibly?
- Do you know how to store the weapon in a way that provides emergency access while keeping it out of the hands of anyone who might steal or misuse it?
- Are you willing to devote the time and expense necessary to develop and maintain a high level of proficiency with the weapon(s) you own?
- Do you understand the level of responsibility and accountability you must accept with weapon ownership?
- Are you willing to forgo alcohol and other intoxicants when carrying your weapon?
- Do you know that your friends and family members will accept your decision?
- Are you willing to assure that everyone who lives with you and may have access to the weapon is trained in safety protocols regardless of whether or not they are authorized to use the weapon?
- Do you qualify for a concealed carry or ownership permit (if required) associated with the weapon(s) you wish to buy?
- Are you willing to change your wardrobe as necessary to carry your weapon in an accessible way that simultaneously keeps it out of public view?
- Do you have appropriate liability insurance?
- Are you prepared to accept the social stigmas that weapon ownership may represent?

For good or ill, owning a lethal weapon can become a life-altering decision. It is a choice that should not be made lightly.

While everyone who practices martial arts has at least some degree of interest in their personal safety, our survey demonstrates that a bit over a third of martial artists carry some form of weapon regularly. Because we only probed deeper with a handful of respondents we cannot know for certain if this is because they simply do not feel the need, found carrying one impractical, or if moral or ethical objections got in the way. We do know, however, that the determination each individual made was well thought out.

Martial Artist Profile – Hermann Bayer, Ph.D.

With degrees in economics, sociology, psychology, and business administration, Hermann worked as scientist, professor, and academic dean for 18 years, and as a CEO for 12 years. He is an Okinawan karate-jutsu *practitioner after studying Japanese* karate-do *earlier. He immigrated from Germany into the United States of America in 2005. Hermann's Karate training began 1981 in Europe with* Doshinkan karate-do *until he, to better understand the arts' true life protection purpose, transitioned to Okinawan* Shorin Ryu karate-jutsu *in the USA. Over the years he spent considerable time with renowned Japanese, Western, and Okinawan teachers, all the while researching the core essence of the style they represent. Now in his 70s, Hermann is still training hard. He practices karate daily and attends four 2-hour training-sessions per week, accompanied by additional training camps in the United States and Okinawa. As the author of several books and numerous articles in his professional fields, he today publishes on* karate-jutsu's *and* karate-do's *socio-cultural roles and developments. His book,* Genuine Karate—Misconceptions, Origin, Development, and True Purpose, *was reviewed by* Hanshi *Patrick McCarthy as "a fascinating exploration," which he in his foreword recommends, "to become a mandatory reading for all serious enthusiasts." You can discover more about Hermann's work on his website* https://hermannbayer.academia.edu/.

What is the best compliment you have ever received?

"There are two different situations, and both times it is more important who said it than what was said. The first one is the characterization of my leadership by the folks I was in charge for. During an employee meeting in December 2016, after they had experienced me for four years, they stated that, 'He supports us, he protects us, and he let us do our job.' The other one is recent: *Hanshi* Patrick McCarthy introduced and recommended my book *Analysis of Genuine Karate* on Facebook and characterized me as 'a remarkable person' whose 'important research, contributions and inspirational leadership have not gone unnoticed.' We communicated quite a bit in the two years before that about my background, my values, my character, my views. Being called a remarkable person by this karate research authority left me speechless."

What's the worst martial arts-related mistake you have ever made?

"Trying to impress. In 1986 some non-martial-arts friends of mine and I had dinner. During our conversation questions about karate and judo were asked. I explained that traditional karate included many moves which are usually attributed to *ju-jutsu*/judo, like throws and groundwork, and I was proud that my friends were eager to learn more. So, being young and stupid, I lost my modesty and I started to brag about the falling and rolling capabilities we learn in our system. To show off, I demonstrated a forward fall/roll over my right shoulder on the apartment's hardwood floor, which would have worked nicely if I had used my right hand and arm correctly to absorb the force of the fall. I did not, and I instead slammed my shoulder on the floor in full force, creating a painful shoulder contusion and joint strain which I still feel today every now and then."

For good or ill, what was the biggest impact of your martial arts training on your life?

"Karate helped me understand the concept of continuous improvement while pursuing an endless path without ever reaching its goal combined with giving your best all the time. This mindset served me well in my professional life; its positive impact was recognized by my superiors and led to promotions into a successful career. It secondly helped me to develop physical strength and overall health, as well as to 'understand' and to control my body and my movements. This strengthened my organs and improved my immune system proven by my current shape and mobility in my seventies. It thirdly allowed me to develop situational awareness and the self-definition of owning enough combat capability to hold my ground in a fight. This helps me to remain calm under pressure in challenging situations and to think before I act proven through my mastering of some extreme situations while sailing through a storm, literally and allegorically."

What single event of the past changed the world for the best?

"The invasion of the Normandy in WWII and the following defeat of Nazi-Germany. This event turned the table not just in a war, but it united the free world against the evil of tyranny and fascism, and it led to the uncovering of unspeakable horror pursued in the name of racial superiority and ethnical cleaning. In a broader sense, it removed the notion of one nation or race being superior to others and it spread the concept of equality of men. Finally, because of the pure dimension of death and destruction in WWII, the world started to realize the true benefit of peace, and maintaining peace became the first goal of politics (even by means of deterrence in the sense of 'if you want peace prepare for war'), whereas before that time war was 'the continuation of politics by another means.'"

What is the best single piece of advice you were ever given?

"It was given to me by a former boss of mine in the early 1990s when I headed an organization in a highly competitive, merciless market. He stated that 'the longer you persist, the less competition you will have, because the longer you hang in, the more competitors will give up. At the end you will be the only one remaining.'. He often supported this advice by his favorite phrase 'there is no shame in falling down, there is only shame in not getting up again.' I immediately connected this advice to what I learned from *Hanshi* Isao Ichikawa about '*do*' in karate. This turned out to be a solid piece of advice, proven true by my personal experience many times; not only in a business environment but in any competitive situation, as well as in any difficult social situation when I had to deal with slander and bad-mouthing."

> "Karate helped me understand the concept of continuous improvement while pursuing an endless path without ever reaching its goal combined with giving your best all the time. This mindset served me well in my professional life."

What single event of the past changed the world for the worst?

"Generally speaking, misusing religion in the sense that, in the name of a God and under the flag of a specific believe system, fighting and killing of non-believers becomes legitimate. The view of one's own religion as the only 'true' (and therefore superior) one de-humanizes non-believers, degrades them into varmints, and morally not only justifies, but even requests, their killing and/or enslavement. In this line of thought I see a path of evil throughout history, from the moral superiority of ancient believe system of gods and demi-gods with following enslavements and human sacrifices over the crusades of Christianity up to Islamic terror in the name of God. Misusing religion did and still does change the world for the worst, and there is no end in sight, because it is easier for individuals to believe than to think."

Who influenced you the most?

"True men embrace their responsibility. They know being a father should be real, not just owning a name."

Ephantus Mwenda, Kenyan novelist

Another open-ended question with surprising unanimity of results, we find that martial artists, both male and female, were strongly influenced by male role models in their lives, with words like "father," "dad," "teacher," "Mr.," or their parent's name prominent in their responses. Fathers represent protectors, providers, and disciplinarians in contemporary society, and as such are critical to the ethical, moral, and emotional development of their children.

In fact, the Bureau of Justice Statistics reports that we incarcerate males at 12 times the rate we imprison females in the United States. According to psychological research, a key reason for this discrepancy is lack of impulse control in males, a trait often found lacking in those who were raised without a father who was active in their life, setting boundaries and modeling acceptable behaviors. This appears to be a worldwide phenomenon though supporting data was both sparse and hard to interpret definitively.

In many ways martial arts instructors, be they *sensei* (Japanese for teacher), *sabom nim* (Korean for grandmaster), *sifu* (Chinese for teacher), *guru* (Sanskrit for master), drill instructor, coach, or whatever honorific they choose to be called, fill a similar role to fathers (and in some cases mothers) in a practitioner's life. These titles were also high on the list selected by our respondents. Since the word *sensei* in Japanese literally translates as "one who has come before," the term implies a coach, mentor, and guide rather than a simple teacher. As such, we can see their influence in their students' lives both inside and outside the *dojo* (training hall) by the prominence of that word in survey responses.

> No matter their gender, martial artists are heavily influenced by strong male role models, particularly fathers and teachers.

These influencers, fathers and teachers, are bound by two common elements: (1) frequency and (2) proximity. The father holds a larger role over the instructor, in most instances, because instructors live apart from and have limited teaching time with their students. While many martial artists practice daily, practitioners typically only participate in some sort of formal class three or four days a week. Even the best-intentioned fathers can be limited in their time available to spend with their families by other duties, especially those who travel for business, are deployed overseas, or otherwise forced to be absent for extended periods of time. Regardless, in two-parent families they tend to spend far more time with their children during their developmental years than any teacher.

According to Parents Plus Kids, a website devoted to effective parenting, qualities of a good father include:

- Leads by example
- Shows patience, compassion, and loyalty
- Loves and protects his partner
- Is dependable, present, and involved
- Loves and supports his child(ren)
- Provides for his family
- Is slow to anger, disciplining from a place of love
- Is proactive, focusing on raising good adults

Compare and contrast the parental attributes above with those of a good martial arts instructor below:

- Leads by example
- Shows patience and compassion
- Is loyal to the precepts of their system
- Is dependable, present, and involved
- Supports their students, teaching both skill and good judgement
- Is slow to anger
- Assures a safe and productive learning environment
- Is proactive, focusing on developing good citizens as well as proficient martial artists

Anecdotally, both author's started training in our youth (ages 6 and 12 respectively), and still see the influence of our instructors in our lives half a century later despite the fact that we have not spoken to some of them in decades and others have long since passed on. Our experience with our own instructors throughout our careers as well as our interactions with other talented teachers and coaches we know well closely matches the above list.

If you find yourself studying from someone who does not portray these qualities, ask yourself if you're training in the right place.

One hypothesis we had in asking this question was that we would find mostly positive influencers in our survey results, which is exactly what we found, but it is important to keep in mind that influences can be negative too. Our parents, teachers, friends, family and relations have significant impact on our self-image, aspirations, and success (or failure) in life. In that vein, motivational speaker Jim Rohn once said, "We are the average of the five people we spend the most time with."

We do not know whether or not Rohn's assertion has been scientifically substantiated, but the statement certainly rings true. Consequently, it is important to consider the folks in our inner circle and ascertain whether or not we're using our time wisely.

Finally, know that influence does not happen by accident. Studies on the psychology of social influence demonstrate that influential people understand themselves, act deliberately, speak thoughtfully, listen actively, set high expectations for themselves, and take action when they believe it is needed. Analysis paralysis has no place in their worlds. They connect with others, act with integrity, and learn constantly. In this fashion they not only set a good example, but also inspire others to follow.

Whether you're a father, a teacher, a mother, or just some yahoo reading this book, consider not only those who have inspired you the most but also those whom you wish to inspire and act accordingly.

Martial Artist Profile – Restita DeJesus

Sifu Restita DeJesus is the Founder and Chief Instructor of Seattle Wushu Center. She has studied martial arts since 1978, and holds black belt certifications in Butokukan *karate,* Wun Hop Kuen Do-Chuan Fa Kajukenbo, Kyudo, *FMAA* Eskrima/Kali, Cacoy Canete's Doce Pares Eskrima, Pangamot, Eskrido, *Chinese contemporary* Wushu, Chen Taijiquan, *and* Yang Taijiquan. *Restita is an inductee to Martial Arts History Museum Hall of Honors, USA Martial Arts Hall of Fame,* Doce Pares *World Federation Hall of Fame, and Masters Hall of Fame. Outside of martial arts, Restita is an ordained Interfaith Minister and Reiki Master Practitioner. In her spare time, her activities include meditation, reading, paracord crafts, knife throwing, bullwhip trick cracking, archery, target blowgun shooting and target slingshot shooting. Her personal philosophy: "Always keep an open enough mind to learn from anything and anyone. Any person can be your teacher." Her website is www.seattlewushu.org.*

What is the best compliment you have ever received?

"After competing at my first national level martial arts tournament, I was approached by a young girl and her parents. The girl's mom said, 'Excuse me, my daughter would like to say something to you.' The girl said, 'When you came out and introduced yourself to the judges, you looked so big… but you're not that tall. How do I do that?' I told her, 'Just be confident and always do your very best, that's how.' The parents went on to explain that she wanted to, 'Someday look as tough without looking tough, just like that lady down there.'"

What's the worst martial arts-related mistake you have ever made?

"When I was a young teen 1st degree black belt, I attended an open tournament and had opinions about other competitors in my open *kata* division. At the time I was so stuck on 'hard style' and thought *kung fu* was 'too soft' to be any good. I came in 3rd place in that tournament (usually placing 1st or 2nd), a *kung fu* stylist taking the 1st place trophy. From that, I saw that the expert judges saw a strength in the *kung fu* stylist that I did not see. I learned from that experience that each martial art teaches the same concepts and strengths, yet may have a different way of expressing them. I've opened my mind since then, and added many aspects of martial arts to my repertoire, that as a young teen, I would not have explored."

For good or ill, what was the biggest impact of your martial arts training on your life?

"Martial arts taught me perseverance. While training in *Wushu*, it was the hardest thing I'd done. I agreed to be trained as my teacher was trained in China. Constantly pulled muscles, puking from the rigorous effort on many occasions, daily 5-hour sessions. There were days where I'd wake up and consider calling in sick, but realized it would just be harder the next day, so I'd 'suck it up' and keep going no matter what."

> *"Martial arts taught me perseverance... There were days where I'd wake up and consider calling in sick, but realized it would just be harder the next day, so I'd 'suck it up' and keep going no matter what."*

When you were a kid, what did you want to be when you grew up?

"As a child, I initially wanted to be a school counselor, then a police officer, then a martial arts instructor. I actually started study in psychology in community college with the intention of college transfer to the University of Washington and getting a degree in psychology to be a counselor/therapist, but dropped out of college 2 years later. Some years later, at 25 years old I tried taking the physical tests for becoming a Seattle Police Officer. I passed the physicals tests but was contacted by a real estate agent about a space I was looking at to start a commercial *dojo*. I made the choice to be a martial arts instructor, knowing that I'd put some of my psychology studies to good use."

Who influenced you the most?

"My High School radio/television instructor, Mr. Jay Wang. He made learning fun and urged us to think creatively outside the box."

Knowing what you know now, would you do it all over again?

"Yes, in a heartbeat. However, knowing what I know now, if I were to re-live my martial arts career, I'd be better able to handle the stress of some of my low points and to better handle the pressure of keeping at top competition condition."

Why did you start training?

"The journey of a thousand miles begins with one step."
Lao Tzu, Chinese philosopher

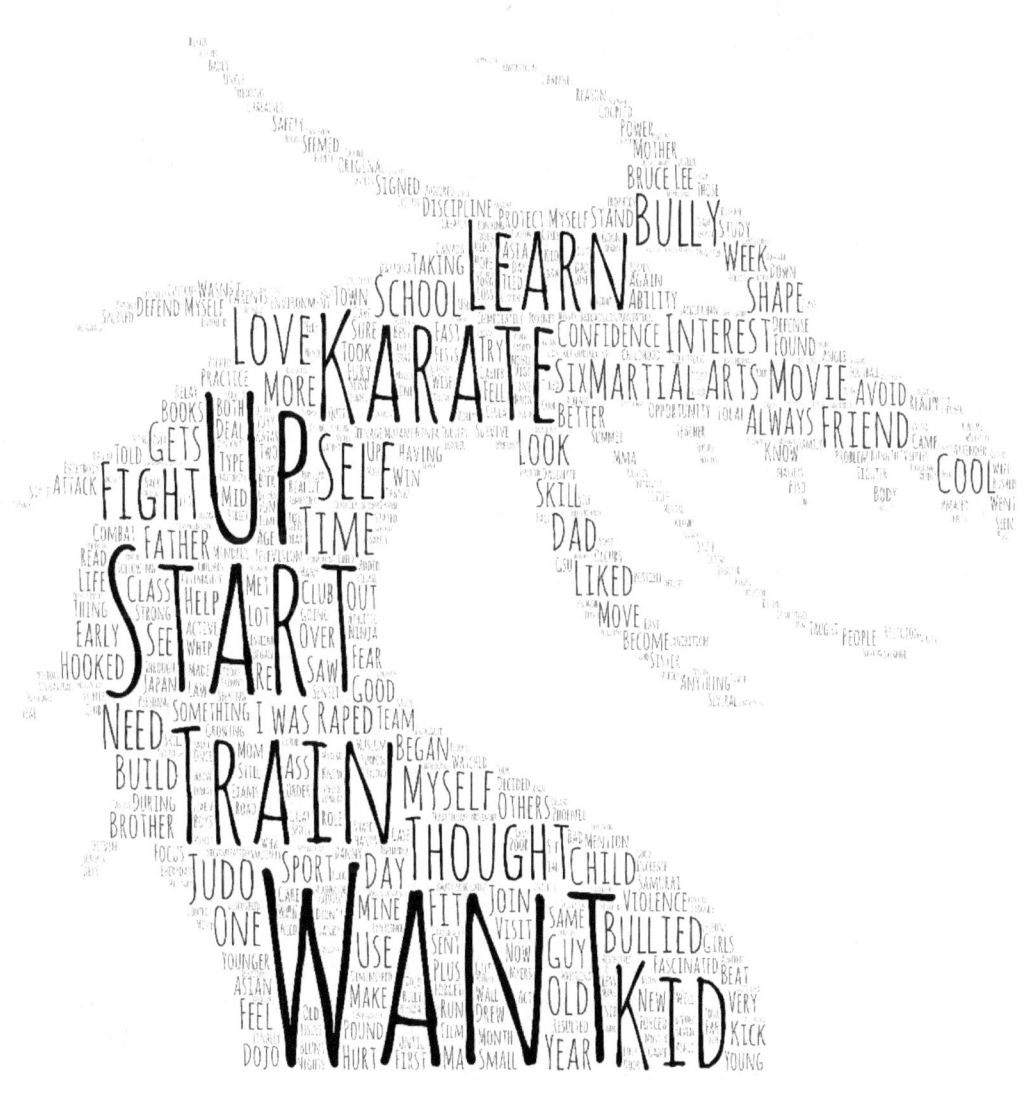

Gordon Ramsay is a famous British chef, restaurateur, television personality, and writer. His global restaurant group, which includes locations in England, France, Singapore, and the United States, has been awarded 16 Michelin stars, one of the hardest to earn and most prestigious awards in the culinary arts. Known for his starring roles in television shows like *Hell's Kitchen*, *MasterChef*, *Next Level Chef*, *Gordon Ramsay Uncharted*, and *Ramsay's*

Kitchen Nightmares, he was awarded an OBE (Order of the British Empire) by Queen Elizabeth II for his contribution to the culinary industry in 2006. And, he has published a number of bestselling books, including his autobiography *Roasting in Hell's Kitchen*.

A lesser-known fact is that, despite his hectic schedule, Chef Ramsay also earned a black belt in karate. In a 2016 interview with BBC Radio, he related that aside from fitness, his karate training provided him improved peace of mind, knowing that he could protect himself should the need arise. Other celebrity martial artists include actress Jennifer Aniston (*Budokon* Mixed Movement Arts), actress Jessica Biel (karate/kickboxing), actor Jack Black (judo), comedian Jim Carrey (Brazilian *jiu-jitsu*), comedian Kevin James (MMA), actor Ashton Kutcher (Brazilian *jiu-jitsu*), and singer/songwriter Demi Lovato (Brazilian *jiu-jitsu*).

These practitioners and countless others worldwide have discovered better cardiovascular health, muscle tone, flexibility, mobility, and coordination, among other physical benefits from their training. The mental discipline inherent in their pursuit of prowess in martial arts no doubt helped them with their careers and everyday lives too. Indeed, the physical and mental benefits of practicing martial arts are widely known, yet as we relayed earlier, the martial arts are still considered something of a niche industry. So, why get started?

Common answers to this question included: "I was bullied." "I got in a fight and I lost, so I needed to be become better at fighting." "I was small." "I was weak." "I was raped." "I needed self-confidence." Almost every response came with a compelling need. The aspiring practitioner found themselves lacking something and looked toward the martial arts to fill that void. The majority of the respondents even pointed to a moment where the switch was flipped, a singular or cumulative event where they thought or were told, "This needs to be fixed."

Interestingly, this moment often came in youth. Although some respondents added age to their description of the moment, phrases such as, "As a kid…" or, "When I was an awkward teen," were more common. The values cited in martial arts study were often specific—self-control, can-do attitude, responsibility, and accountability—these attributes form an incomplete but powerful list of frequent phrases used by our study participants. Nevertheless, at a 30,000-foot view of the value of proposition, we find that martial arts provide a flexible framework, one that is adaptable to the needs of aspiring practitioners at most any age or situation in life.

Here are a few examples from survey respondents:

John Leylegian wrote, "The discipline and mindset I acquired through my training has helped me look at the world differently, and I believe it helped me deal with my recent bout with Covid-19. It helped moderate my fear and anxiety about having to go to the hospital for it. In addition, I also believe my relative fitness helped pull me through the illness and get me back to training that much sooner."

Parul Verma, Ph.D. related, "Martial arts training improved my understanding of the human body in general and my body in particular. Consequently, I have become more aware of potential self-defense strategies that are more suited for my body type. Because of this, my confidence has increased, and I am able to handle my fears better. There are many other subtler aspects that are practiced in training and have impacted my philosophy in general. One in particular is seeking perfection, which I try to practice in my professional as well as personal life."

Sean Canonica reported, "The biggest impact that martial arts training has had on my life is that it has given me a positive outlet and something to be passionate about. Before starting karate, I had never been good at sports and had really only played video games as a hobby. Now, I have something I can focus on that entails physical movement and where there is always something new to learn. My karate training also allows me the opportunity to escape from the stresses of day-to-day life and just focus only on what is going on in the moment. In this way, my martial arts training gives me a positive activity to focus on and be passionate about in my life."

Benefits of martial arts are myriad. Even though many of our survey respondents described getting started in their youth, we are never too old to begin training. One of the most amazing things about martial arts, unlike most other sports, is that the longer we train the stronger we can become regardless of age. This is especially true for those who practice traditional arts rather than fighting sports where safety rules and weight classes favor younger athletes.

> While practitioners often begin training in their youth, there are no age limits to the myriad of mental and physical benefits we can gain by practicing martial arts.

Clearly, disease or injury can derail progress, but proper technique requires very little in the way of brute force to be effective. That is why the iconic little old man with a black belt, the real-life version of Mr. Miyagi from the movie *The Karate Kid*, can and often does readily defeat younger, stronger, and more agile opponents. Several individuals fitting that description participated in our survey, though one of them is actually an 80-year-old woman, Veena Grover, who has thirty years' experience teaching karate, taekwondo, and yoga under her well-worn and somewhat faded black belt.

Scientific research shows that rigorous exercise programs can slow the effects of aging, helping us live better, more fulfilling, and, oftentimes, longer lives. Studies suggest that even moderate exercise can delay the onset of Alzheimer's disease and other forms of dementia, demonstrating mental as well as physical benefits. In fact, many of the best active martial artists in the world are over the age of 40, many well into their 50s, 60s, 70s, or even 80s. Names like Grandmaster Dan Anderson, Grandmaster Loren Christensen, *Hanshi* Peter Consterdine, *Kiyoshi* Hoch Hochheim, Dr. Sang Kim, Grandmaster Chuck Norris, and Dr. Yang Jwing-Ming come to mind.

Look to *Guru* Dan Inosanto by way of example. Considered the foremost student and leading protégé of Bruce Lee, he is proficient in *Jeet Kune Do* but also holds advanced rank in *Muay Thai, Pentjak Silat,* and Brazilian *jiu-jitsu*. A talented Filipino martial artist and weapons practitioner, he showcased his skills in movies like *Game of Death, Sharky's Machine, Big Trouble in Little China,* and *Out for Justice*. His daughter, Diana Lee Inosanto, an accomplished martial artist in her own right, is a stunt woman, writer, director, and producer in Hollywood. And, as of this writing, he still actively teaches martial arts at the age of 85, running The Inosanto Academy in Marina Del Rey, California.

No matter what age you are, you are never too old to begin training if you're so inclined. Once you begin, there is really no limit to how long you can participate if you set your mind to it and take good care of yourself.

Martial Artist Profile – Josh Amos

Josh was born and raised in Washington State. He grew up in the 70s and 80s. He started archery when he was five, hunting at eight, and karate when he was twelve. At the age of 18, he joined the United States Marine Corps. In the service, he got a Logistics Military Occupation Specialty (MOS) and chose Okinawa as his first duty station. He went to automatic weapons, terrorism counter-action, and chemical warfare schools to add to his martial skills, and studied several different kinds of karate. Picking up a copy of Marc MacYoung's book Cheap Shots, Ambushes, and other Lessons: A Down and Dirty Book on Streetfighting & Survival *was a game changer. Josh was transferred Yuma, Arizona where he studied yet more martial styles briefly, instructors transferred in and out, so it was catch as catch can. Unfortunately, he got crunched up in the Marines and has a lasting disability from it. Afterwards he moved back to Washington, took up pistolcraft, and has been training in various ways ever since.*

When you were a kid, what did you want to be when you grew up?

"When I was a kid, I always wanted to be a Marine. Which is funny since I was not athletically gifted and I was pretty laid back about life. But something deep down inside me needed to do that. And I did. I joined at 17 and went to boot camp at 18. I was the youngest Marine in my first unit, and I was honorably discharged two months after my 22nd birthday after a four-year enlistment."

Who influenced you the most?

"My son influenced me the most. I was a non-custodial teen dad, so I had to calculate my action's potential impact on him before doing anything."

What is the best single piece of advice you were ever given?

"The advice was, 'Behavior is truth.' It came from the lawyer/child advocate/gritty author Andrew Vachss. This advice has kept me from being taken advantage of by bad bosses, politicians, salesmen, and while in bad relationships. What are they actually doing? To take this a step further, this advice meant that I had to study more people and more situations that were outside of my comfort zone so I could identify what they meant by what they were saying or what they were doing."

What's the best compliment you have ever received?

"Marc MacYoung and I were having cigars, he said 'I have met your son and your daughter, and I am really proud of you… but then I always have been.' Marc has known me for decades, and saw the struggle I had to get custody of my son from the WA State Family Courts. Marc also knew that I had informally adopted my daughter and helped her through some rough teenage years."

> "'Behavior is truth.' This advice has kept me from being taken advantage of by bad bosses, politicians, salesmen, and while in bad relationships."

What's the worst martial arts-related mistake you have ever made?

"As a young man, I thought that being a Marine, reading a few books on martial arts, having been in a few brawls, and taking a few shooting seminars was enough to make me a professional level instructor. I thought my learning was complete and I could teach just as good as the professional instructors out there."

For good or ill, what was the biggest impact of your martial arts training on your life?

"The impact of the martial arts was the journey that it led me on. I have met and connected with so many people, studied so many topics, (history, politics, philosophy, criminology, fitness, various types of arms), travelled to places (Okinawa, gun ranges, seminars), and had so many singular experiences, that never would have happened if I hadn't started training in martial arts at a young age. I suppose that it's a similar calling to music. I process and understand things from the point of view of a trained and skilled combatant, and it sets me apart from those who haven't followed the same path. For example, watching office workers scurry before an office bully is odd to me, not that I plan to fight the bully, but if it comes down to it, the option is there. Above all, training reminds me that life is awesome and its worth fighting for."

For good or ill, what was the biggest impact of your martial arts training on your life?

"I thought to myself, join the army, it's free. So, I figured while I'm here I'll lose a few pounds, and ya got what, a six-to-eight-week training program? A real tough one, which is perfect for me! I'm gonna walk out of here a lean mean fightin' machine."

John Candy (as Dewy Oxburger from the movie *Stripes*)

When martial arts schools market their service offerings, they often focus on positive benefits that can come with training like developing good character, improving self-confidence, learning focus, or developing discipline, as well as physiological changes that practitioners experience such as muscle gain, improved cardiovascular health, agility, flexibility, and calmness. They might also point out how their system staves off undesirable behaviors or threats, in other words how they can contribute to students' personal safety, help them face their fears, lose weight, or find coping mechanisms for stress relief. Military and law enforcement agencies speak to many of these same points along with appealing to those who have the desire to serve their country or community (e.g., servant leadership), and also add information about pay, benefits (such as healthcare and education), and enlistment bonuses.

These potential benefits are how the outside world tends to see the martial arts. Much in the same way that Dewy Oxburger, played by actor John Candy (1950–1994) in the 1981 movie *Stripes*, saw the United States Army. His character had no grounding in what the army experience would entail, and this naiveté was represented in his answer that we quoted at the beginning of this chapter. That movie was a comedy, hence his character's amusing response to the drill sergeant who asked who he was and why he wanted to join the military.

Oxburger demonstrated in one short paragraph a fundamental misunderstanding of the commitment he had made upon enlisting. His goal, "lose a few pounds," demonstrated misplaced priorities. Similarly, the items listed earlier, such as weight loss or muscle gain, feeling more empowered, or improving one's self-defenses skills are the common entry points to the world of martial arts, but that's not the whole story…

The entry points appear to distill into a theme around the discipline of mind and body, with highlights on particular items, actions, and emotions that resonate with potential students such as increased confidence. These are all desirable benefits, but many can as easily be achieved by joining a gym or hiring a personal trainer. They are not exclusive to martial arts. More often than not, a broader experience that morphs and changes throughout one's martial journey is part and parcel to the experience.

Clearly knowing and articulating one's objective before beginning training is valuable, but oftentimes the reason we think we're training turns out to not be the same reason why we continue our martial journey. For example, violence professionals know that the best defense is not being there when the other guy wants to fight, so awareness, avoidance, and de-escalation are far more important than fighting skills for folks who are primarily concerned with their personal safety. After all, fighting is what we do when we've screwed up our self-defense, so when prospective students come to the *dojo*, *dojang*, *kwoon*, or whatever the system calls their training hall solely to learn to how to punch or kick they tend to quickly adopt a broader perspective or walk away disappointed.

Further, any significant pauses in training can reset our expectations or intentions. And, of course, our goals tend to evolve over time…

For example, as children many folks may be drawn to the martial arts simply because they are fun. Building strength, balance, and coordination is definitely rewarding, yet the most beneficial aspect for adolescents is often the enhancement of self-esteem that comes from surmounting challenges and receiving promotions throughout the training. Parents tend to appreciate the discipline and conditioning aspects more than their children do, and many discover that their youngster pays better attention in school as a result of their training as well. Parents often join in order to spend more time with their offspring.

As teenagers, practitioners tend to become more concerned with the competitive aspects of the training, with trophies, medals, and win/loss records of paramount interest. Social interactions and the body-sculpting impact of physical conditioning become more important for older youths. The ability to defend ourselves from potential adversaries is often a draw, especially for those who live in high-crime areas or who have sought out training after surviving physical violence or sexual assault.

As martial artists reach their late 30s or early 40s, many practitioners begin looking for something deeper, such as *ki* (internal energy) training, character development, or spiritual enlightenment. For those in military or law enforcement, career aspirations may supersede the initial draw toward giving back to the community through service, either by coalescing in a desire to learn certain specialized skills, seek promotions, or improve oneself in a variety of other ways not originally anticipated in the early stages of their vocation. Many move away from operational responsibilities into mentoring, coaching, or leadership roles.

In breaking down the results of this "biggest impact" question, we find two broad categories: (1) seeking behaviors and (2) fleeing behaviors. Our respondents report that they found the biggest impact on the seeking side of the ledger, discovering that their training helped them find something in themselves that was positive which may not necessarily have extinguished a negative behavior or trait.

> Most martial artists report that their training revealed hidden character traits, helping them discover something positive in themselves they did not know existed prior to beginning their journey.

Here's a real-life example from one of our military respondents, Lieutenant Carissa Jenkins, who wrote that the biggest impact of martial arts training on her life was learning how to face fear:

"I will never forget the first time I got punched in the face. It's a scary thing to confront an opponent and know that, no matter how high you keep your hands, you're most likely going to get hit one way or another. There were many things I had to do during my military training that required me to overcome my natural instinct of flight, and fight instead. During combatives I had to literally fight. During my survival swim class, I had to jump off the top of a 10-meter diving board in full kit and swim the length of the pool under water through three hoops. Despite my inherent fear of heights, I was able to step off the diving board. My military training has taught me to fight my natural tendencies to shy away from challenges and prepared me to boldly face my fears."

If you stopped or took a long break from training, why?

"Rise and rise again until lambs become lions"
Robin Hood, English archer/folk hero

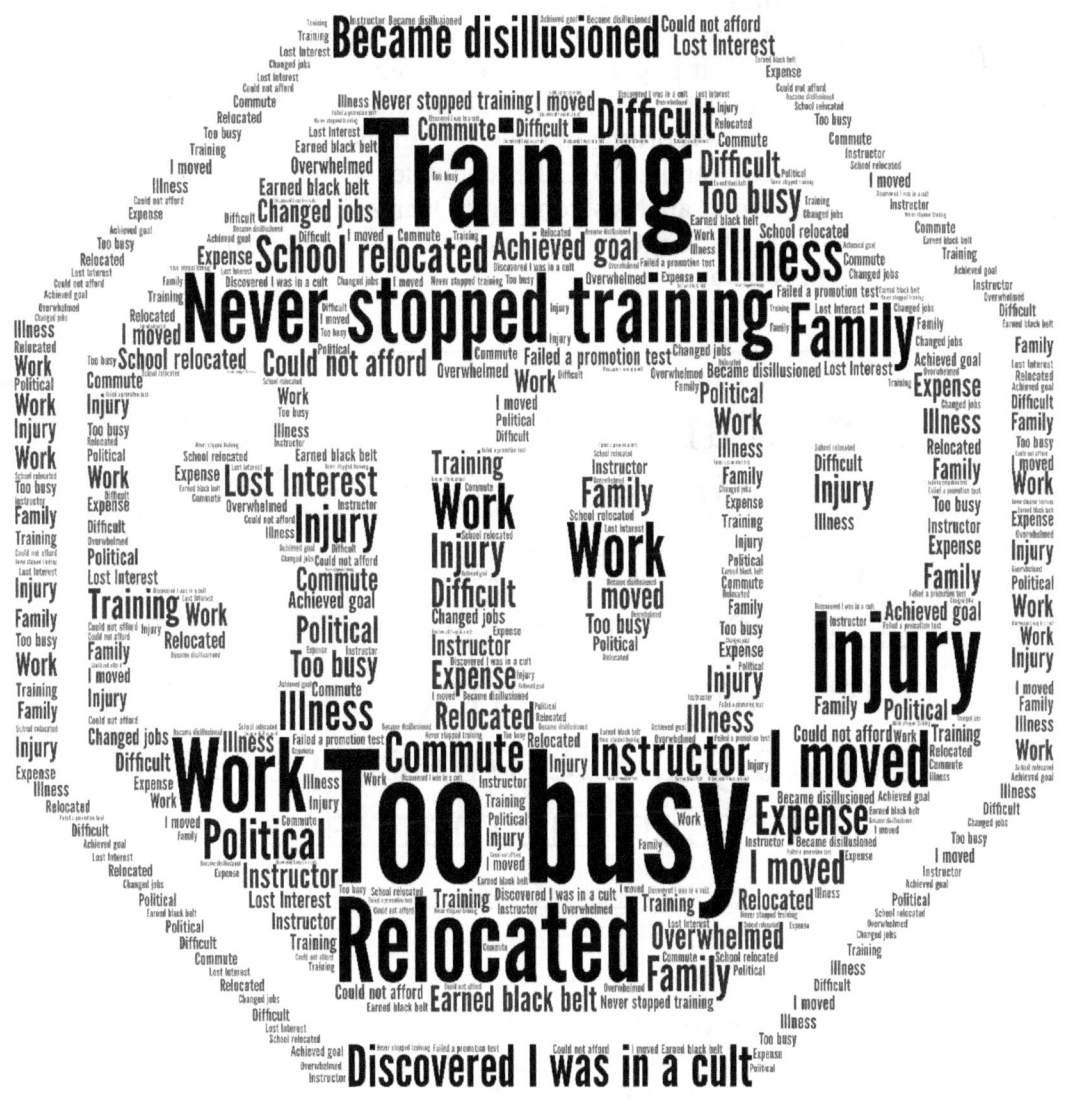

We purposely did not assign a number to quantify what a "long" break actually entails. To some six months may seem like a long interruption, yet to others it may not. For instance, some might not consider taking a leave for the birth of a child or aiding a family member in need as an extended break. Consequently, this question has a contextual quality to it, not a hard quantity. With this in mind, a significant number of respondents stated they never stopped training when responding to the question.

A common theme for those who did take a long break had to do with either the practitioner or their instructor relocating, which isn't horribly surprising considering the fact that about 10% of the adult population of the United States moves every year due to job transfers, changes in marital status, or to find a better neighborhood or purchase a home, among other reasons. According to the U.S. Census Bureau, 29,780,000 people in the U.S. moved between 2019 and 2020. Other countries where citizens move frequently, according to global economic analysis company Quartz, include New Zealand, South Korea, Australia, Fiji, Canada, Argentina, Panama, Chile, Switzerland, Senegal, France, Finland, Paraguay, and Norway.

> Martial arts training can last a lifetime. While extended breaks may become necessary due to changes in circumstances or priorities, these pauses do not inevitably undermine a person's success in the martial arts.

Other survey participants accomplished their goals or objectives, such as earning a black belt, picking up needed skills, or the like, and then decided to move on to other endeavors they considered more valuable. This may have meant reaching a plateau in their development, realizing that the art was no long as rewarding or fun as it once was, or simply discovering that life changes and other priorities had gotten in the way. In many instances these pauses eventually led to a change in system or style, but did not cause the practitioner to quit martial arts altogether.

Sadly, some respondents cited disillusionment due to politics, or listed bureaucracy as a secondary issue that made an already present or impending matter that ultimately made dropping out an easier choice. This could be expressed as, "I was not happy with the direction of the school and then a new opportunity opened up at work that interfered with my training schedule."

Suffice it to say that the human dynamic of policymaking, governance, and authority is ever-present, even in martial arts. A step further, a handful of respondents discovered they were in a cult and subsequently changed direction to escape that toxic environment. Charismatic, authoritarian leadership in martial arts cults takes ordinary politics to the next level and beyond... These organizations are dangerous—mentally, physically, and financially—with rigid doctrine, fervent pressure to conform, and social isolation that can make it very challenging to escape.

Outside the much-loathed politics, there are two main categories that drove survey respondents to take an extended break in their training or even quit altogether: (1) circumstances and (2) priorities. Circumstances are things that are generally out of the practitioner's ability to control, whereas priorities are their choice. Here are some common examples from our survey:

Circumstances:

- Injured
- Relocated/moved
- Instructor stopped teaching
- Instructor/school moved
- Instructor died

Priorities:

- Family responsibilities
- Work commitments
- School obligations
- Community duties

While martial arts can enhance practitioners lives in numerous ways, many of the reasons to quit reported by our survey respondents were admirable. For example, placing family needs over training goals is a worthy choice. Taking a long break until a serious injury has completely healed so as not to interfere with the recovery process, particularly while studying books or videos on one's art or performing visualization exercises to minimize knowledge loss, is prudent. And, bettering oneself with education that requires an extended break from training is also held in high regard.

Whatever their reasons for pausing, the majority of respondents when faced with any or many of the issues listed above eventually found a path to continue their training after their break. Taking a pause, even an extended one, does not mean that one's martial journey must come to an end. If you have the will to train, you will eventually find a way to make it happen.

Martial Artist Profile – Karl Duff, Ph.D., J.D.

Karl was born in an old mill town in rural North Georgia in the early 1950's. His father died when he was 4. His mother remarried when he was 6 and his stepfather did the heavy lifting of being the father-figure in the house. A veteran of serious WWII combat (Monte Casino and other battles), he unfortunately self-medicated his PTSD with alcohol. Karl didn't know he was very near-sighted, so sports activities dwindled to nothing as he got older because he couldn't see the ball. Near the end of undergrad school in 1975, he found a Burmese Bando *class taught by Dr. Geoff Willcher, who was working on his doctoral degree at Georgia State University. Karl started attending and trained 6 to 7 days a week for 3 years, and heavily thereafter. He was awarded his black belt by Bando Great-Grandmaster Dr. U Maung Gyi, PhD, BL, and remains one of Dr. Gyi's senior students today. Karl continued to train while earning his master's degrees and a doctoral and law degree. He was also exposed to* tai chi *and various Okinawan and Japanese styles. His law school exit thesis was published in 1984 as,* The Law and Martial Arts *by Ohara Publications. At one point he had a tempestuous presentation concerning the interstate shipment of martial arts weapons before the United States Senate Judiciary Committee, tangling with Senator Ted Kennedy (1932–2009). He has taught a small, private, non-profit class since 1982. Karl has practiced law since 1983 and specializes in corporate law, insurance, and risk management for large construction projects, focusing on the professional liability of design professionals.*

What energizes you outside of work?

"Working as an anti-terrorism officer in our State Guard, helping our unit backstop the Georgia National Guard in disasters (e.g., COVID, hurricanes, etc.). I would be remiss if I failed to list playing drums with some buddies of mine; we've played together on and off since 1967 and that's where the tinnitus comes from."

What is the best compliment you have ever received?

"Aside from praise from my wife, it has to be the time I had a client in the early days of practicing law tell me that after I had successfully argued his case (for free, 'pro bono') that he had never seen someone speak and move with such assurance."

Knowing what you know now, would you do it all over again?

"Yes, I have received much more from my training that it has required of me, and it has required a great deal. Friends, brotherhood, skill, patience, persistence, discipline, courage, determination, the ability to learn and to teach—and to learn and improve as a result of harsh criticism. Yep, a total plus."

> "I have received much more from my training that it has required of me, and it has required a great deal... Who knew that sweating and getting beaten up could be interesting and challenging and satisfying?"

Why did you start training?

"To be blunt: the purpose was to attack a 'beer gut' resulting from too many fraternity parties. My first quarter in the Georgia State University Bando class resulted in a weight loss of 30 pounds. I was hooked. Who knew that sweating and getting beaten up could be interesting and challenging and satisfying?"

When you were a kid, what did you want to be when you grew up?

"I wanted to be an astronaut. That meant being an Air Force pilot. When I learned that my lack of depth perception and terrible eyesight precluded that path, I was crushed."

For good or ill, what was the biggest impact of your martial arts training on your life?

"For good: the qualities of positive motivation, discipline and focus. I still use these qualities/skills to this day. Those qualities are why I was able to complete my doctoral exams and dissertation, pass my law school work, pass the notoriously tough Georgia Bar Exam (over 80% failure rate at that time), have a chapter of my dissertation published at UCLA, complete my 1st level black belt studies and earn my black belt while also authoring an exit thesis from law school which would later become a martial arts book published by Ohara. All this happened in roughly 30 months."

How have you made money from your martial arts?

"Wealth consists not in having great possessions, but in having few wants."
Epictetus, Greek Stoic philosopher

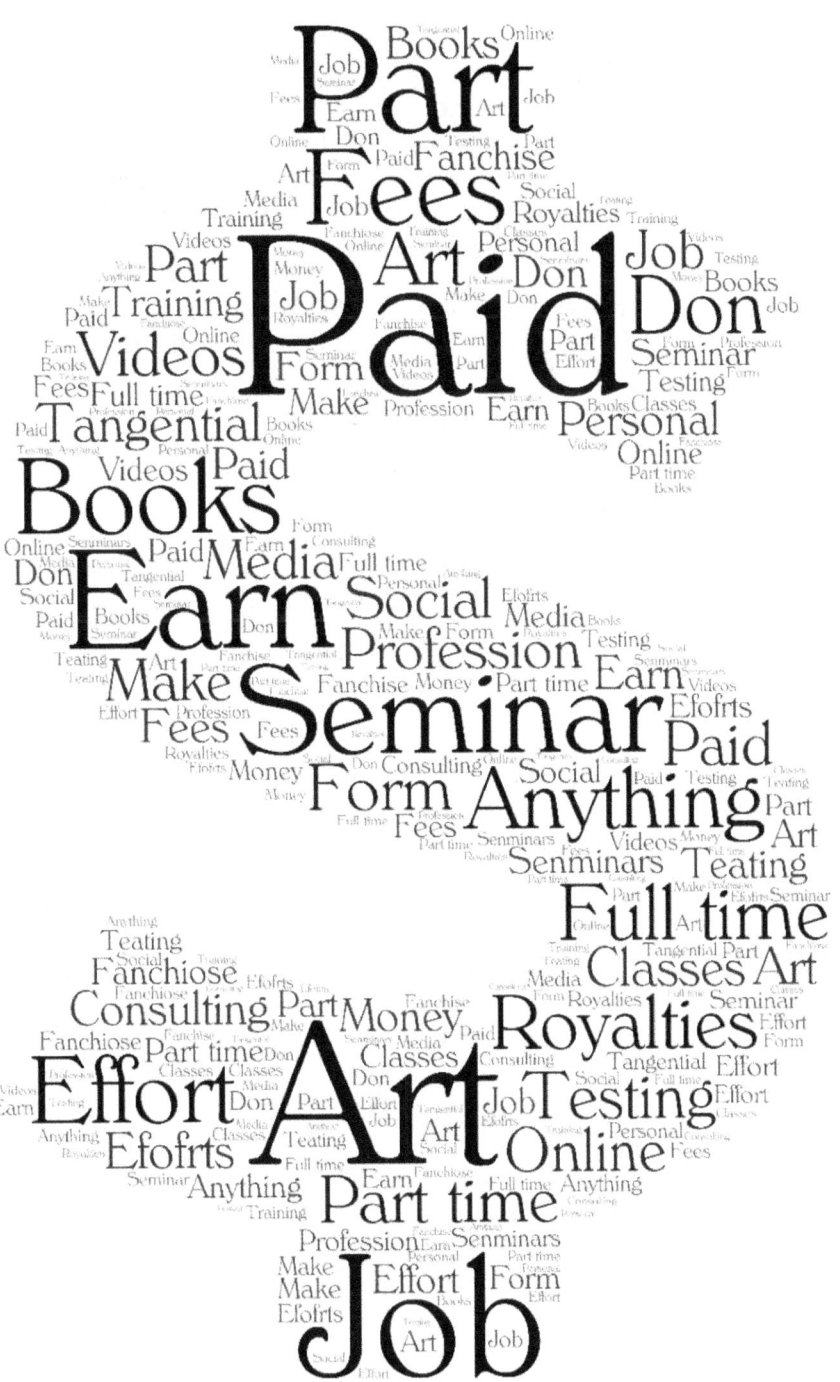

Despite martials arts being a multibillion-dollar industry, it is exceedingly difficult to earn a living solely from teaching martial arts. It's exhausting, physical work, with a median pay of just $37,388 a year in the United States according to Salary.com. That equates to about to about $17.97 an hour, which is barely above minimum wage in many cities, a mere 40% of what the average IT manager is paid in that country. This remuneration can vary depending on certifications, specialized skills, and experience, yet the 90th percentile martial artist is paid $65,855 a year, which is still 30% less than an average IT manager by way of comparison.

Those who coach popular fighting sports like MMA or those found in the Olympic games can do somewhat better financially than those who teach traditional martial arts, however it's still not a good field for folks whose top career priority is making money.

While salaries in this industry are low, it can be even tougher to work for oneself. Depending on one's location, a commercial school often needs upwards of 20 to 30 students per class and multiple classes a day to cover rent, utilities, business licenses, insurance, advertising, staff, and the like, and still leave enough money left over for the head instructor to bring something home to her family at the end of the day. Mainstream styles often have an easier time finding affordable liability insurance, yet anyone who includes ancient or modern weapons in their training may find insurance one of their highest costs of doing business.

Instructors who are able to franchise their business or own multiple schools have the best opportunity of making significant income from the art, but that is a long-term business plan that may take years to come to fruition. And, such actions may come with a bit of a stigma.

The term "McDojo" is a pejorative for a martial arts school that is overly focused on making money, sacrificing quality in the name of income. While there is nothing wrong with earning a living from martial arts instruction, common attributes of schools that have over-rotated on quantity versus quality include things like an overweight instructor who drives a luxury car, annual or long-term contracts, adolescent black belts, inability to fail a promotion test, little to no sparring or physical contact, limited if any focus on real world self-defense, and the guaranteed ability to earn a black belt in only one to two years.

This challenging environment is why most respondents reported that they made no income from their martial art. For those who actually earn remuneration of some type from their practice, the majority reported that it was as a part-time job, not an occupation. Only a handful of respondents stated that teaching martial arts was their full-time vocation.

Let's break these findings down: The survey did not allow for any comments on the selection of, "I don't earn anything from my art." While we do not know for certain why participants were unwilling or unable to generate income, common reasons we find in conversations with fellow practitioners include:

- I have not earned a high enough rank to be authorized teach
- I do not believe that martial arts should be a money-making proposition
- Turning it into a job would ruin the martial arts for me
- Martial arts are a hobby not a job
- Another career provides enough for me and/or my family
- Teaching seems like a daunting proposition

> **Despite working in a multibillion-dollar industry, the average martial arts instructor earns $37,388 a year in the United States, barely over minimum wage in many cities.**

Of those who do make money from their martial art, revenue comes from two subsets, (1) internal and (2) external. Internal income is defined as revenue generated by the martial arts school itself, whereas external income is everything derived from sources outside the straining hall. Here are a few examples:

Internal income:

- Membership dues (similar to a health club)
- Testing fees (tied with rank advancements or certifications)
- Uniform sales (including patches, belts, jackets, shirts, etc.)
- Additional training material sales (such as pads, gloves, targets, and weapons)
- Franchise fees (paid by other schools in one's system)
- Sub-leasing the facility, or portions thereof, to others when not in use

External income:

- Paid consulting
- Teaching seminars and conferences
- Royalties from print books, e-books, and audiobooks
- Royalties from videos
- Royalties from online courses
- Paid social media (such as a YouTube channel)
- Tangential effort (such as personal training, modeling, acting, choreography, or performing movie stunts)

Because it is so hard to make a living teaching martial arts, practitioners should cherish talented instructors when they find them. These folks typically dedicate themselves to their art, sacrificing a higher standard of living in other professions in favor of doing something they love and find inherently rewarding. This choice is not necessarily fundamentally altruistic, but rather a refreshing perspective that money isn't everything or even the primary thing of importance in a person's life.

There is both honor and value in this devotion to the martial arts, if not renumeration. Given the myriad of physical, mental, and emotional benefits of martial arts study and practice, we believe that it is safe to say that these individuals make a positive impact on their communities, helping in a small way to make the world itself a better place.

Which one of your senses are you most willing to sacrifice?

"All we have to believe is our senses: the tools we use to perceive the world, our sight, our touch, our memory. If they lie to us, then nothing can be trusted."

Neil Gaiman, English author

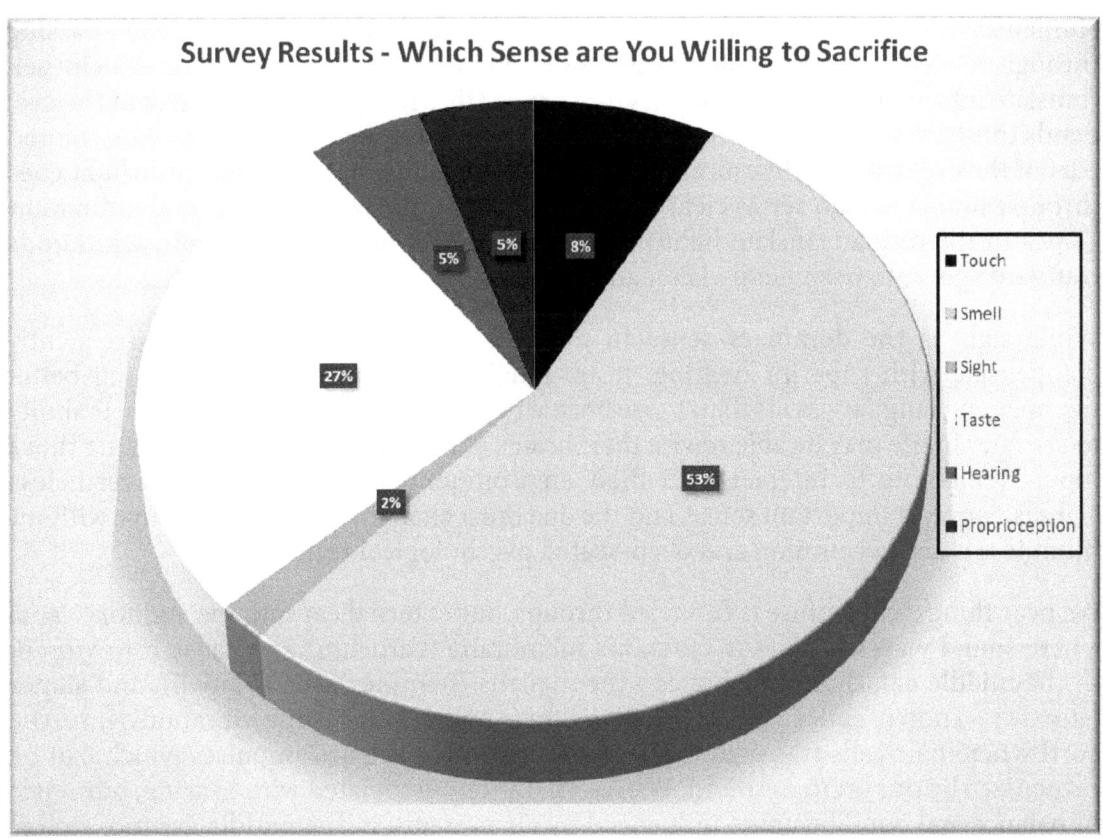

The most dominant sense to human beings is (1) vision, followed in order of prominence by (2) hearing, (3) smell, (4) taste, (5) touch, and (6) proprioception. This is logical from a survival of the species perspective; after all vision and hearing are the senses that best allow us to recognize potential threats, identifying friends or foes at a distance. Touch and taste, on the other hand, are about close contact. Depending on the context, this contact could be life-giving, life-threatening, or even completely innocuous, yet if we have not identified what's coming before it is up close and personal it can be difficult to react appropriately.

The sense of smell, although important, lies in between the others, as our olfactory sense can be used to identify a wildfire in the distance or a lingering scent of cologne in the same room. Proprioception, our sense of our bodies in space, helps us respond in a coherent and graceful manner to whatever our other five senses have detected, but it is more internal-facing than the others and not even considered a sense by some (hence the common term "five senses" or "five senses plus one").

Human sight is complex, with light reflecting off of objects in our field of vision passing through the lens of our eye and landing on optic nerve cells in the retina which then translate information into our brain. Our cornea (the transparent outer layer of the eye) bends this light as it travels through the pupil onto the retina, with our iris (the colored part of the eye) working like a camera lens to control how much or how little light goes through so that we can see as clearly as possible in both dazzling and dim illumination. Cones in the retina translate light into colors, central vision, and details, while rods translate light into peripheral vision and motion.

While sight is the dominant sense in most humans, people born blind frequently compensate with superior hearing, taste, touch, and smell, often developing better memory and language skills than those born with sight. Even those who lose their ability to see later in life may be able rewire their brains similarly with practice, utilizing those inputs remaining to interact with their environment more effectively. Nevertheless, sight is our most important sense, and the one most challenging for folks to live without. Blindness is also a common and deep-seated psychological fear.

We hear things when noise is funneled through our external ear into the auditory canal where sound waves reach our tympanic membrane (eardrum) and cause it to vibrate. In the middle ear, three tiny bones—the malleus (hammer), incus (anvil), and stapes (stirrup)—known collectively as the auditory ossicles, transmit vibrations into the corti where hair cells translate these vibrations into electrical impulses which can be recognized by our brain as sound. While not directly associated with hearing, our sense of balance and equilibrium is influenced by air pressure in the middle ear too, so this system is important for a variety of purposes.

Scientists believe that touch is the first sense that humans develop in the womb, with sensations communicated to the brain through specialized neurons in the skin. These receptors allow us to identify pressure, temperature, vibration, texture, and various other sensations. Our sense of touch conveys both intimacy and intimidation, pleasure and pain, and is an important element of our ability to manipulate objects, use tools, and defend ourselves effectively. People born with congenital insensitivity, the inability to perceive sensations via touch, or who experience diminished sensitivity as they age often suffer burns, bruises, broken bones, and other serious health issues as a result of this loss.

Our sense of smell is generated by sensitive nerve endings in the olfactory cleft inside our nasal cavities that transmit aromas to the brain. Humans have 400 smelling receptors, far less than other animals, but are able to detect over a trillion scents nonetheless. Smell is also an important component of taste (a process called olfactory referral) which is why folks with allergies or nasal congestion often have trouble tasting food properly. Due to psychological links between olfaction, memory, and emotion people who experience anosmia, the complete loss of one's sense of smell, often suffer impaired memory and degraded quality of life. They are unable to detect the warning signs of spoiled foods, gas leaks, or other hazards too. Distorted or decreased olfactory sense is also symptomatic of illness, aging, or depression.

> **Martial artists' perception of their senses is consistent with the general population. Most people when choosing to give up a sense, select smell or taste before touch, hearing, proprioception, or sight.**

Our sense of taste can be broken down into the perceptions of salty, sweet, sour, savory, and bitter. Spiciness is actually not a taste, but rather a pain signal. Scientists believe that our sense of taste aided in human evolution by warning our ancestors of poisonous or rotten foods which tasted bitter or sour. Salty or sweet, on the other hand, often meant the food was rich in nutrients, which is why we are drawn to these flavors today. Sinusitis, nasal polyps, smoking, traumatic brain injuries, certain medications including beta blockers and angiotensin-converting enzyme (ACE) inhibitors, Alzheimer's, and Parkinson's disease can contribute to loss of taste which often leads to decreased appetite and poor nutrition.

Proprioception (or kinesthesia) is how our brain understands where our body is in space, including the sense of movement and position of our limbs and muscles. People with poor proprioception are often clumsy and uncoordinated, which is obviously a bad thing when it comes to combat or self-defense. This includes balances issues, inability to climb stairs or navigate uneven surfaces, poor postural control, and the inability to control one's own strength. Impairment can stem from drugs, alcohol, and certain medical conditions such as peripheral neuropathy, amyotrophic lateral sclerosis (ALS), multiple sclerosis

(MS), strokes, Parkinson's, or Huntington's disease, with symptoms including the inability to control limb movements, touch your nose with your eyes closed (which is why this is often used as a sobriety test), walk without looking at your feet, or move freely without consciously thinking about your environment.

It is not surprising that our survey responses we very much in line with this hierarchy of the senses, with only two percent of respondents willing to sacrifice their vision compared to over half who believed they could live without their sense of smell. Martial artists would rather see an attacker than smell their assailant, which not only aligns with the evolutionary importance of the human senses but also with the proximity of threats as well. In other words, the dominant senses for the human species remain consistent in the martial artist population. So, heroic fairytales of blind monks/swordsmen aside, we may safely conclude that when it comes to our six senses a human is a human is a human, regardless of martial arts experience or training.

Martial Artist Profile – Thomas Tobin

Based in Portland, Oregon, Thomas Tobin holds advanced black belts in two separate martial arts, Chinese Kempo *and* Danzan Ryu Jujitsu, *and has spent over two decades teaching and training martial arts and self-defense. He has guided multiple students through the rank of black belt and is a volunteer Marketing and Special Events officer in the American Judo & Jujitsu Federation. He also runs a martial arts and self-defense education and consulting business and has provided guidance to many school owners in the martial arts community. He is currently developing a start-up company to make personal safety education more accessible and provide skilled individuals with a platform to share their knowledge and experience with the public. When not teaching or training, he enjoys exploring the Pacific Northwest with his dog Cricket, reading, and taking on excessive amounts of new hobbies. His website is www.sandalwoodmountain.com.*

What's the worst martial arts-related mistake you have ever made?

"When I first started training, I discovered that I had a natural talent for it. Learning the moves and remembering the *kata* came fairly easy and I had enough of a physical aptitude that the learning curve was fairly shallow. At least in the beginning. As a result, my study habits developed poorly and formed inaccurate ideas about how hard I needed to work to progress. I am still struggling with some of the after effects. I regret the loss of progress from the early years and wonder where my skill set would be now if I had taken things more seriously in the beginning. I also look back to older revisions of forms and techniques and have difficulty remembering past lessons because I wasn't as diligent as I should have been in my note taking. Even after working to improve, I still think about the lost time."

What is the best compliment you have ever received?

"After a particularly grueling group black belt test I was standing with the other instructors congratulating the candidates as they were called up. As one of my students came up to receive his promotion one of our high-level instructors next to me complimented him on his performance. He shook my students had and told him, 'You did a really excellent job, very impressive.' My student smiled and pointed to me and replying, 'That's because he is my teacher.'"

If you could go back in time, what advice would you give to your teenage self?

"You don't have to do it all on your own. Take advantage of the help that is available, be it from friends, coworkers, school etc. There no shame in reaching out for assistance or admitting that you are in over your head. The people that are offering their hands are doing it because they want to. Accepting help is gifting others the opportunity to give it, don't deny them that."

> "There no shame in reaching out for assistance or admitting that you are in over your head... Accepting help is gifting others the opportunity to give it, don't deny them that."

What single event of the past changed the world for the worst?

"Social media is designed to be addictive and behavior altering. It has been directly linked to a rise in depression and anxiety disorders as well as other negative mental health indicators. Technology that was originally intended to make us more connected has instead contributed to a decline of interpersonal skills and left us feeling more isolated."

When you were a kid, what did you want to be when you grew up?

"My mother says I always wanted to be Superman. Unfortunately, I can only leap medium-sized buildings so that was out. In my preteen/teen years I wanted to teach martial arts which I did for quite a long time and still do on a smaller scale. Being able to be a resource for my friends and family and teaching and empowering my students does occasionally make me feel like a super hero."

What is the best single piece of advice you were ever given?

"'Root before you grow.' – Suzanne Duran. Having an established support system makes you capable of branching out and taking risks and if they don't pan out you have something to lean against while you get your bearing. Establishing that support structure is the first step in any process. Make sure that you have something solid before trying to expand beyond your base."

Knowing what you know now, would you do it all over again?

"At the age of six I wanted to be a cook. At seven I wanted to be Napoleon. And my ambition has been growing steadily ever since."

Salvador Dali, Spanish artist

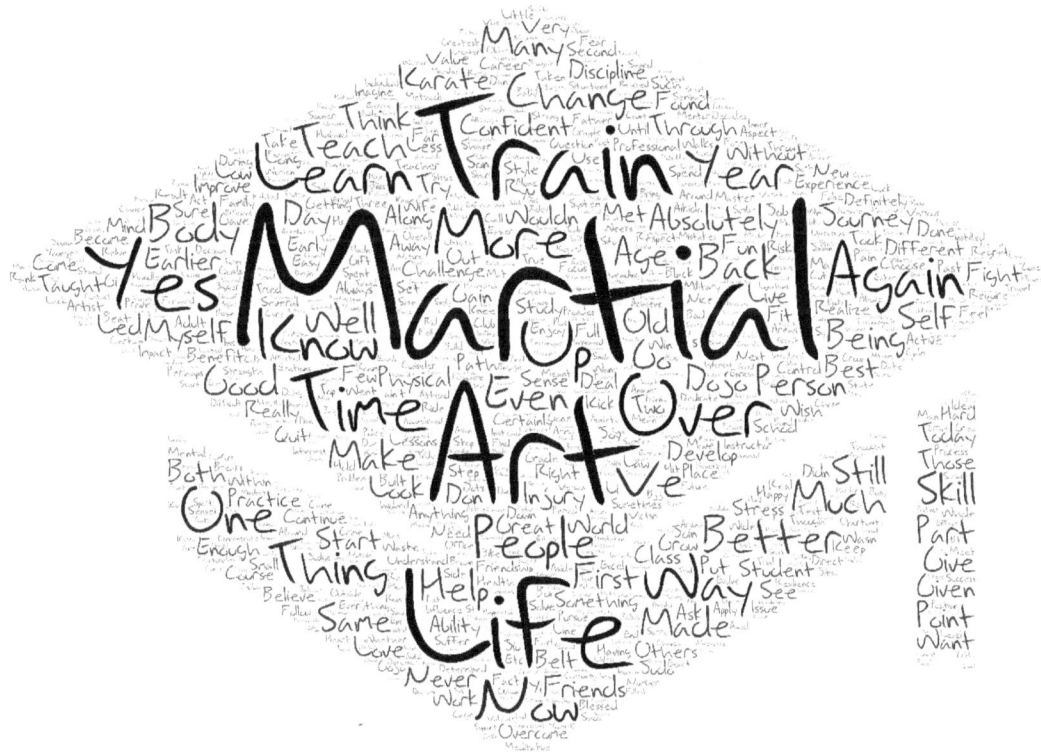

The old saying, "hindsight is 20/20," implies that history is easier to assess than the future. In other words, after we know how our choices turned out we are able to determine whether or not we chose wisely in the past. Nevertheless, it is not uncommon for people to say, "I wouldn't change a thing," even if an independent observer would objectively identify many reasons why we should have. This dichotomy creates an interesting and important dynamic, which is why we asked this question on our survey...

Let's begin analyzing these findings by pointing out that while teaching young children can be a lot like filling empty vessels with facts and ideas, teaching experienced teenagers or adults is far more complex. Concepts can no longer simply be poured in; they must be fitted into and meshed together with what is already there. This means that, right or wrong, our preconceived expectations and biases impact how we view and understand the world.

Psychologists call this condition "confirmation bias," the human tendency to process information by looking for or interpreting data that is consistent with our preexisting beliefs while simultaneously ignoring any inconsistent evidence. We not only have this inherent predisposition, but are also social animals, and as such are instinctively reliant on our tribe for safety, support, and security. This means that once we've bonded with a group it can become very difficult to leave or even express a divergent opinion from the consensus for fear of being cast out of the assembly. Social media only exacerbates this dynamic.

> Knowing what they know now, 94.4% of martial artists surveyed report that they would travel their same path again.

In other words, the need to validate choice is human nature. It is simultaneously human nature to want more of a good thing. With few exceptions, martial arts have been a very good thing in the survey respondents' lives. Consequently, it is unsurprising that most participants responded to this question with a resounding "yes." Several related that their study of martial arts had literally saved their lives, while others gained immeasurable value and personal growth from their training.

Those few respondents who said "no," or provided caveats to an otherwise positive response, related in large part that they would have been more conscientious about injury prevention, taken things a little slower, strived for more balance, or otherwise ensured that all their parts and pieces still worked properly in their old age. There is definitely wisdom in that perspective. For example, Todd Durgan related:

"I would do it again, but I would do things differently for sure. Some of the people along my journey had damaging training methods and practices. While it is impossible to acquire the same attributes, physical or mental, with alternative training methods, I would certainly have looked to try some things that are a little gentler on the body. Getting old is hard enough without lifelong injuries to expedite the crippling and aging process. Train smart, and train hard just don't be hard on your body, those injuries will catch up to you eventually. That being said, my life has been enriched immeasurably through the arts and the study thereof. I cannot imagine not having the very precious relationships and people in my life, many of whom are my dearest friends and especially my wife who joins me on the mat to enrich her and others lives through karate."

Do you recommend your system/style to your friends or family?

"The geographical pilgrimage is the symbolic acting out of an inner journey. The inner journey is the interpolation of the meanings and signs of the outer pilgrimage. One can have one without the other. It is best to have both."

Thomas Merton, American Trappist monk and theologian

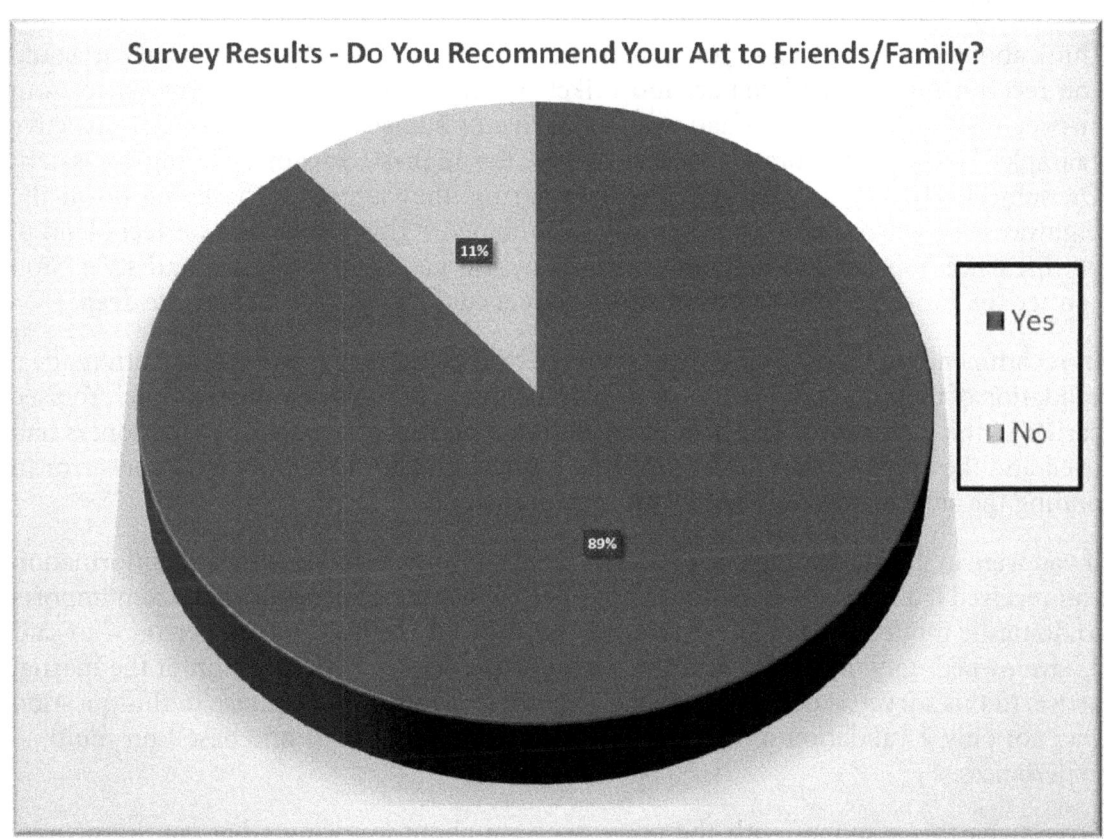

We asked this question in the binary positive, so avoidance is not an aspect of any survey participant's response nor is an explanation as to why or why not they answered the way that they did. In other words, if somebody were to similarly ask you about the best way to get from point A to point B under these ground rules, your answer could only be "take path A." The hazards of path B, such as that tribe of cannibalistic, machinegun-toting trolls who've developed a taste for human flesh living under the bridge along that route, could not addressed.

Regardless of how we set it up, there is an undertone to this yes/no question. The obvious choice is, "Yes!" After all, who wouldn't want to recommend something they have personally found valuable? One way to think about this is that by recommending something you do, own, or spend a lot of time with you find validation in your choice. We've already discussed confirmation bias in the previous chapter, but let's take a different spin on things here…

Think about a major purchase you have made recently. If a friend asked, "What car would you recommend for me?" you are most likely going to default to your experience. Your answer may include a combination of objective or subjective responses. An objective example, "I chose this brand because it had the highest consumer rating for safety." Or, subjectively, "These cars look simply amazing, they appear to be flying down the highway even when they're standing still." Combined, "This vehicle is a perfect blend of performance, top-tier fuel economy with its hybrid gas-electric engine, and style." You can see the various permutations of such answers could be as wide as they are deep.

In recommending their system or style to others, these survey respondents both made a validation of their choice as well as declared, "Let me save you some wasted time." You see, earlier in the survey we asked how many different martial arts systems practitioners had tried and the average came back 5.79. That number equates to a lot of trial-and-error in finding the art that best resonated with each individual.

If you were in the market for a new car, you would almost certainly weigh the information you received from somebody who said, "I have owned six different brands, from imports to domestic models, and I believe that this car is by far the best" over a person who said, "I have owned only this brand and I'm sticking by it for life." The position of the martial artists in this survey is that of the former. In other words, their response to this question was not only a validation of their choice, but also a thoughtful one based on multiple experiences.

Overlaying this response with the prior question about knowing what you know now, would you do it all over again, and it is reasonable to assume that if respondents could have explained their answer they would have. And, they would have done so with the intention of saving aspiring practitioners time, heartache, and money.

Clearly, respondents stood ready and able to assist budding martial artists begin their journey as effectively as possible. But, what about the other 11 percent? Why wouldn't they recommend to someone they care about the same path that they have worked so hard to find and cultivate? That's a good question, one we pondered before cheating a bit and talking one of the respondents who answered this way, asking the question, "Why not?" His conclusion can be condensed to one phrase, "Everybody has to find their own way." It was not a negation of the martial arts or the training.

Our conclusion… in the simplest of terms, is that 89% of the respondents are concrete in their response with an actionable recommendation while the other 11% are supportive but ambiguous in direct recommendation. This means that the best way to begin one's martial arts journey, or to change course if you find yourself on the wrong path, is to talk to an experienced practitioner and get their recommendations.

> Survey respondents overwhelmingly recommended their art to others, citing experience with multiple systems or styles to add conviction to their answers.

Clearly a veteran martial artist's advice is your best bet to begin or accelerate your journey, but what if you don't know what to ask or who to talk to? Well, as American poet Henry David Thoreau (1817–1862) once wrote, "People seldom hit what they do not aim at." This means that you need to start by knowing your objective…

What do you want to learn? No matter how good of a system or instructor you find, you will only find value if the curriculum addresses your goals. Are you looking for a career in law enforcement or military service, competency in civilian self-defense, or ability to participate in sporting competition? Do you seek physical conditioning, mental discipline, or character development? Are you interested in ancient weapons forms or modern combatives? Are many of the above important to you or are you after something completely different?

In our experience, finding the right teacher or agency is more important than choosing the perfect martial art to study. Since there are only a limited number of vital areas on the body that can be manipulated, struck, or otherwise damaged by a martial practitioner, and there are only a limited number of ways that each joint in the body can move, martial systems tend to share common components. Emphasis and strategies will differ, of course, but techniques such as empty-hand punching, kicking, grappling, or throwing overlap multiple systems and styles.

But, skill in martial arts does not always equate to competency in teaching. Gifted athletes often have trouble articulating what comes naturally. Consequently, so long as a system you select matches your goals and objectives, choose the best instructor you can find. The following advice on how to find a great martial arts instructor applies more to traditional martial arts, fighting sports, and RBSD than to any law enforcement agency or military branch as you'll rarely get to choose your teachers in such institutions:

Once you have put some thought into it and know what you are looking for, google a list of local schools, see if what you find on their website resonates with your goals, and make appointments to visit the ones that appear to be a good match. Most instructors will let you observe a class so long as you stay out of the way, and many offer a free introductory session, so take advantage of those opportunities when presented and note what you observe.

Are students standing around looking confused or does everyone appear to be actively engaged in the learning process? Are they talking or working? Do students and teachers interact respectfully? Are students corrected in positive ways when they make mistakes? Is there an appropriate level of supervision? Is there adequate attention to safety?

You should be able to briefly interview the instructor while you're there and get an idea of that person's vision, methods, and practices. There is no perfect instructor, we all have strengths and weaknesses, but in virtually every locale you will discover that some teachers are clearly superior to others. You will likely discover that some resonate better than others when it comes to your learning style too.

To find the best teacher available, look for the following traits:

- A passion for teaching
- A sense of direction and purpose for the school or system
- A high degree of perception regarding the needs and interests of students
- A deep, well-rounded knowledge of martial arts
- A high enough skill level in their art to be able to meet your development needs
- A broad understanding of the legal, moral, and ethical implications of conflict and fighting
- A demonstrated ability to communicate effectively
- An emphasis on safety
- A high degree of integrity and personal honor

To a certain degree you get what you are paying for, but a higher price does not always indicate better quality of instruction. Be wary of long-term contracts. In fact, if someone offers you a "special" one-time only deal (typically for several thousand dollars) that covers all your training and equipment through black belt or equivalent thereof, you are probably in the wrong place. McDojo aren't just a meme, they're a genuine phenomenon.

When it comes to paying for instruction, month-to-month arrangements are best. In addition to your dues, you may expect to pay a moderate initiation fee when you first begin and will likely have to purchase a uniform and/or protective equipment. Where rank systems are followed, most schools require a nominal charge that covers the cost of each new belt, sash, badge, or certificate for each rank you achieve, with higher fees for black belt (or equivalent) tests. However, most schools only charge the testing fee once regardless of whether or not you pass a promotion test on the first try.

Most students discover that their martial arts experience transforms their lives in ways they never expected. Finding the right instructor, someone who can help you fulfill your goals, is the first and most important step in that journey.

Martial Artist Profile – Wendell A. Goins, MD, FACS

Wendell Goins is both a Medical Doctor and a Fellow of the American College of Surgeons. His martial arts journey began in 1976 while attending Howard University College of Medicine in Washington D.C. While there, he came to the conclusion that if he was to have a successful and fulfilling life, a "warrior lifestyle" would be necessary. He was awarded his first black belt in 1983 in tang soo do *by Grandmaster Ki Whang Kim and remained at Kim Studio until 1993. He began learning CMC-Yang style* tai chi chuan *in 1992. After moving to South Carolina in 1996, he began training with Universal (White Brothers) Karate and received his black belt there in 1998. The discipline of martial arts has helped him stay on the path of warriorship and has optimized his surgical career (equanimity under duress), interpersonal relations (humble team player and leader, family and friends), and his physical health. He still remains very active in martial arts, currently associated with Universal Karate-Do in Lancaster, South Carolina where they practice a combination of* shotokan *karate and Okinawan* kempo *including* kobudo *(Odo Sensei lineage).*

When you were a kid, what did you want to be when you grew up?

"At age 10, I wanted to be either a medical doctor, astronaut, or park ranger. Becoming an astronaut got ruled out pretty fast since I had bad ears, although I considered it again in the 80s as a Mission Specialist for the Space Shuttle. I also reasoned that I could enjoy the great outdoors without being a ranger. Since I had a deep interest in the human condition, I decided on a career in the medical field. While in college at Georgetown University I became employed at the National Institute of Health. I studied hard and was admitted into Howard University Medical School after 3 years. I worked with the U.S. Public Health Service for 2 years before starting my surgical training. I became a Trauma-Critical Care-General-Cancer Surgeon to save lives. I am fortunate and blessed to have been able to live out my aspirations."

What is the best single piece of advice you were ever given?

"My earliest mentor was my Scoutmaster, Colonel James C. Queen who was a retired U.S. Army Green Beret Paratrooper. He taught me how to become comfortable and survive in the great outdoors. I have backpacked in many remote places and continue to do so. During one of our long 50-mile weekend hikes, he would advise us to keep 'putting one foot in front of the other' and that persistence and perseverance would get us to our goal despite momentary discomfort. I have followed this advice my whole life."

What is the best compliment you have ever received?

"There is no greater compliment that a surgeon can receive, than that from another surgeon who wants you to perform a major life-saving operation on either them or their immediate family. This is quite humbling because there are no guarantees in life. I have had many such opportunities since my surgical residency and up to the present. My medical-surgical career and martial arts training are intertwined and have both provided me with a sense of quiet self-confidence, gratefulness, and humbleness. This has resulted in a profound fearless compassion for my fellow man and a deep sense of brotherhood among family, friends, and acquaintances."

> "There is no greater compliment that a surgeon can receive, than that from another surgeon who wants you to perform a major life-saving operation on either them or their immediate family."

What's the worst martial arts-related mistake you have ever made?

"Not sure if I have ever had a 'worst' mistake, though I am sure that I have made mistakes along this martial arts journey. However, I did have a misunderstanding when thinking that internal-soft martial arts styles (e.g., *tai chi chuan*) were markedly different from the external-harder styles (e.g., karate, taekwondo). On the surface, the internal and the external styles do appear very different, however the martial applications when in a 'real fight for your life' are very similar. I have concluded that the differences between the internal and external arts have to do with orientation, attitude, and training methods. Some styles will have a more rapid learning curve for practical application, but at the end, they all use the same striking, kicking, joint manipulation, and take-downs or throws to get the job done."

What single event of the past changed the world for the worst?

"If you consider the total history of mankind and the many atrocities that have occurred over the eons, it is hard to single out one event as changing the world for the worst. If this question was brought before the United Nations, undoubtedly you will get a multitude of answers. We all look at things from our own perspective, based on what we learned from our parents and social-cultural groups and from our individual life experiences. Plus, a truly negative event can also have positive outcome, such as, most would agree, that the events of WWII (Hitler/Holocaust/Japan) were horrible, however the world changed for the better after this (standard of living) and resulted in man reaching the moon 20 years later. If I had to pick one event that happened during my lifetime, it would have to be the events of 9/11."

Knowing what you know now, would you do it all over again?

"Absolutely, yes I would do it again. Knowing what I know now, if I had a second chance, I would find a way to start while in high school. I would also include more grappling, judo, or *aikido* early on while still flexible and nimble. I started my 3 daughters (ages 4 to 10) early. Of course, there have been challenges along the way. During the course of 40 years in martial arts, I was diagnosed with arthritis and with a cardiac condition. I was also injured several times: orbit and toes fractured, ruptured a lumbar disc while performing a jump spinning hook kick, and rib fracture from a side kick. I have had two back operations and a knee replacement. I determined early in my 20s that for me to have a successful fulfilling life, I would have to adopt a 'warrior lifestyle' and martial arts have facilitated that."

Survey demographics – Gender mix

"I originally came to this country (China) to transmit the Dharma and save deluded beings. When the single flower opens into five petals, then the fruit will ripen naturally of itself."

Bodhidharma, Buddhist monk

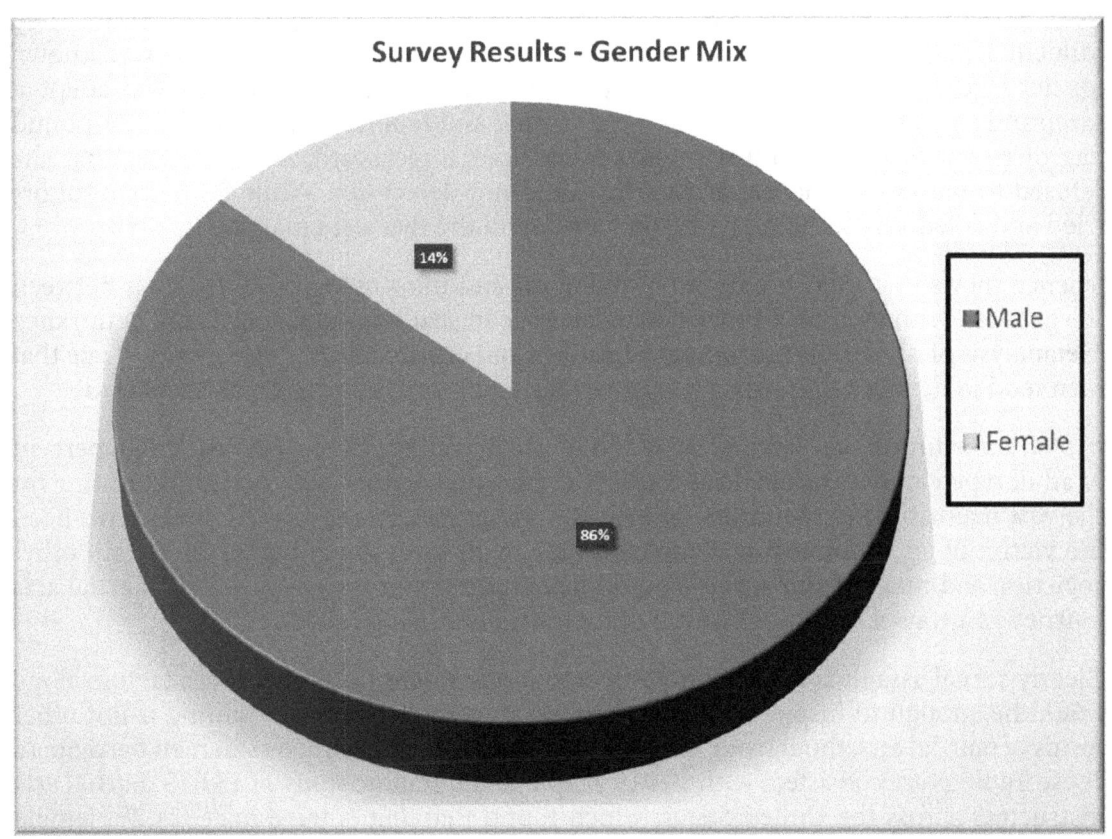

Historically women have played important roles in the development, promotion, and proliferation of martial arts. For example, Ng Mui (or Ng Mei), a Chinese *shaolin* abbess, created *wing chun* kung fu in the 1700s in order to enable smaller, weaker people such as herself to quickly defeat bigger, stronger adversaries. Her name, which translates as "five plum," is a poetic allusion to the five-petal blossom about which the legendary Bodhidharma (who founded the *shaolin* temple) prophesized in the quote above, foretelling five generations of master martial artists who would follow him.

Starting in southern China, *wing chun* soon became famous for its effectiveness, spreading throughout Asia and eventually to much of the rest of the world. It is the system that Bruce Lee practiced prior to inventing his own style.

While women tend to be smaller and weaker on average than men, effective martial arts training can more than make up for these differences. For example, Sokon "Bushi" Matsumura, the founder of *Shuri-te* karate, was one of Okinawa's most famous and influential martial arts masters. He fell in love with Yonamine Chiru, who was well known for her love of fighting. Nicknamed *no bushi tsuru*, or "crane warrior," she was adept at *sumo* and *tegumi* wrestling as well as weightlifting and reportedly picked up a 130-pound bag of rice with one hand just to sweep the floor underneath. Legend states that she refused to marry any martial artist who could not defeat her. While numerous suitors tried and failed, Matsumura proved her equal, and the two were married in 1818.

Science shows that there are both physiological and morphological differences between the genders, with men on average having an edge in size, strength, speed, and endurance. Metanalysis of numerous psychological studies and crime statistics also demonstrate that men tend to be more aggressive, less agreeable, and more prone to break the law too.

In fact, according to the National Sexual Violence Resource Center (NSVRC), 90% percent of adult rape victims are female as are 82% of juvenile victims, with males accounting for the vast majority of perpetrators. Nearly 20% of women in the United States have been the victim of an attempted or completed rape, with rates much higher in certain other societies, and many of our survey respondents related that they began their martial arts journey as a way of regaining control of their life after being raped.

Clearly sexual assault is not the only threat, but one might think that these factors alone would be enough to inspire women to at least pursue self-defense training if not other forms of martial arts, though our survey found that far fewer women than men participate. These findings are consistent with a 2019 Zippia demographic study of 13,025 martial arts instructors across the United States, which found that 74.6% were male, 21.2% female, and 4.2% unknown. Although there is no information available, one would presume that these ratios are generally consistent with student demographics as well.

According to the World Bank, women made up 49.6% of the world's population in 2020, whereas according to the United States Census Bureau women accounted for 50.8% of the population of the country in 2019. Clearly, this data demonstrates a disproportionate underrepresentation of women in martial arts where three of every four of participants are male.

Interestingly, women don't just under-participate in martial arts, they watch far fewer fighting sports too. Despite the success of superstars like Amanda Nunes, Cat Zingano, Cristiane Justino (a.k.a. Cris Cyborg), Gina Carano, Holly Holm, Miesha Tate, Paige VanZant, Ronda Rousey, Satoko Shinashi, and Zhang Weili, women's boxing, wrestling, and MMA has 96% less audience worldwide than equivalent men's sports.

Clearly women can benefit from martial arts, arguably more so than men, so how can we change this dynamic?

> While women make up 49.6% of the world's population they are underrepresented at all levels in martial arts, including instruction, participation, and viewership.

As a community we may be able to draw more women into to the martial arts by emphasizing positive aspects such as fitness, discipline, self-confidence, and spiritual development. While violence prevention is a laudable goal, many women are intimidated by the idea of grappling or sparring with strangers, especially strange men, which can be a big hurdle to overcome in an industry dominated by male instructors, even when women-only self-defense classes are offered.

It is important to teach to the strengths and weaknesses of individual students, as instructors tend to over-rotate on imparting what they have found effective personally, which is great for those with the same physical attributes and somatotype, but not so good for practitioners of either gender who have a different body type. Finally, we must assure a code of conduct that precludes any form of harassment or sexualization in the training hall so that everyone can feel confident that they will be practicing in both physical and psychological safety.

The female martial artists who participated in our survey all reported finding value in their training. When asked if knowing what they know now would they do it over again, the answer was resoundingly affirmative. We hope that the examples set by these role models, some of whom we have highlighted throughout the book, will help encourage others of their gender to become involved in martial arts as well.

Martial Artist Profile – Steven Almendarez

Born and raised in Brooklyn, New York, Steven started practicing martial arts at the age of 10 to escape the streets and survive them. He joined the United States Marine Corps at the age of 17 and also served in the U.S. Army National Guard, leaving both branches as a Sergeant. Afterward, he worked 5 years on the U.S. Capitol Police, serving on the Hazardous Materials Response Team and Dignitary Protection. He then transferred to a local police agency where he served in the following capacity: Tactical Patrol, Intelligence, Narcotics, SWAT, Gang Investigations, Undercover operations, Defensive Tactics/Firearms/Water Survival instructor, Recruitment, Crisis Intervention, and Hostage Negotiations. He holds a second-degree black belt in Israeli Combat Systems and mid to high level ranks in Jiu-Jitsu, Capoeira, Muay Thai, *judo and various weapon systems. His website is* www.masadatactical.com.

When you were a kid, what did you want to be when you grew up?

"When I was a kid, I wanted to be a soldier and a *ninja* after watching the movie *American Ninja* with Michael Dudikoff. It was one of my first introductions to martial arts. With the release of the *Karate Kid* and *The Last Dragon*, it further fueled my desire to practice martial arts and be able to protect myself and others. I lived in a dangerous neighborhood and was constantly tormented by bullies. After watching some NYC Police Officers and Firefighters subdue a suspect who was beating on a woman, I knew I wanted to become a first responder after I served in the military. Now, at the age of 41 I have accomplished that and then some. Now I mentor and train the future in martial arts, military and civil service."

What is the best single piece of advice you were ever given?

"When I first started training martial arts, I was afraid, weak, and struggled with self-esteem issues. While sparring, my partner kicked and made contact causing me to retreat and start to cry. *Shihan* Vazquez (now *O'Sensei*) pulled me to the side and told me, 'In martial arts we must learn to control our emotions. We cannot show weakness. Understand that pain will always be a part of your life both physically and emotionally. learn to anticipate it so you can control it and it does not control you.'"

What is the best compliment you have ever received?

"When I pursued a career in law enforcement, it eventually led me to the Police Academy as the Lead Defensive Tactics Instructor. I was given orders to make the current system more efficient and practical. Utilizing my empirical experiences in life, the military and years of martial arts training, I was able to create a program that was effective, simple and fun to learn. That being said, during my career I have received messages from officers I trained who were involved in significant use-of-force situations. Two in particular thanked me after these situations for my determination and commitment in training them to overcome and win in these situations that could have been deadly if they were not trained properly."

> "Martial arts weren't just about winning the next fight, but overcoming adversity in everyday life... This mindset created a work ethic and determination that perpetuated very successful careers for me."

Knowing what you know now, would you do it all over again?

"Yes, I would. Martial arts were a saving grace for me growing up in Bushwick, Brooklyn N.Y., and most importantly a lifeline. Struggling with fear, anxiety, and self-esteem issues in a crime-ridden neighborhood could have been considered a death sentence in retrospect, but I decided not to be a victim and empower myself through the martial arts. As I grew and studied various disciplines and systems, I became more refined in both body and mind. Martial arts weren't just about winning the next fight, but overcoming adversity in everyday life. I entered my military and law enforcement career with some understanding of discipline in body and mind. This martial arts mindset created a work ethic and determination that perpetuated very successful careers for me. It furthermore structured me and helped me as a husband and father of three children who are now my students as well."

What's the worst martial arts-related mistake you have ever made??

"I grew up in a rough neighborhood so learning martial arts was key to my survival. That and watching *American Ninja* set me on a course to train *Koga Ryu Ninjitsu* under Shihan Felix Vazquez in Brooklyn NY. One day in junior high school outside of band class, I was attacked by three bullies who had it in for me. With a few classes under my belt, I proceeded to prepare for 'combat.' I quickly realized my ego and emotions had gotten the better of me and I was quickly overpowered. I had no choice but to grab my trumpet and start swinging. When it was all said and done, I realized martial arts was more than just physical techniques and bravado. I had to develop and control my mind and emotions as well and not let them control me. I did have to pay for the damaged trumpet."

What single event of the past changed the world for the best?

"I believe a single event of the past that changed the world for the better was the 16th century reformation. The reformation led to individuals thinking more broadly and openly. No longer were tradition and authority figures going to be followed mindlessly. Just as in martial arts, we must question our body and minds in order to understand our weaknesses and strengths so we should question and understand those appointed over us and always challenge the mantra of 'this is the way it's always been done.' We cannot progress forward and reach a state of *bushido* (virtuous warriors) if we do not overcome adversity, be it physical, mental, or political."

Survey demographics – Affinity group mix

"First there is a time when we believe everything, then for a little while we believe with discrimination, then we believe nothing whatever, and then we believe everything again—and, moreover, give reasons why we believe."

Georg Christoph Lichtenberg, German physicist and philosopher

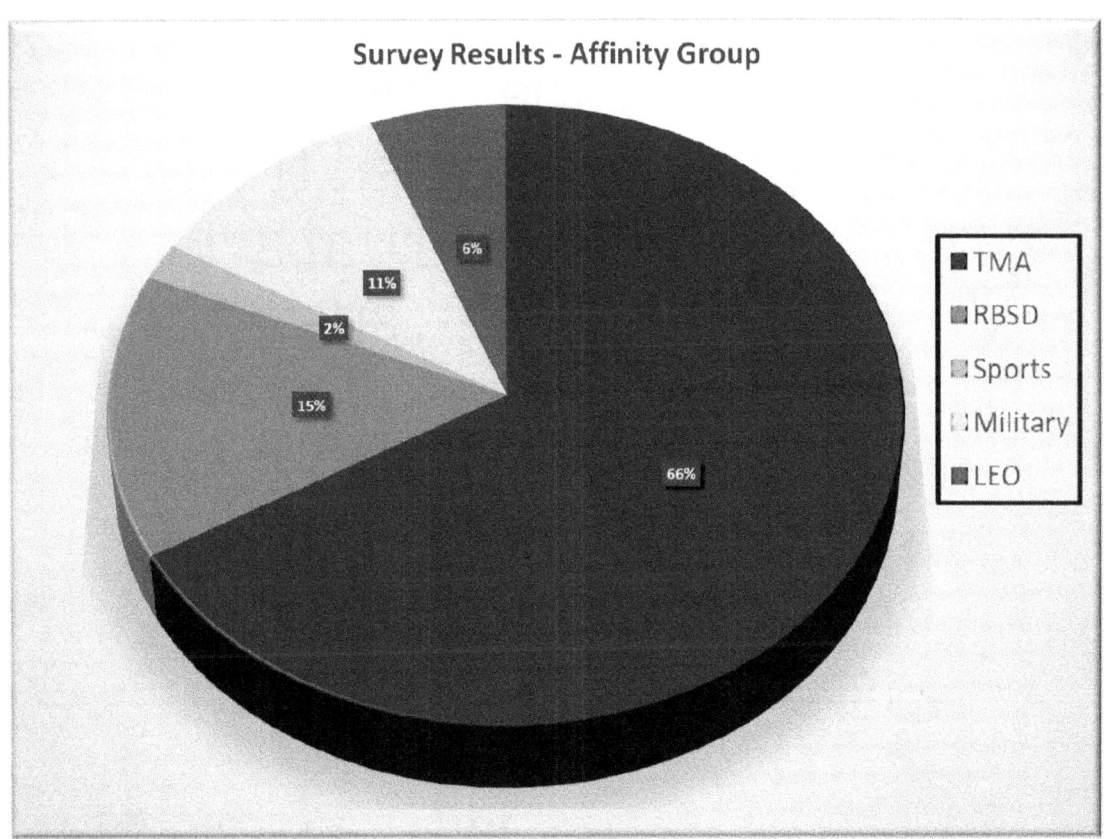

It is challenging to discern the world's most popular martial arts systems, in part because there is little consensus on the exact definition of the term "martial art." For example, some methodologies only count traditional styles and fighting sports like arnis, boxing, judo, karate, kung fu, taekwondo, and wrestling, considering pursuits like fencing, archery, shooting sports, law enforcement, and military training beyond the scope, whereas others have a more holistic appraisal. Obviously, we cast a broad net in our survey, though that approach caused a bit of a challenge in creating distinct affinity groups.

You see, many of our contributors have practiced more than one system, with the average respondent having experienced 5.79 martial arts, yet we only allowed a single affinity group entry per person for classification purposes. So, for instance, a practitioner who spent four years in Golden Gloves boxing, six competing in judo, and three as a professional MMA fighter, followed by fourteen practicing karate was placed in the traditional martial arts column rather than the fighting sports column based on where he spent the propensity of his time.

> On average, survey respondents reported trying 5.79 different martial arts during their career, spanning traditional martial arts, reality-based self-defense, military, law enforcement, and fighting sports.

One way of gauging interest in any subject is by studying internet search results. Uplifter, a Canadian company that caters to club management software, used google analytics to determine consumer interest trends between 2004 and 2019 and identify the five most "popular" martial arts in the world. Their findings in rank order include:

1. Mixed Martial Arts (MMA)
2. Karate
3. Taekwondo
4. Judo
5. Kung fu

Other arts that ranked near the top of the list included *Muay Thai*, Brazilian *jiu-jitsu*, *aikido*, and *Krav Maga*. An examination of our affinity group data closely matches these results, with overrepresentation by traditional martial arts followed by reality-based self-defense, military, law enforcement, and fighting sports.

There is clear misalignment in the prominence of MMA, which we consider a fighting sport, though in part that is a factor of our aforementioned affinization methodology. And, search results do not necessarily equate to participation; folks conducting those google searches might just as easily have been watching MMA as practicing in it.

The bottom line is that we can never know with certainty that our sample reflects the totality of opinion worldwide, but we believe that it is statistically significant nonetheless. In other words, we feel confident that our results are real, not a matter of luck (or misfortune) in receiving a certain mix of respondents to our questionnaire. Certainly, our findings are interesting and useful if not entirely scientific.

Martial Artist Profile – Charlie Lampshire

Charlie is a karateka with 27 years of experience. He started in Wado-Ryu karate and earned a 2nd dan grade before exploring other styles, clubs, and systems including Wing Chun, Krav Maga, Muay Thai, and Koryu Uchinadi Kempo Jutsu under the instruction of a student of Hanshi Patrick McCarthy. He has worked a variety of roles including as a personal fitness instructor for 15 years, a group exercise instructor specializing in Boxercise (hitting things), strength conditioning (lifting things) and kettlebells (swinging things). He has also been a school sports coach, a youth mentor, a police officer, and an auditor in the aviation industry. He is a loving husband and a father of two (soon to be three) fantastic kids. He has very rarely stood still.

What's the worst martial arts-related mistake you have ever made??

"One afternoon after 10 years training in *Wado Ryu* karate I stupidly let my ego drag me into a fight. Three youths in the street insulted my hair and my anger flared. Before I knew it a brawl was upon me. I held my own but my punches were not stopping them. I was pulling my punches as I do in sparring practice. I was hitting them but it was just making them angrier. It was only once some strangers intervened and wrenched us all apart that I realized that my training had set me up to fight in competitions but my self-defense skills sucked. I let my ego drag me into the fight and my 'fighting' skills did little. It was just luck that some passersby helped me out. It was at that point that I knew something had to change. First thing to go was my mullet."

What is the best single piece of advice you were ever given?

"Stop caring about what others think about you. You're not that special mate, nobody gives a fuck about you. Nobody cares enough about anyone but themselves to even notice you! The only one who notices when you fuck up is yourself! Most people on this planet are so self-involved that there's no chance they care if you succeed or fail and you're letting that stop you from even trying?! Do you not see how stupid that is? If you want to do something then just go ahead and bloody do it! Don't let the thoughts of others bother you as I guarantee they aren't even giving you a second thought."

What is the best compliment you have ever received?

"'You seem like such a brilliant dad.' I don't really feel I need to add anything more to this. Of all the titles and roles that I have held throughout my life, *Sensei*, Teacher, Coach, Manager, Officer, the only one that matters to me is 'Dad.'"

> "Of all the titles and roles that I have held throughout my life, Sensei, Teacher, Coach, Manager, Officer, the only one that matters to me is 'Dad.'"

For good or ill, what was the biggest impact of your martial arts training on your life?

"The confidence in my own skills and ability to both de-escalate a violent situation and deal with it when that failed stood me in great stead during my short law enforcement career. It gave me the ability to quickly assess a situation, analyze the threats and develop a strategy for minimizing any potential harm to either myself, a third party or the screaming 'roid monster off his face on cocaine. This in turn gave me the confidence to face pretty much any difficult situation head on. I had a particularly memorable job interview in which towards the end the panel told me 'You are remarkably confident; most people are very nervous when facing a panel like this.' I replied, 'Well to be fair I've had big guys try and take my head off both on the mats and off. Why should I be nervous about a conversation?'"

What energizes you outside of work?

"I'm the opposite to a social butterfly. I get my energy from being left on my own to recharge in peace. I love to lose myself in a mindless movie or a *Lord of The Rings* marathon. Give me a quiet room, a big screen and a decent whisky please."

What is your guilty pleasure?

"I do not have guilty pleasures. I no longer feel guilty about my love for cheesy disco music, stupidly fruity cocktails, and colorful Hawaiian shirts. Life is way too short to be embarrassed by anything."

Conclusion

"I find that the very things that I get criticized for, which is usually being different and just doing my own thing and just being original, is the very thing that's making me successful."

Shania Twain, Canadian singer and songwriter

385

Everyone likes to think that they're special, that they are exceptional. As it turns out, data indicates that in many ways martial artists actually are. You see, martial artists are ordinary folks who study disciplines that give them a different perspective, endure hardships that build a different strength, and in embracing their art manage to reveal their character in ways that are different from everybody else. It's not an easy path, but that's the way we like it. Knowing what they know now, 94.4% of respondents would travel their same path again. In other words, it's an arduous journey but it's totally worth it.

Most martial artists are process-focused and often drawn toward service, with a higher-than-normal distribution of Diplomat and Analyst MBTI personality types, folks who are able to make good judgements under stress, counted among our members. While only a third of the general population is comprised of early risers, with most folks preferring to stay up late when given the choice, martial artists are a different breed. Two-thirds of us are early birds. This chronotype reduces the risk of certain mental and physical health issues and is indicative of people who do far better in structured environments than the norm. Our suprachiasmatic nuclei help assure that we get enough sleep on a regular basis, leading to more energy, higher productivity, and a generally more positive outlook on life.

Striving to continuously challenge and improve ourselves, martial artists focus more on self-development and less on pure relaxation during our time off than average citizens. For example, while most people prefer to vacation by relaxing at the beach, martial artists have a higher propensity for rugged adventures in the mountains. We have a healthy, realistic, and often humorous view of our shortcomings too. Despite the fact humans tend to fear change, most martial artists are more introspective, continuously seeking to habituate ways of improving ourselves.

While martial artists study violence, we do not become violent from our training. Practitioners learn how to set and achieve challenging goals, develop good character, and use our skills wisely. In other words, we not only learn how to fight, but also know when it's appropriate to do so, and we understand the true cost of taking or not taking action far more than ordinary citizens. This helps account for the fact that as a community, martial artists are incarcerated at half the rate of the general public.

It's not just the practitioners, the martial arts themselves are unique too. Defined as any system or tradition of combat practiced for competition, cultural heritage, spiritual development, self-defense, military, or law enforcement application, unlike many athletic endeavors it is not the participant's size, age, somatotype, or gender that predicts success. In fact, anyone with the right desire and determination can become a proficient martial artist. Throughout our journey the same knowledge, skills, and experience we learn that help us overcome larger, stronger adversaries can be directed toward most any challenge. While practitioners often begin training in their youth, there are no limits to the myriad of mental and physical benefits we can gain by practicing martial arts over our lifetime.

> While everyone likes to think that they're exceptional, data indicates that martial artists actually are. The personal and societal benefits of martial arts are significant which helps in explaining why it has become a multi-billion-dollar industry.

To paraphrase Shania Twain's quote above, we are different, we're original, and now we have the data that proves it. As a community, these differences honed by our martial arts training are what makes us successful. So, while everyone likes to believe that they are extraordinary, as it turns out, martial artists genuinely are.

"Absorb what is useful, discard what is useless and add what is specifically your own."

Bruce Lee
(1940 – 1973)

Rogues' gallery

"Silent gratitude isn't very much use to anyone."
Gertrude Stein, American novelist, poet, and playwright

Thanks to all the traditional martial artists, RBSD practitioners, fighting sports competitors, law enforcement officers, and military personnel who responded to our survey. This indispensable, one-of-a-kind information wouldn't exist without you!!

A rogues' gallery is defined as a collection of dangerous people or things, at designation we found fitting if not a touch ironic since the term can also refer to villains which describes no one listed here, for the folks who filled out our questionnaire. Everyone who completed our survey had the option of making their name public or responding anonymously. These participants ranged in age from a 15-year-old high school athlete (wrestling, karate) to an 80-year-old martial arts instructor (karate, taekwondo, yoga) with over 30 years of teaching experience under her belt. Here's our participant register displaying the names of our respondents:

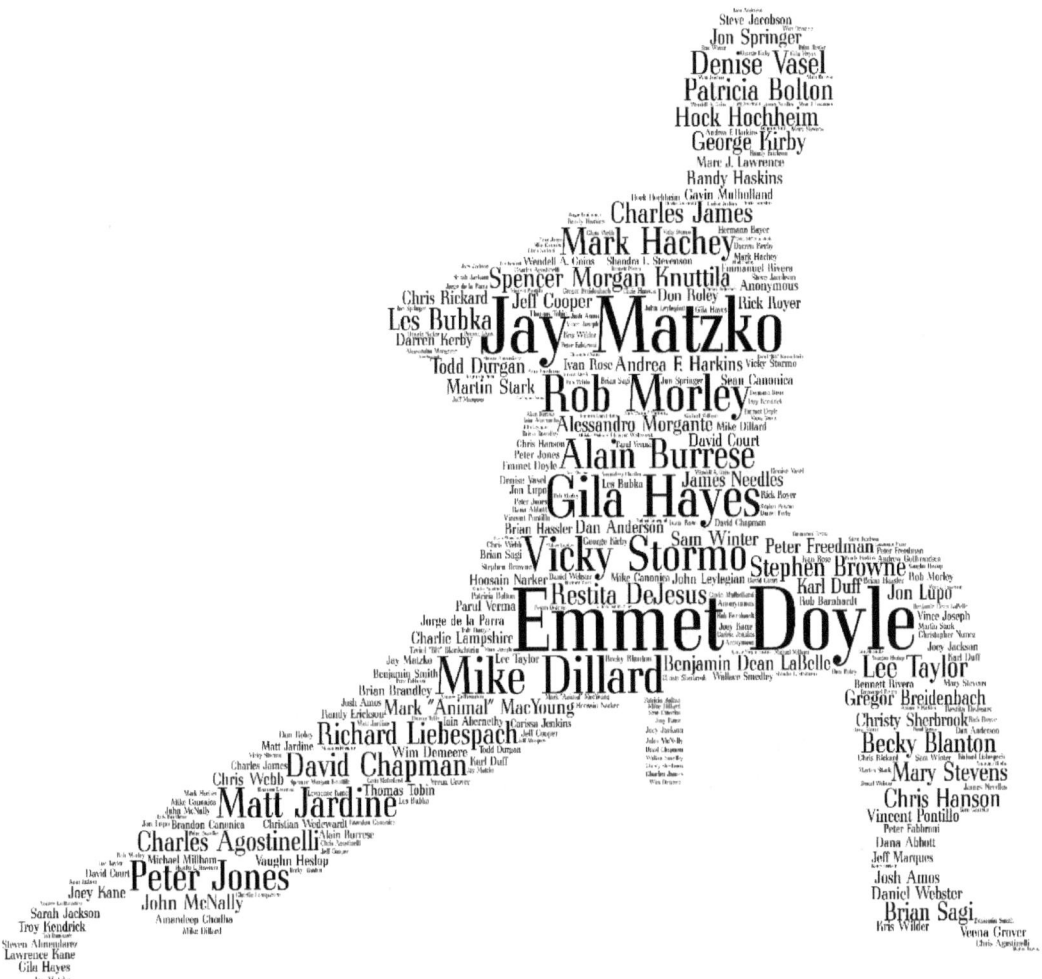

Those who wished to be recognized in the book were also asked to provide a photo so that we could best honor their contribution. Many participants did not choose to provide a picture, while others sent in small or low-resolution images that were either unusable or unscalable, so the size and placement of the photos we were able to include below were entirely based on the quality/resolution of pictures submitted by participants and has nothing to do with any individual's contribution to the book. They're all exceedingly appreciated! Our rogues' mugshots are displayed below in more than less, but not really alphabetical order…

Alain Burrese  Andrea Harkins  Benjamin LaBelle

Armandeep Chodha  Andrew Gulbrandsen  Alessandro Morgante

Benjamin Smith Becky Blanton Bennett Rivera

Christopher Nunez   Dana Abbott   Dan Anderson

Denise Vasel   Darren Kerby   Daniel Webster

Emmanuel Rivera   Emmet Doyle   Gavin Mulholland

W. Hock Hochheim Gregor Breidenbach George Kirby

Iain Abernethy Hermann Bayer Hoosain Narker

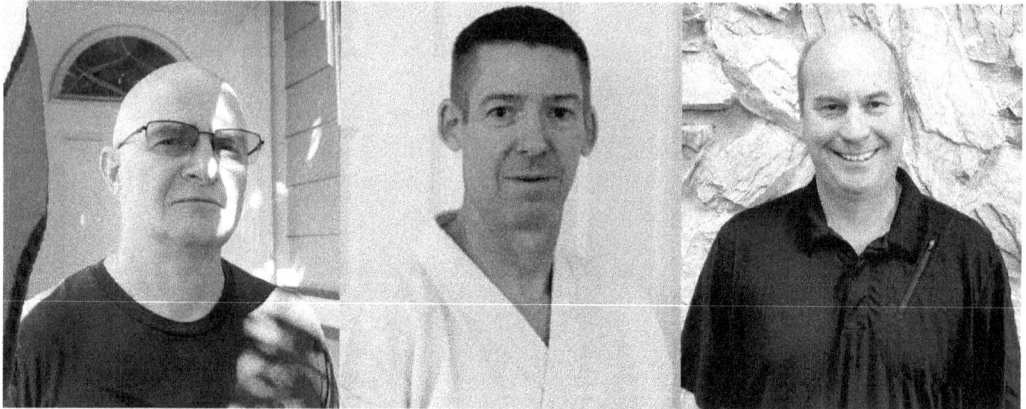

James Needles Ivan Rose Jay Matzko

Restita DeJesus

Rick Royer

Sarah Jackson

Rob Barnhart

Randy Haskins

Sean Canonica

Steve Jacobson

Shandra Stevenson Michael Millham

Steven Almendarez   Gila Hayes   Troy Kendrick

Spencer Knuttila   Stephen Browne   Todd Durgan

Sam Winter   Thomas Tobin   Vaughn Heslop

Don Roley　　　Rob Morley　　　David Chapman

Jeff Marques　　　David Court　　　Charles James

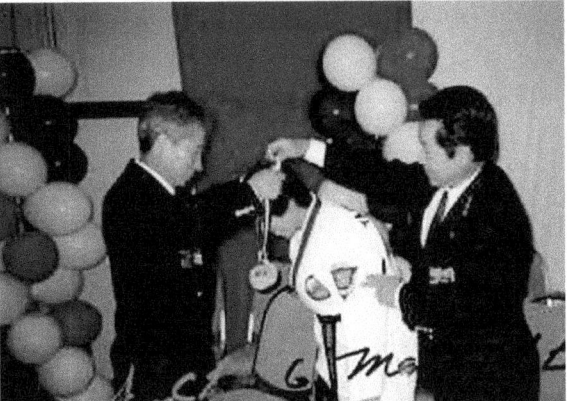

Veena Grover

Appendix A – Survey Methodology

How the survey was conducted and results created: We contacted 572 martial artists from around the world and invited them to take part in this survey. These included practitioners of traditional martial arts, Reality-Based Self-Defense (RBSD), fighting sports, military, and law enforcement disciplines. Of these 572 contacts, 107 chose to take part. While we provided the option for distinct or anonymous feedback, most participants chose to be named and stand behind their feedback, which afforded us the opportunity to ask clarifying questions when necessary.

This study differs from a poll. Polls can be scientific or unscientific. For example, a poll of likely voters for a presidential election spread out across the United States is simple in its line of inquiry, using questions such as, "If the election were held today, are you more likely to vote for Candidate X or Candidate Y?" The sample selected for such studies may be comprised of only voters with a record of voting in all four of the last four elections, making them likely to cast a ballot in the next presidential election. Demographic information such as gender and age are often components of such interviews, but may not be asked of participants in simple polls like this as they are already known due to database from which the sample group was created. Outcomes of these types of polls often result in statements of findings we see reported in the news such as, "In a recent poll of likely voters, Candidate Y has a 7-point lead over Candidate X."

A social medial poll, such as one conducted on Twitter, Instagram, Facebook, or LinkedIn by way of comparison, is not scientific. All commenters are allowed to cast responses should they be interested in doing so. The only need for a response is a person who uses the social media platform. Further, the inquiry may very well include leading questions designed to steer the proverbial witness, such as, "Why are dogs better than cats?" as opposed to more scientific and neutral queries. There is no demographic data, gender, age, income, education, political affiliation, or location attached to the feedback. That means that this type of poll is pure entertainment. It is really nothing more than a shootout from America's wild west, statistically meaningless and as reckless as a drunken cowboy staggering from the pay wagon to the casino.

The Stanford Review reported on a survey done on the campus of Stanford University during the Covid-19 Pandemic of 2021 (https://stanfordreview.org/stanford-bicycles-helmets-masks/). For an hour on Wednesday, September 22nd, surveyors observed 400 bicyclists on Lasuen Mall on the campus to determine that Stanford university students were more likely to wear masks on bicycles than helmets irrespective of their respective safety benefits.

Of the 400 hundred bicyclists viewed, they had four observations: 195 wearing no mask and no helmet (49%), 134 with masks but no helmet (34%), 42 with helmets but no mask (10%), and 29 wearing both mask and helmet (7%). This Stanford Survey is an example of a simple survey of a select group. They wanted to understand what combination of helmets and masks bicyclists in the area were wearing. Clearly it was assumed that any person bicycling on campus at that time had a relationship with the University, either as students, faculty, or staff.

The Martial Arts and Your Life survey was comprised of 107 respondents, a little over one-quarter of the sample size of the Stanford survey. Yet, unlike the simple observations at Stanford, our survey had 40 questions (listed in Appendix B) that were reviewed in depth. Additionally, we gathered demographic information from respondents in their bio and background information that supplemented the questions and facilitated additional findings.

Our survey used both closed- and open-ended questions. Closed questions are multiple-choice queries such as, "What is your somatotype?" with the three options of Mesomorph, Ectomorph, or Endomorph being the only responses allowed. The open-ended questions, on the other hand were queries like, "What is the greatest compliment you have ever received?" These open-ended queries allowed for self-selection of words and ideas, identifying what is most important in the respondents' lives. The combination of these open-ended questions in conjunction with the closed questions allows for a rich analysis across responses.

Once all this data was received and validated, we created an extensive database that allowed for question-by-question analysis, cross-correlation, and in-depth comparison and contrast with information from other polls, surveys, and data sources related to the subject matter. Because most respondents provided contact information, in a few instances we followed up with additional questions or clarifications. In this fashion we were able to create the charts and graphs you found in each chapter. Additionally, it allowed us to examine findings at multiple levels, testing and validating or disproving our initial hypotheses about what martial makes martial artists' tick. In this fashion we were able to generate a comprehensive review of the subject matter.

Appendix B – Questionnaire

Our survey included the following questions (in addition to each respondent's name, title, rank, contact information, biography, and other demographic data which we've excluded here)…

1. How does your system organize rank?

Note: Please refer to the system you practice now (or last practiced if you no longer train). If there is no formal rank in your system type N/A here. Please limit this response to 150 words or less:

2. What is the highest rank you have ever achieved in the martial arts?

Note: Please select the highest rank you have earned in any system, not necessarily the one you are practicing right now, by placing an **X** after the appropriate level below. The answers to this question will be used to create a graph, hence cannot accommodate all possible rank variations. Since there is no universal rank system that span all martial arts across the globe, please pick the closest equivalent to your ranking. For example, if you have a black sash with three stripes that would most likely be equivalent to Dan (black belt) – 4. Choose **only one** response to this question:

Kyu (colored belt) – 1	Kyu (colored belt) – 6	Dan (black belt) – 1	Dan (black belt) – 6
Kyu (colored belt) – 2	Kyu (colored belt) – 7	Dan (black belt) – 2	Dan (black belt) – 7
Kyu (colored belt) – 3	Kyu (colored belt) – 8	Dan (black belt) – 3	Dan (black belt) – 8
Kyu (colored belt) – 4	Kyu (colored belt) – 9	Dan (black belt) – 4	Dan (black belt) – 9
Kyu (colored belt) – 5	Kyu (colored belt) – 10	Dan (black belt) – 5	Dan (black belt) – 10
N/A – My system(s) has no rank			

3. How many different martial systems have you tried?

Note: Please enter a **number** in the space below. Do not explain why, editorialize, or name the art(s) We want to keep the answer crisp:

4. If you did not practice the martial art you are involved in now, what other martial art(s) would you do?

Note: Please name the art or arts, with no explanation or editorialization. N/A is an acceptable answer. Please limit this response to **30 words or less**:

5. What is your Myers-Briggs personality type?

Note: Understanding your personality type via the Myers-Briggs Type Indicator (MBTI) supports your emotional well-being, athletic performance, and professional goals by leveraging scientific insight into your predilections, strengths, and weaknesses. If you do not already know your personality type, please take the free test at www.16personalities.com. You can also spend time on that site to better understand the various types and what they mean if you so desire. Please enter your **4-letter personality type** (e.g., INTJ, ESTP, ENFP, etc.) in the space below:

6. What is your somatotype, (a) ectomorph, (b) mesomorph, or (c) endomorph?

Note: These three somatotypes (body types) were categorized in the 1940s by psychologist William Herbert Sheldon (1898 – 1977). While some aspects of his work have been discredited, modern research shows that a person's body type impacts their athletic performance and how best to achieve their fitness goals. **Ectomorphs** tend to be naturally lean, with narrow shoulders and hips, and faster metabolisms, and often struggle to gain muscular weight or body fat. **Mesomorphs** tend to have wider shoulders, narrower waist/hips, small joints, and long limbs, and fit in the middle between the other two somatotypes. **Endomorphs** tend to have heavier bone structures, wider waist/hips, squarer torsos, and slow metabolisms, and often have an easier time gaining both muscular weight and body fat. Please place an **X** next to the appropriate choice below:

Ectomorph	Mesomorph	Endomorph

7. Have you ever applied your martial art outside the training hall or competition/tournament ring?

Note: Answers to this question **will only be shown in aggregate** and will not be attributed to any individual respondent. Real life applications can include any time you used your skills working as a bouncer, security professional, law enforcement officer, or military operative as well as street fights, barroom brawls, assaults, and other endeavors that **do not** include a specified **venue** with codified **safety rules** and **referees**. Please place an **X** next to the appropriate answer below:

Yes	No

8. If you answered yes to question # 7 above, how many times?

Note: Answers to this question **will only be shown in aggregate** and will not be attributed to any individual respondent. If you answered yes, please place an **X** next to the appropriate number of times you have used your art in a real-life application below. Please choose **only one box** to check:

1	11 to 15	31 to 40	61 to 70
2 to 5	16 to 20	41 to 50	71 to 80
6 to 10	21 to 30	51 to 60	81 or more

9. What's the worst martial arts-related mistake you have ever made?

Note: Martial arts are defined as any codified system or tradition of combat practiced for competition, cultural heritage, spiritual development, self-defense, military, or law enforcement applications. Please limit your response to **150 words** or less:

10. Are you a night owl or an early bird?

Note: Please place an **X** next to the appropriate answer below:

Night owl	Early Bird

11. What attributes do you admire most?

Note: The response to this question should reflect admirable qualities you have seen in martial arts practitioners. Think about values (e.g., honesty, integrity, courage, etc.), principles (e.g., coaching, perseverance, giving back to the community, etc.), and skills (e.g., ability to hit a target from a mile away with a rifle, break bricks with a punch, or consistently win a tournament), or anything else you feel is appropriate, and identify the attributes that you admire most. Please keep this response to **15 words** or less:

12. What superpower do you wish you had?

Note: Please list only **one** power (e.g., telepathy, superhuman strength, invisibility, ability to walk through walls, etc.) with no explanation or editorialization below. Limit this response to **5 words** or less:

13. If wrote a book about your life, what would the title be?

Note: Please be creative. Limit this response to **15 words** or less:

14. What is the best compliment you have ever received?

Note: The response to this question does not necessarily have to be martial arts-related, though some sort of tie back to what you have internalized from practicing the arts (e.g., confidence, courage, determination, self-discipline, perseverance, politeness, mindfulness, etc.) would be appropriate. Please limit this response to **150 words** or less:

15. What is the best single piece of advice you were ever given? Who was it from?

Note: The response to this question does not necessarily have to be martial arts-related. Consider both solicited and unsolicited advice like mentoring, life coaching, career counseling, investment tips, alternatives analysis, decision guidelines, or whatever made a lasting impact. Please limit this response to **150 words** or less:

16. If you had to pick one age to be permanently, which age would you choose? Why?

Note: Please be specific, such as "15-years-old" as opposed to "teenage." Limit this response to **50 words** or less:

17. If you could go back in time, what advice would you give to your teenage self?

Note: The response to this question does not necessarily have to be martial arts-related. Think of anything you wish you had known in your younger years (and might reasonably have listened to or taken action on had you been given the advice). If you are still a teenager, think of something you wish you had known months or years ago. Please limit this response to **150 words** or less:

18. When you were a kid, what did you want to be when you grew up? Did you follow that path? Why or why not?

Note: The response to this question does not necessarily have to be martial arts-related. Please limit this response to **150 words** or less:

19. What energizes you outside of work?

Note: The response to this question does not necessarily have to be martial arts-related. Answers can include things like reading a book, consuming certain foods or drinks, meditation, movies, massages, participating in various hobbies/events, or even taking a good nap. Please be creative. Limit this response to **50 words** or less:

20. What is your favorite weekend activity?

Note: The response to this question does not necessarily have to be martial arts-related. Please be creative and do not duplicate your response to Question #19 above. Name the action or activity but do not editorialize or explain why. Limit this response to 25 words or less:

21. What is your guilty pleasure?

Note: The response to this question does not necessarily have to be martial arts-related. Please be creative and do not duplicate either of your last two responses (Questions #19 and #20). Limit this response to **50 words** or less:

22. Would you rather visit the beach or the mountains?

Note: Please place an **X** next to the appropriate answer below. Choose only one option:

Beach	Mountains

23. Have you ever spent a night in jail?

Note: Answers to this question **will only be shown in aggregate** and will not be attributed to any individual respondent. Please place an **X** next to the appropriate answer below:

Yes	No

24. What three words would your friends use to describe you?

Note: Please respond with **exactly 3 words**, no more no less:

25. What is one thing, big or small, that you are truly bad at?

Note: The response to this question does not necessarily have to be martial arts-related. Be creative. Responses can include skills you do not possess (e.g., cooking, painting, singing in tune) situations that make you uncomfortable (e.g., small talk, confrontations, public speaking), sports you do not play well (e.g., bowling, golf, ice skating), or anything else you perform poorly. Please list the **one thing** you are bad at, limiting this response to **25 words** or less:

26. What is one thing you are currently trying to make a habit?

Note: The response to this question does not necessarily have to be martial arts-related. Be creative. Consider positive things you may be trying to grow like improving your morning routine, better managing your time, or more actively listening to others, as well as negative things you may wish to reduce such as cutting back on social media, minimizing multitasking, or eliminating certain foods from your diet. It could also relate to your temperament, outlook on life, or priorities. Do not explain why, simply list the **one thing** you are trying to make a habit. Please limit this response to **25 words** or less:

27. Who is/was the greatest athlete of all time?

Note: Please list that person's name below. If your choice someone who many folks may not recognize (e.g., Polydamas, Milo of Croton, Cú Chulainn, Pheidippides, etc.) please elaborate with no more than **25 words** so that readers will understand who you are referring to and what sport they play/played or athletic endeavor they undertook:

28. What single event of the past changed the world for the best?

Note: Think broadly, everything from the discovery and use of fire by early humans to the invention of the wheel, discovery of penicillin, or any turning point that you feel was pivotal to course of human history in a positive way. Please limit this response to **150 words** or less:

29. What single event of the past changed the world for the worst?

Note: Think broadly, everything from the fall of the Roman empire to the bubonic plague, various world wars, or any turning point that you feel was pivotal to course of human history in a negative way. Please limit this response to **150 words** or less:

30. Who is your favorite musician (or band)?

Note: Please name the musician or band but do not editorialize or explain why. Respond in the box below. Please limit this response to **15 words** or less:

31. What terrifies you?

Note: The response to this question does not necessarily have to be martial arts-related. This can include things like public speaking, flying, heights, snakes, certain insects, small enclosed spaces, dying, darkness, or blood, among other things. Please list your biggest fear in the box below. Limit this response to **15 words** or less:

32. Do you regularly carry a weapon?

Note: Answers to this question **will only be shown in aggregate** and will not be attributed to any individual respondent. For the purpose of this question, a weapon is defined as any instrument or device specifically designed for use in attack or defense such as pepper sprays, stun guns, knives, or firearms. It does not include makeshift implements that could be used as weapons but are not designed as such, like a set of car keys, belt, or boot. Please place an **X** next to the appropriate answer below:

Yes	No

33. Who influenced you the most?

Note: This might include martial artists, philosophers, religious figures, parents, teachers, or even unknown individuals whose actions or compassion you witnessed who inspired you. Please list that person's name below. If your choice is someone who many folks may not recognize (e.g., Tenzin Gyatso, etc.) please elaborate with no more than **25 words** so that readers will understand who you are referring to:

34. Why did you start training?

Note: Think back on why you started. This can include a wide variety of things like making new friends, standing up to bullies, getting in shape, building self-confidence, avoiding victimization, improving mindfulness, competing in tournaments, etc. Please limit this response to **25 words** or less:

35. For good or ill, what was the biggest impact of your martial arts training on your life?

Note: This could include discipline, mindset, values, confidence, courage, fitness, physical skills, injuries, lawsuits, jail time, job opportunities, or anything else that you believe is relevant. Please limit this response to **150 words** or less:

36. If you stopped or took a long break from training, why?

Note: Please determine your own definition of "long break" when answering. You may select **more than one** reason. Place an **X** next to each applicable box below:

Earned my black belt	Lost interest	Could not afford the expense
Achieved my goal(s)	Too busy with work	My instructor/school relocated
Illness	Too busy with school	My school changed instructors
Injury	Too busy with family	I relocated/moved
Felt overwhelmed	Commute too difficult	My school became too political
Curriculum too easy	Failed a promotion test	Fear of other practitioners
Became disillusioned	Discovered I was in a cult	N/A – I never stopped training

37. How have you made money from your martial arts?

Note: You may select **more than one** method. Please place an **X** next to each applicable box below:

It's my full-time profession	Royalties from books
It's a part-time job	Royalties from videos
Paid seminars	Royalties from online classes
Paid consulting	Paid social media
Testing fees	Tangential effort (e.g., personal training)
Franchise fees	N/A – I do not earn anything from my art

38. Which one of your senses are you most willing to sacrifice?

Note: N/A is <u>not</u> an option here, you must **choose one**. Proprioception, also known as kinesthesia, is a person's ability to sense their location, movements, and actions (awareness of their body in space). Please do not editorialize or explain why. Place an **X** next to your choice below:

| Touch | Sight | Hearing |
| Smell | Taste | Proprioception |

39. Knowing what you know now, would you do it all over again? Why?

Note: Please keep this answer martial arts-related. Think about the highs and lows of your training, the tests you endured, challenges you overcame, things you learned, how you used your skills, and all the various ways in which your martial journey impacted your life. Limit this response to **150 words** or less:

40. Do you recommend your system/style to your friends or family?

Note: Please refer to the system or style you practice today or to the last one you practiced before quitting if you no longer train. Do not editorialize or explain. Place an **X** next to the appropriate answer below:

| Yes | No |

Bibliography

Books:

- Ayoob, Massad. *The Truth About Self-Protection.* New York, NY: Bantam Books (Police Bookshelf), 1983.
- Baron-Cohen, Simon. *The Essential Difference: Men, Women and the Extreme Male Brain.* New York, NY: Penguin Publishing, 2007.
- Carroll, Pete (with Yogi Roth). *Win Forever: Live, Work, and Play Like a Champion.* New York, NY; Penguin Publishing, 2010.
- Christensen, Loren and Dr. Alexis Artwohl. *Deadly Force Encounters: What Cops Need To Know To Mentally And Physically Prepare For And Survive A Gunfight.* Boulder, CO: Paladin Enterprises, Inc., 1997.
- Christensen, Loren. *Far Beyond Defensive Tactics: Advanced Concepts, Techniques, Drills, and Tricks for Cops on the Street.* Boulder, CO: Paladin Enterprises, Inc., 1998.
- Christensen, Loren. *Warriors: On Living with Courage, Discipline and Honor.* Boulder, CO: Paladin Enterprises, Inc., 2004.
- Covey, Stephen M. R. and Rebecca R. Merrill. *The Speed of Trust: The one Thing that Changes Everything.* New York, NY: Simon & Schuster, 2008.
- Covey, Stephen R. and David K. Hatch. *Everyday Greatness: Inspiration for a Meaningful Live.* Nashville, TN: Thomas Nelson, 2006.
- Covey, Stephen R. *The 7 Habits of Highly Effective People: Powerful Lessons in Personal Change.* New York, NY: Simon & Schuster, 1989.
- DeBecker, Gavin. *The Gift of Fear: Survival Signals That Protect Us From Violence.* New York, NY: Dell Publishing, 1998.
- Drucker, Peter F. *The Effective Executive.* New York, NY: Harper & Row, 1966.
- Dungy, Tony (with Nathan Whitaker). *Quiet Strength: The Principles, Practices, and Priorities of a Winning Life.* Winter Park, FL: Legacy LLC, 2007.
- Greenleaf, Robert K. *The Servant as Leader.* Westfield, IN: The Greenleaf Center for Servant Leadership, 2008.
- Grossman, David A. and Loren Christensen. *On Combat: The Psychology and Physiology*

- *of Deadly Conflict in War and Peace*. Belleville, IL: PPCT Research Publications, 2004.
- Grossman, David A. *On Killing: The Psychological Cost of Learning to Kill in War and Society*. New York, NY: Little, Brown, and Company, 1995.
- Hartley, Gregory and Maryann Karinch. *Get People to Do What You Want: How to Use Body Language and Words for Maximum Effect*. Newburyport, MA: Career Press, 2019
- Kane, Lawrence A. *Martial Arts Instruction: Applying Educational Theory and Communication Techniques in the Dojo*. Boston, MA: YMAA, 2004.
- Kane, Lawrence A. *Surviving Armed Assaults: A Martial Artists Guide to Weapons, Street Violence, and Countervailing Force*. Boston, MA: YMAA, 2006.
- Kane, Lawrence A., and Kris Wilder. *The Little Black Book of Violence: What Every Young Man Needs to Know About Fighting*. Wolfeboro, NH: YMAA, 2009
- Kane, Lawrence A., and Kris Wilder. *The Way to Black Belt: A Comprehensive Guide to Rapid, Rock-Solid Results*. Wolfeboro, NH: YMAA, 2015
- Kane, Lawrence A., and Kris Wilder. *The Way of Kata: A Comprehensive Guide for Deciphering Martial Applications*. Wolfeboro, NH: YMAA, 2005
- Kano, Jigoro. *Kodokan Judo: The Essential Guide to Judo by Its Founder Jigoro Kano*. Tokyo, Japan: Kodansha International, Ltd., 1986
- Lott, Jr. John R. and William M. Landes. *Multiple Victim Public Shootings, Bombings, and Right-to-Carry Concealed Handgun Laws: Contrasting Private and Public Law Enforcement*. University of Chicago, 1999.
- Lovret, Fredrick J. *The Way and the Power: Secrets of Japanese Strategy*. Boulder, CO: Paladin Enterprises, Inc., 1987
- MacYoung, Marc. *A Professional's Guide to Ending Violence Quickly*. Boulder, CO: Paladin Enterprises, Inc., 1993.
- MacYoung, Marc. *Cheap Shots, Ambushes, and Other Lessons: A Down And Dirty Book On Streetfighting and Survival*. Boulder, CO: Paladin Enterprises, Inc., 1989.
- MacYoung, Marc. *Fists, Wits, and a Wicked Right: Surviving On the Wild Side of the Street*. Boulder, CO: Paladin Enterprises, Inc., 1991.
- MacYoung, Marc. *Floor Fighting: Stompings, Maimings, and Other Things to Avoid When a Fight Goes to the Ground*. Boulder, CO: Paladin Enterprises, Inc., 1993.
- MacYoung, Marc. *Knives, Knife Fighting, And Related Hassles: How to Survive A Real Knife Fight*. Boulder, CO: Paladin Enterprises, Inc., 1990.
- MacYoung, Marc. *Pool Cues, Beer Bottles, & Baseball Bats: Animal's Guide to Improvised Weapons for Self-Defense and Survival*. Boulder, CO: Paladin Enterprises, Inc., 1990.
- MacYoung, Marc. *Street E & E: Evading, Escaping, and Other Ways to Save Your Ass When Things Get Ugly*. Boulder, CO: Paladin Enterprises, Inc., 1993.
- Miller, Rory A. *Facing Violence: Preparing for the Unexpected*. Wolfeboro, NH: YMAA Publication Center, 2011.

- Miller, Rory A. *Force Decisions: A Citizen's Guide to Understanding How Police Determine Appropriate Use of Force*. Wolfeboro, NH: YMAA Publication Center, April 2012.
- Miller, Rory A. *Meditations on Violence: A Comparison of Martial Arts Training and Real-World Violence*. Wolfeboro, NH: YMAA Publication Center, 2008.
- Miller, Rory and Lawrence A. Kane. *Scaling Force: Dynamic Decision Making Under Threat of Violence*. Wolfeboro, NH: YMAA Publication Center, 2012.
- Miller, Rory. *Conflict Communication A New Paradigm in Conscious Communication*. Washougal, WA: Wyrd Goat Press, 2014.
- Miller, Rory. *Drills: Training for Sudden Violence (A Chiron Manual)*. Washougal, WA: Wyrd Goat Press, 2011.
- Niednagel, Jonathan P. *Your Key to Sports Success*. Laguna Miguel, CA: Laguna Press, 1997.
- Panné, Jean-Louis and Andrzej Paczkowski, Karel Bartosek, Jean-Louis Margolin, Nicolas Werth, Stéphane Courtois, Mark Kramer, and Jonathan Murphy. *The Black Book of Communism: Crimes, Terror, Repression*. Cambridge, MA: Harvard University Press, 1999.
- Peterson, David B. and Mary Dee Hicks. *Development First: Strategies for Self-Development*. Minneapolis, MN: Personnel Decisions International, 1995.
- Peterson, David B. and Mary Dee Hicks. *Leader as Coach: Strategies for Coaching and Developing Others*. Minneapolis, MN: Personnel Decisions International, 1996.
- Pink, Daniel H. *Drive: The Surprising Truth about What Motivates Us*. New York, NY; Penguin Publishing, 2009.
- Quinn, Peyton. *Real Fighting: Adrenaline Stress Conditioning through Scenario-Based Training*. Boulder, CO: Paladin Enterprises, Inc., 1996.
- Rath, Tom and Barry Conchie. *Strengths Based Leadership: Great Leaders, Teams, and Why People Follow*. New York, NY: Gallup Press, 2008.
- Rosenthal, Robert and Lenore Jacobson. *Pygmalion in the Classroom: Teacher Expectation and Pupils' Intellectual Development*. Norwalk, CT: Crown House Publishing Company, LLC, 1992
- Scott, Susan. *Fierce Conversations: Achieving Success at Work and in Life, One Conversation at a Time*. New York, NY: The Berkley Publishing Group, 2002.
- Senge, Peter M. *The Fifth Discipline: The Art and Practice of the Learning Organization*. New York, NY: Currency Doubleday, 1990.
- Siddle, Bruce K. *Sharpening the Warrior's Edge: The Psychology and Science of Training*. Millstadt, IL: PPCT Research Publications, Inc., 1995.
- Sockut, Eugene. *Secrets of Street Survival – Israeli Style: Staying Alive in a Civilian War Zone*. Boulder, CO: Paladin Enterprises, Inc., 1995.
- Stouffer SA, Lumsdaine A. A., Lumsdaine M. H., et al. *The American Soldier*. Princeton, NJ: Princeton University Press; 1949.
- Suarez, Gabe. *The Combative Perspective: The Thinking Man's Guide to Self-Defense*. Boulder, CO: Paladin Enterprises, Inc., 2003.

- Taubert, Robert K. *Rattenkrieg! The Art and Science of Close Quarters Battle Pistol*. North Reading, MA: Saber Press, July 1, 2012.
- Thompson, George. *Verbal Judo: The Gentle Art of Persuasion*. New York, NY: HarperCollins, 1993.
- Wilder, Kris and Lawrence A. Kane. *10 Rules of Karate: The Immutable Path to Victory*. Seattle, WA: Stickman Publications, 2021.
- Wilson, William Scott and Tsunetomo Yamamoto. *Hagakure: The Book of the Samurai*. Boston, MA: Shambhala Press, 2002.

Websites:

- 16 Personalities (www.16personalities.com)
- 19FortyFive (https://www.19fortyfive.com/)
- Analytics Vidhya (https://www.analyticsvidhya.com/)
- AP News (www.apnews.com)
- Bowker (https://www.bowker.com/)
- CNN News (www.cnn.com)
- Encyclopedia Britannica (www.britannica.com)
- Fine Japanese Calligraphy (www.takase.com)
- Force Science Institute (www.forcescience.org)
- Fox News (www.foxnews.com)
- Harvard Business Review (www.hbr.org)
- History Net (www.historynet.com)
- How Stuff Works (www.howstuffworks.com)
- IBISWorld (https://www.ibisworld.com/)
- Khan Academy (www.khanacademy.org)
- Kodokan Judo Institute (http://kodokanjudoinstitute.org/en/)
- Life Hacker (www.lifehacker.com)
- London Center for Policy Research (https://www.londoncenter.org/thought-to-action)
- Marc MacYoung (www.nononsenselfdefense.com)
- National Institute of Mental Health (www.nimh.nih.gov)
- National Sexual Violence Resource Center (https://www.nsvrc.org/)
- NiemanLab (https://www.niemanlab.org/)
- Olympic Games (https://olympics.com/en/olympic-games)
- Our World in Data (https://ourworldindata.org/)
- Parents Plus Kids (https://parentspluskids.com/)
- Psychology Today (www.psychologytoday.com)
- Quartz (https://qz.com)

- Scribe Media (https://scribemedia.com/)
- Smithsonian Channel (https://www.smithsonianchannel.com)
- Society for Human Resource Management (www.shrm.org)
- Society for Organizational Learning (www.solonline.org)
- Stratfor Geopolitical Intelligence Platform (www.stratfor.com)
- Stock Kanji (www.stockkanji.com)
- Surveyon (https://www.surveyon.com)
- The Bureau of Justice Statistics (www.bjs.gov)
- The Daily Mail (https://www.dailymail.co.uk/)
- The Federal Bureau of Investigation (www.fbi.gov)
- The Healthy (https://www.thehealthy.com/)
- The History Channel (www.history.com)
- The Myers & Briggs Foundation (https://www.myersbriggs.org/)
- The New York Times (www.nytimes.com)
- The People History: (www.thepeoplehistory.com)
- The Quotations Page (www.quotationspage.com)
- The Seattle Times (www.seattletimes.com)
- The Stanford Review (www.stanfordreview.org)
- The Wall Street Journal (https://www.wsj.com/)
- The World Bank (https://www.worldbank.org/en/home)
- Unified Crime Reports (www.fbi.gov/about-us/cjis/ucr/ucr)
- United States Army Combined Arms Center (https://usacac.army.mil)
- United States Bureau of Labor Statistics (www.bls.gov)
- United States Census Bureau (https://www.census.gov/)
- United States Department of Justice (https://www.justice.gov/)
- United States Department of Transportation (https://www.transportation.gov/)
- Uplifter (https://www.uplifterinc.com/)
- Warfare History Network (www.warfarehistorynetwork.com)
- Wikipedia (https://en.wikipedia.org/wiki/Main_Page)
- Washington Post (https://www.washingtonpost.com)
- World Population Review (https://worldpopulationreview.com/)
- YouTube (www.youtube.com)
- Zippia (https://www.zippia.com/)

Thank you!

Thank you for your purchase! Publishing is an arduous process and it's folks like you who make our efforts worthwhile. With roughly 4 million new titles created every year, unbiased customer reviews are indispensable in helping readers identify books that are worth buying. To that end, if you found value from this work, please let other people know. Publish an Amazon review and send us the link at http://www.stickmanpublications.com/contact/ along with your contact information and you will be entered into a drawing to win autographed versions of our four bestselling titles.

About the Authors

Lawrence A. Kane, COP-GOV, CSP, CSMP, CIAP

Lawrence was inducted into the Sourcing Industry Group (SIG) Sourcing Supernova Hall of Fame in 2018 for pioneering leadership in strategic sourcing, procurement, supplier innovation, and digital transformation. An Executive Certified Outsourcing Professional, Certified Sourcing Professional, Certified Supplier Management Professional, and Certified Intelligent Automation Professional, he currently works as a senior leader at a Fortune® 50 corporation where he gets to play with billions of dollars of other people's money and make really important decisions.

A martial artist, judicious use-of-force expert, and the bestselling author of 22 books, he has won numerous awards including an Independent Press Award, a Beverly Hills Book Award and Presidential Prize, a USA Best Book Award, two National Indie Excellence Awards, a NYC Big Book Award, and a Next Generation Indie Book Award, among other honors.

Since 1970, Lawrence has studied and taught traditional Asian martial arts, medieval European combat, and modern close-quarter weapon techniques. Working stadium security part-time for 26 years he was involved in hundreds of violent altercations, but got paid to watch football. A founding technical consultant to University of New Mexico's Institute of Traditional Martial Arts, he has also written hundreds of articles on martial arts, self-defense, countervailing force, and related topics.

He has been interviewed numerous times on podcasts (e.g., Art of Procurement, Negotiations Ninja Podcast), nationally syndicated and local radio shows (e.g., Biz Talk Radio, The Jim Bohannon Show), and television programs (e.g., Fox Morning News) as well as by reporters from Computerworld, Le Matin, Practical Taekwondo, Forbes, Traditional Karate, and Police Magazine, among other publications. He was once interviewed in English by a reporter from a Swiss newspaper for an article that was published in French, and found that oddly amusing.

Lawrence lives in Seattle, Washington. You can contact him directly at lakane@ix.netcom.com or connect with him on LinkedIn (www.linkedin.com/in/lawrenceakane).

Kris Wilder, BCC

Kris was inducted into the U.S. Martial Arts Hall of Fame in 2018. He runs the Cheney Karate Academy, a frequent destination for practitioners from around the world which also serves the local community. He has earned black belt rankings in three styles, karate, judo, and taekwondo, and often travels to conduct seminars across the United States, Canada, and Europe. His book, *The Way of Sanchin Kata*, was translated into Japanese, a rare honor for a Western karate practitioner.

A Nationally Board-Certified Life Coach and prolific author, Kris has lectured at Washington State University and Susquehanna University, and served as club advisor for the Eastern Washington University Karate Club. He spent about 15 years in the political and public affairs arena, working for campaigns from the local to national level. During this consulting career, he was periodically on staff for elected officials. His work also involved lobbying and corporate affairs. And, he was also a member of The Order of St. Francis (OSF), one of many active Apostolic Christian Orders.

Kris is the bestselling author of 24 books, including a Beverly Hills Book Award and Presidential Prize winner, a USA Best Book Awards winner, a National Indie Excellence Awards winner, an Independent Press Award winner, and a Next Generation Indie Book Awards winner. He has been interviewed on CNN, FOX, The Huffington Post, Thrillist, Nickelodeon, Howard Stern, and more.

Kris lives in Cheney, Washington. You can contact him directly at Kriswilder@kriswilder.com, follow him on Twitter (@kris_wilder), on Facebook (www.facebook.com/kris.wilder) or Instagram (https://www.instagram.com/thekriswilder/).

Amalgamated Works by the Authors

Non-Fiction Books:

1. Musashi's Dokkodo (Kane/Wilder)

    "The authors have made classic samurai wisdom accessible to the modern martial artist like never before!" – **Goran Powell**, award winning author of *Chojun* and *A Sudden Dawn*

    Shortly before he died, Miyamoto Musashi (1584 – 1645) wrote down his final thoughts about life for his favorite student Terao Magonojō to whom *Go Rin No Sho*, his famous *Book of Five Rings*, had also been dedicated. He called this treatise *Dokkodo*, which translates as "*The Way of Walking Alone*." This treatise contains Musashi's original 21 precepts of the *Dokkodo* along with five different interpretations of each passage written from the viewpoints of a monk, a warrior, a teacher, an insurance executive, and a businessman. In this fashion you are not just reading a simple translation of Musashi's writing, you are scrutinizing his final words for deeper meaning. In them are enduring lessons for how to lead a successful and meaningful life.

2. The Musashi Field Manual (Kane/Wilder)

    "The authors' reading of the *Dokkodo* makes the work accessible and applicable to our modern lives. You've made a smart move in getting this book. Don't let it collect dust on your bookshelf, put it into action!" – **Iain Abernethy**, British Combat Association Hall of Fame member

    Shortly before he died in 1645 Miyamoto Musashi, the venerable "Sword Saint" of Japan, passed along his wisdom. He called this treatise Dokkodo, which translates as "The Way of Walking Alone." Dokkodo was a short essay, a mere 21 passages, yet both profound and lifechanging for the lucky few who were able fathom and follow it. When scrutinized it proves as extraordinary today as when Musashi first wrote it centuries ago. Musashi blazed the trail, now you have the privilege of following in the Sword Saint's footsteps. This manual aligns your heart and mind. It guides you toward insightful discernment and enduring self-improvement. As a result, you will walk away stronger and more prepared for all of life's tests.

3. <u>10 Rules of Karate (Wilder/Kane)</u>

"Since losing isn't an option on or off the mat, this is an absolute must read for karateka." – **Christian Wedewardt**, Founder & Head of Karatepraxis

All ten precepts in this concise book cut to the heart of ending physical confrontations as quickly as possible with empty-hand techniques. Our definition of "ending" is to make the attack stop. There is no running after the now fleeing assailant to catch and strike him down. There is no lesson, no teaching, no therapy, no epiphany. There is only making that bad guy stop what he is doing instantly so that you and those you care about will be safe. These ten principles are style agnostic, all about ending fights immediately. They define how to best apply your skills and training in the real world. Those who work with these principles will find swiftness, clarity, and victory in so doing.

4. <u>The Little Black Book of Violence (Kane/Wilder)</u>

"This book will save lives!" – **Alain Burrese**, J.D., former U.S. Army 2nd Infantry Division Scout Sniper School instructor

Men commit 80% of all violent crimes and are twice as likely to become the victims of aggressive behavior. This book is primarily written for men ages 15 to 35, and contains more than mere self-defense techniques. You will learn crucial information about street survival that most martial arts instructors don't even know. Discover how to use awareness, avoidance, and de—escalation to help stave off violence, know when it's prudent to fight, and understand how to do so effectively when fighting is unavoidable.

5. <u>Sh!t Sun Tzu Said (Kane/Wilder)</u>

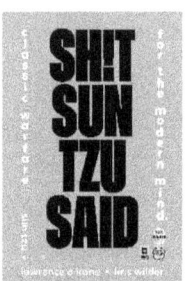

"If you had to choose one variant of Sun Tzu's collected work, this one should be at the top of the pile… I loved it!" – **Jeffrey-Peter Hauck**, MSc, JD, Police SGT (Ret.), LPI, CPT USA, Professor of Criminal Justice

Sun Tzu was a famous Chinese general whose mastery of strategy was so exceptional that he reportedly transformed 180 courtesans into skilled soldiers in a single training session. While that episode was likely exaggerated, historians agree that Sun Tzu defeated the Ch'u, Qi, and Chin states for King Ho-Lu, forging his empire. In 510 BC, Master Tzu recorded his winning strategies in Art of War, the earliest surviving and most revered tome of its kind. With methods so powerful they can conquer an adversary's spirit, you can use Master Tzu's strategies to overcome any challenge, from warfare to self-defense to business negotiations. This book starts with the classic 1910 translation of *Art of War*, adds modern and historical insight, and demonstrates how to put the master's timeless wisdom to use in your everyday life. In this fashion, the *Art of War* becomes accessible for the modern mind, simultaneously entertaining, enlightening, and practical.

6. The Big Bloody Book of Violence (Kane/Wilder)

"Implementing even a fraction of this book's suggestions will substantially increase your overall safety." – **Gila Hayes**, Armed Citizens' Legal Defense Network

All throughout history ordinary people have been at risk of violence in one way or another. Abdicating personal responsibility by outsourcing your safety to others might be the easy way out, but it does little to safeguard your welfare. In this book you'll discover what dangers you face and learn proven strategies to thwart them. Self-defense is far more than fighting skills; it's a lifestyle choice, a more enlightened way of looking at and moving through the world. Learn to make sense of "senseless" violence, overcome talisman thinking, escape riots, avert terrorism, circumvent gangs, defend against home invasions, safely interact with law enforcement, and conquer seemingly impossible odds.

7. Dude, The World's Gonna Punch You in the Face (Wilder/Kane)

"As an emergency room physician, I see a lot of injuries. This book can save you a lot of pain and trauma, not just physical but also emotional and financial as well. Do yourself a favor, read it, and stay out of my Emergency Room." – **Jeff Cooper**, MD

We only get one shot at life. And, it's really easy to screw that up because the world wants to punch us all in the face. Hard! But, what if you knew when to duck? What if you were warned about the dangers—and possibilities—ahead of time? Here is how to man-up and take on whatever the world throws at you. This powerful book arms young men with knowledge about love, wealth, education, faith, government, leadership, work, relationships, life, and violence. It won't prevent all mistakes, nothing will, but it can keep you from making the impactful ones that you'll regret the most. This book is quick knowledge, easy to read, and brutally frank, just the way the world gives it to you, except without the pain. Read on. Learn how to see the bad things coming and avoid them.

8. Sensei Mentor Teacher Coach (Wilder/Kane)

"Finally, a book that will actually move the needle in closing the leadership skills gap found in all aspects of our society." – **Dan Roberts**, CEO and President, Ouellette & Associates

Many books weave platitudes, promising the keys to success in leadership, secrets that will transform you into the great leader, the one. The fact of the matter is, however, that true leadership really isn't about you. It's about giving back, offering your best to others so that they can find the best in themselves. The methodologies in this book help you become the leader you were meant to be by bringing your goals and other peoples' needs together to create a powerful, combined vision. Learn how to access the deeper aspects of who you are, your unique qualities, and push them forward in actionable ways. Acquire this vital information and advance your leadership journey today.

9. Dirty Ground (Kane/Wilder)

"Fills a void in martial arts training." – **Loren W. Christensen**, Martial Arts Masters Hall of Fame member

This book addresses a significant gap in most martial arts training, the tricky space that lies between sport and combat applications where you need to control a person without injuring him (or her). Techniques in this region are called "drunkle," named after the drunken uncle disrupting a family gathering. Understanding how to deal with combat, sport, and drunkle situations is vital because appropriate use of force is codified in law and actions that do not accommodate these regulations can have severe repercussions. Martial arts techniques must be adapted to best fit the situation you find yourself in. This book shows you how.

10. Scaling Force (Kane/Miller)

"If you're serious about learning how the application of physical force works—before, during and after the fact—I cannot recommend this book highly enough." – **Lt. Jon Lupo**, New York State Police

Conflict and violence cover a broad range of behaviors, from intimidation to murder, and require an equally broad range of responses. A kind word will not resolve all situations, nor will wristlocks, punches, or even a gun. This book introduces the full range of options, from skillfully doing nothing to employing deadly force. You will understand the limits of each type of force, when specific levels may be appropriate, the circumstances under which you may have to apply them, and the potential costs, legally and personally, of your decision. If you do not know how to succeed at all six levels covered in this book there are situations in which you will have no appropriate options. More often than not, that will end badly.

11. Surviving Armed Assaults (Kane)

"This book will be an invaluable resource for anyone walking the warrior's path, and anyone who is interested in this vital topic." – **Lt. Col. Dave Grossman**, Director, Warrior Science Group

A sad fact is that weapon-wielding thugs victimize 1,773,000 citizens every year in the United States alone. Even martial artists are not immune from this deadly threat. Consequently, self-defense training that does not consider the very real possibility of an armed attack is dangerously incomplete. You should be both mentally and physically prepared to deal with an unprovoked armed assault at any time. Preparation must be comprehensive enough to account for the plethora of pointy objects, blunt instruments, explosive devices, and deadly projectiles that someday could be used against you. This extensive book teaches proven survival skills that can keep you safe.

12. The 87—Fold Path to Being the Best Martial Artist (Kane/Wilder)

"The 87—Fold Path contains unexpected, concise blows to the head and heart... you don't have a chance, but to examine and retool your way of life."
– **George Rohrer**, Executive and Purpose Coach, MBA, CPCC, PCC

Despite the fact that raw materials in feudal Japan were mediocre at best, bladesmiths used innovative techniques to forge some of the finest swords imaginable for their samurai overlords. The process of heating and folding the metal removed impurities, while shaping and strengthening the blades to perfection. The end result was strong yet supple, beautiful and deadly. As martial artists we utilize a similar process, forging our bodies through hard work, perseverance, and repetition. Knowing how to fight is important, clearly, yet if you do not find something larger than base violence attached your efforts it becomes unsustainable. *The 87-Fold Path* provides ideas for taking your training beyond the physical that are uniquely tailored for the elite martial artist.

13. How to Win a Fight (Kane/Wilder)

"It is the ultimate course in self-defense and will help you survive and get through just about any violent situation or attack." – **Jeff Rivera**, bestselling author

More than 3,000,000 Americans are involved in a violent physical encounter every year. Develop the fortitude to walk away when you can and prevail when you must. Defense begins by scanning your environment, recognizing hazards and escape routes, and using verbal de-escalation to defuse tense situations. If a fight is unavoidable, the authors offer clear guidance for being the victor, along with advice on legal implications, including how to handle a police interview after the altercation.

14. Lessons from the Dojo Floor (Wilder)

"Helps each reader, from white belt to black belt, look at and understand why he or she trains." – **Michael E. Odell**, Isshin-Ryu Northwest Okinawa Karate Association

In the vein of Dave Lowry, a thought-provoking collection of short vignettes that entertains while it educates. Packed with straightforward, easy, and quick to read sections that range from profound to insightful to just plain amusing, anyone with an affinity for martial arts can benefit from this material. This book educates, entertains, and ultimately challenges every martial artist from beginner to black belt.

15. Martial Arts Instruction (Kane)

"Boeing trains hundreds of security officers, Kane's ideas will help us be more effective." – **Gregory A. Gwash**, Chief Security Officer, The Boeing Company

While the old adage, "those who can't do, teach," is not entirely true, all too often "those who can do" cannot teach effectively. This book is unique in that it offers a holistic approach to teaching martial arts; incorporating elements of educational theory and communication techniques typically overlooked in *budo* (warrior arts). Teachers will improve their abilities to motivate, educate, and retain students, while students interested in the martial arts will develop a better understanding of what instructional method best suits their needs.

16. The Way of Kata (Kane/Wilder)

"This superb book is essential reading for all those who wish to understand the highly effective techniques, concepts, and strategies that the *kata* were created to record." – **Iain Abernethy**, British Combat Association Hall of Fame member

The ancient masters developed *kata*, or "formal exercises," as fault—tolerant methods to preserve their unique, combat-proven fighting systems. Unfortunately, they also deployed a two-track system of instruction where only the select inner circle that had gained a master's trust and respect would be taught the powerful hidden applications of *kata*. The theory of deciphering *kata* was once a great mystery revealed only to trusted disciples of the ancient masters in order to protect the secrets of their systems. Even today, while the basic movements of *kata* are widely known, the principles and rules for understanding *kata* applications are largely unknown. This groundbreaking book unveils these methods, not only teaching you how to analyze your *kata* to understand what it is trying to tell you, but also helping you to utilize your fighting techniques more effectively.

17. The Way of Martial Arts for Kids (Wilder)

"Written in a personable, engaging style that will appeal to kids and adults alike." – **Laura Weller**, Guitarist, *The Green Pajamas*

Based on centuries of traditions, martial arts training can be a positive experience for kids. The book helps you and yours get the most out of every class. It shows how just about any child can become one of those few exemplary learners who excel in the training hall as well as in life. Written to children, it is also for parents as well. After all, while the martial arts instructor knows his art, no one knows his/her child better than the parent. Together you can help your child achieve just about anything... The advice provided is straightforward, easy to understand, and written with a child-reader in mind so that it can either be studied by the child and/or read together with the parent to assure solid results.

18. The Way of Sanchin Kata (Wilder)

"This book has been sorely needed for generations!" – **Philip Starr**, National Chairman, Yiliquan Martial Arts Association

When karate was first developed in Okinawa it was about using technique and extraordinary power to end a fight instantly. These old ways of generating remarkable power are still accessible, but they are purposefully hidden in *sanchin kata* for the truly dedicated to find. This book takes the practitioner to new depths of practice by breaking down the form piece-by-piece, body part by body part, so that the very foundation of the *kata* is revealed. Every chapter, concept, and application is accompanied by a "Test It" section, designed for you to explore and verify the *kata* for yourself. *Sanchin kata* really comes alive when you feel the thrill of having those hidden teachings speak to you across the ages through your body. Simply put, once you read this book and test what you have learned, your karate will never be the same.

19. Journey: The Martial Artist's Notebook (Kane/Wilder)

"Students who take notes progress faster and enjoy a deeper understanding than those who don't. Period." – **Loren W. Christensen**, Martial Arts Masters Hall of Fame inductee

As martial arts students progress through the lower ranks it is extraordinarily useful for them to keep a record of what they have learned. The mere process of writing things down facilitates deeper understanding. This concept is so successful, in fact, that many schools require advanced students to complete a thesis or research project concurrent with testing for black belt rank, advancing the knowledge base of the organization while simultaneously clarifying and adding depth to each practitioner's understanding of his or her art. Just as Bruce Lee's notes and essays became *Tao of Jeet Kune Do*, perhaps someday your training journal will be published for the masses, but first and foremost this notebook is by you, for you. This is where the deeper journey on your martial path toward mastery begins.

20. The Way to Black Belt (Kane/Wilder)

"It is so good I wish I had written it myself." – **Hanshi Patrick McCarthy**, Director, International Ryukyu Karate Research Society

Cut to the very core of what it means to be successful in the martial arts. Earning a black belt can be the most rewarding experience of a lifetime, but getting there takes considerable planning. Whether your interests are in the classical styles of Asia or in today's Mixed Martial Arts (MMA), this book prepares you to meet every challenge. Whatever your age, whatever your gender, you will benefit from the wisdom of master martial artists around the globe, including Iain Abernethy, Dan Anderson, Loren Christensen, Jeff Cooper, Wim Demeere, Aaron Fields, Rory Miller, Martina Sprague, Phillip Starr, and many more, who share more than 300 years of combined training experience. Benefit from their guidance during your development into a first-class black belt.

21. Wolves in Street Clothing (Wilder/ Hollingsworth)

"Teaches folks to rekindle tools that are already in us—already in our DNA—and have been there for thousands of years." – **Ron Jarvis**, Tracker, Outdoorsman, Self-Defense Instructor

This book gives you a new light in which to see human predatory behavior. As we move farther and farther from our roots insulating ourselves in technology and air-conditioned homes we get disconnected from the inherent and innate aspects of understanding the precursors to violent behavior. Violence is not always emotionally bound, often and in the animal kingdom is simply a tool to access a needed resource—or to protect an essential resource. Distance, encroachment, and signals are keys to avoiding a predator. Why would a cougar attack a man after a bike ride? Why would a bear attack a man in a hot tub? Why would a thug rob one person and not another? The predatory animal mind holds many of the keys to the answer to these questions. Learn drills that will help you tune your focus and move through life safer and more aware of your surroundings.

22. 70-Second Sensei (Kane/Wilder)

"I'll let you in on a secret. The *70-Second Sensei* is a gateway drug. It's short, easy to read, and useful. It has stuff in it that will make you a better instructor. Even a better person." — **Rory Miller**, Chiron Training

Once you have mastered the physical aspects of your martial art, it is time to take it to the next level—to lead, to teach, to leave a legacy. This innovative book shows you how. Sensei is a Japanese word, commonly translated as "teacher," which literally means "one who has come before." This term is usually applied to martial arts instructors, yet it can signify anyone who has blazed a trail for others to follow. It applies to all those who have acquired valuable knowledge, skills, and experience and are willing to share their expertise with others while continuing to grow themselves. After all, setting an example that others wish to emulate is the very essence of leadership. Clearly you cannot magically become an exemplary martial arts instructor in a mere 70-seconds any more than a businessperson can transform his or her leadership style from spending 60-seconds perusing The One Minute Manager. You can, however, devote a few minutes a day to honing your craft. It is about giving back, offering your best to others so that they can find the best in themselves. And, with appreciation, they can pay it forward...

23. The Contract Professional's Playbook (Nyden/Kane)

"While early career practitioners may understand the value of drafting, negotiating, and managing exceptional contracts, they often struggle to master the requisite skills. This comprehensive manual helps structure the negotiation process, thereby minimizing the perilous process of trial-and-error, expediting competency with leading practices and tools that can help reduce risk and speed outcomes for both buy-side and sell-side alike." — **Gregg Kirchhoefer**, P.C., IAOP Leadership Hall of Fame Member

Ever increasing demand for performance- and outcome-based agreements stems from pressure for enterprises to drive greater value from their strategic customer/supplier relationships. To achieve expected performance, contractual relationships are increasingly complex and interdependent, requiring more stakeholders be involved in the decision making. Unfortunately for contract professionals held accountable to these requirements there has been little in the way of resources that answer their "how to" questions about drafting, negotiating, and managing performance- and outcome-based agreements. Until now! *The Contract Professional's Playbook* (and corresponding eLearning program) walks subject matter experts who may be new to complex contracting step-by-step through all aspects of the contract life cycle. Invaluable competencies include identifying and managing risk, increasing influence with stakeholders, developing pricing models, negotiating complex deals, and governing customer-supplier relationships to avoid value leakage in the midst of constant change. It's an invaluable resource that raises the bar for buy-side and sell-side practitioners alike.

24. There are Angels in My Head! (Wilder)

"This is not a book on doctrine, dogma or collection of creeds to memorize in order to impress others with knowledge. This is a practical application of your participation in a new experience. Here you will find your questions answered even before they are asked." – **Br. Rich Atkinson**, Order of St. Francis

The unexplainable has happened. A prayer has been answered, a gift has been given, a communication has occurred... Is it the voice of God, or the voices in your head? Here's how to find out: In this groundbreaking book, you will discover the organization of the mystical experience. Based on the classic works of G. B Scaramelli, an 18th Century Jesuit Priest, Wilder brings modern relevance to any person to apply to their journey as they seek the Divine. Using examples and principles from Christianity and other religions, Wilder demonstrates that mankind's profound mystical experience crosses all cultures and religions.

Fiction Books:

1. Blinded by the Night (Kane)

   "Kane's expertise in matters of mayhem shines throughout." – **Steve Perry**, bestselling author

   Richard Hayes is a Seattle cop. After 25 years on the force, he thinks he knows everything there is to know about predators. Rapists, murderers, gang bangers, and child molesters are just another day at the office, yet commonplace criminals become the least of his problems when he goes hunting for a serial killer and runs into a real monster. The creature not only attacks him, but merely gets pissed off when he shoots it. In the head. Twice! Surviving that fight is only the beginning. Richard discovers that the vampire he destroyed was the ruler of an eldritch realm he never dreamed existed. By some archaic rule, having defeated the monster's sovereign in battle, Richard becomes their new king. When it comes to human predators, Richard is a seasoned veteran, yet with paranormal ones he is but a rookie. He must navigate a web of intrigue and survive long enough to discover how a regular guy can tangle with supernatural creatures and prevail.

2. Legends of the Masters (Kane/Wilder)

   "It is a series of (very) short stories teaching life lessons. I'm going to bring it out when my nephews are over at family dinners for good discussion starters. A fun read!" – **Angela Palmore**

   Storytelling is an ancient form of communication that still resonates today. An engaging story told and retold shares a meaningful message that can be passed down through the generations. Take fables such as *The Boy Who Cried Wolf* or *The Tortoise and the Hare*, who hasn't learned a thing or two from these ancient tales? This book retools Aesop's lesser-known fables, reimagining them to meet the needs and interests of modern martial artists. Reflecting upon the wisdom of yesteryear in this new light will surely bring value for practitioners of the arts today.

DVDs:

1. <u>121 Killer Appz (Wilder/Kane)</u>

    "Quick and brutal, the way karate is meant to be." - **Eric Parsons**, Founder, Karate for Life Foundation

    You know the *kata*, now it is time for the applications. *Gekisai (dai ni), Saifa, Seiyunchin, Seipai, Kururunfa, Suparinpei, Sanseiru, Shisochin*, and *Seisan kata* are covered. If you ever wondered what purpose a move from a *Goju Ryu* karate form was for, wonder no longer. This DVD contains no discussion, just a no-nonsense approach to one application after another. It illuminates your *kata* and stimulates deeper thought on determining your own applications from the *Goju Ryu* karate forms.

2. <u>Sanchin Kata: Three Battles Karate Kata (Wilder)</u>

    "A cornucopia of martial arts knowledge." - **Shawn Kovacich**, endurance high—kicking world record holder (as certified by the Guinness Book of World Records)

    A traditional training method for building karate power, *sanchin kata* is an ancient form. Some consider it the missing link between Chinese kung fu and Okinawan karate. This program breaks down the form piece by piece, body part by body part, so that the hidden details of the *kata* are revealed. This DVD complements the book *The Way of Sanchin Kata*, providing in-depth exploration of the form, with detailed instruction of the essential posture, linking the spine, generating power, and demonstration of the complete *kata*.

3. <u>Scaling Force (Miller/Kane)</u>

    "Kane and Miller have been there, done that and have the t-shirt. And they're giving you their lessons learned without requiring you to pay the fee in blood they had to in order to learn them. That is priceless." – **M. Guthrie**, Federal Air Marshal

    Conflict and violence cover a broad range of behaviors, from intimidation to murder, and they require an equally broad range of responses. A kind word will not resolve all situations, nor will wristlocks, punches, or even a gun. Miller and Kane explain and demonstrate the full range of options, from skillfully doing nothing to applying deadly force. You will learn to understand the limits of each type of force, when specific levels may be appropriate, the circumstances under which you may have to apply them, and the potential cost of your decision, legally and personally. If you do not know how to succeed at all six levels, there are situations in which you will have no appropriate options. That tends to end badly. This DVD complements the book *Scaling Force*.

www.ingramcontent.com/pod-product-compliance
Lightning Source LLC
Chambersburg PA
CBHW081213170426
43198CB00017B/2602